We no longer live in the seventeenth century. Wars no longer serve the purpose of raising up or casting down the gloire *of privileged individuals, they are universal catastrophes, and the writer who does not devote his talent to combating their menace, far from following the example of great predecessors, is turning away from it; far from protecting their heritage, he is helping to destroy it. No contemporary novelist has the right to cite as a precedent Jane Austen, who, living at the time of the Napoleonic Wars, does not make a single reference to them in all her books.*

We have been arguing that literature, far from incurring a risk by mixing itself with what is of deepest concern for the Age that produces it, draws its very strength from such involvement. . . . We cannot determine what the questions of our time shall be, but we can determine that what we write shall be an answer. Whether or not our answers come to be considered "literature" is not the point, because in any case there will be no literature apart from them. However "universal" we attempt to make ourselves, it is not within our power to live in any century but our own, and if it is one which requires that literature give way before journalism, there is nothing we can do—except transform journalism. It was after all precisely in such a way that Milton's Areopagitica *and Pascal's* Lettres Provinciales *came into being.*

—Chapter 2, From Baudelaire to Sartre

EVERETT W. KNIGHT

LITERATURE AS

AS

CONSIDERED PHILOSOPHY

The French Example

COLLIER BOOKS
NEW YORK, N.Y.

This Collier Books edition is published by arrangement with The Macmillan Company.

Collier Books is a division of The Crowell-Collier Publishing Company.

First Collier Books Edition 1962

TO CHRISTINE

Contents

Acknowledgments

I wish to thank the Belgian American Educational Foundation for granting me a fellowship which made possible a year's study at Brussels and Louvain.

I wish also to express my gratitude to the Carnegie Trust for the Universities of Scotland for so generously making possible the publication of this book.

Introduction

THERE IS in each of us an artist—called memory—who mysteriously and unbidden transforms our past into a thing of beauty. Curiously, however, it is an artist that works best with the poorest material, doing very little with the years of well-fed peace while miraculously transforming those of obscure toil and perhaps even of hunger and cold into something absurdly precious. It is the same for the race which looks back to its "golden age," the same for the intellectual who looks back upon other centuries and sees not the plagues, the famines, the superstition and the cruelty but only the cathedrals, the poems, the great men. It has often been the case that the more arduous and painful the existence of men, the more magnificent the monuments they leave to their descendants. What if our own difficult times were breeding greatness, or at least something astonishingly new? It will not be the sort of greatness we are accustomed to, but that is a poor excuse for allowing a generation or a century to go by before recognizing it. How easily we imagine a Florentine platonist perhaps not totally uninterested in the work of a certain craftsman of the town, Michelangelo, but nevertheless convinced of the superiority of whatever ancient created this or that marble torso freshly disentombed. The platonist could not know that he was a "Renaissance man," but he might have known that something extraordinary was going on about him. In what concerns ourselves, we risk not only overlooking great art, but a means of quitting the wasteland where our writers and intellectuals, not without complacency have been growing thin.

The person who invented the term "existentialism" rendered both the philosophy that now goes by that name and the reading public a great disservice. It is of minor importance that the existentialists themselves should criticize the

9

philosophical accuracy of the word and accept it only because circumstance has forced it upon them; what does
matter is that, given the term, people suppose that it desig-
nates something reasonably precise. In fact it does not.
Hence the perpetual question "What is existentialism?,"
which never receives a satisfactory answer.[1]

If existentialism, unlike for example Spinozism or relativity, cannot be adequately defined, it is because like
rationalism, like romanticism, it is not an idea but a *movement*. We identify a novel as belonging to the romantic
period less by the ideas it contains than by the unmistak-
able intellectual and moral atmosphere which it revives for
us. Hence we can talk about romanticism, but defining it
is apt to be a long and never entirely satisfactory undertaking. It is true, of course, that in general it was literature
that contributed most heavily to romanticism, while in the
case of existentialism it is philosophy; and we may feel
that while literature does not lend itself very willingly to
definition, philosophy should. However, particularly in
what concerns philosophy, existentialism is not only a
movement but a revolutionary one; and the condemnation
of philosophy as the construction of systems (in the case
of empiricism the existence of system is implied), as faith
in the possibility of defining the universe, is precisely one of
the most important aspects of the revolt. Classical philosophy considers existence a secondary phenomenon, an
appearance behind which it should be possible to discover
a rational order, invisible on the surface. However, it appears in retrospect that the perpetually renewed hostilities
between the philosophic or scientific mind and the religious
(we are at the moment in the midst of a truce) amount
fundamentally to very little, it being no more absurd to
suppose that man was created after the image of God than
to believe the universe created after the image of man's

[1] The word "existentialism" will always refer to the philosophy of Sartre and
his school, although some of our remarks will, of course, have a much wider
relevance.

intelligence. Rationalism is as much a matter of faith as are the articles of the believer. There is, moreover, a sense in which the philosopher more than the believer merits the reproach of turning away from existence. Existence cannot be *thought*, but it can be taken to be a manifestation of God's will. The Christian is free to believe *because of* the absurdity of existence, the philosopher must believe *in spite of* it. Consequently, two of existentialism's greatest precursors, Pascal and Kierkegaard, were religious thinkers. The rationalist's mistrust of existence is a tacit admission of the absurd, and the existentialist revolt consists very largely in asserting that if existence is absurd, it at least *exists;* an advantage not shared by the "essences" invented by the philosophers to make it thinkable. But to espouse existence as the ultimate reality, to deny that it is a mere appearance, is to affirm that the Truth is not formulated, but lived. Given sufficient faith, one can demonstrate that the Creation conforms to a Plan, divine or scientific; one cannot demonstrate that it does not; one can only, as Gide does in *Corydon*, offer series of notable exceptions to the rules proposed. The absurd is less proved than it is experienced—existed. Life, unorganized by the novels and treatises written about it, is eminently ambiguous; but existentialism, instead of attempting to explain away what does not make sense, has been justly called a "philosophy of the ambiguous."[2] Classical philosophy tries to make life conform to thought, existentialism seeks to make thought conform to life.

The traditionalist, of course, has already broken off relations with the existentialist, whom he accuses of irrationality. This familiar reproach is justified; but what the rationalist does not want to recognize is that it is justified only from the rationalist point of view, which for the past half a century has been becoming increasingly untenable

2 Alphonse de Waelhens, *Une Philosophie de l'Ambiguité: l'Existentialisme de Maurice Merleau-Ponty*, Louvain, 1951. The existentialism of Sartre is, in a somewhat different way, equally a philosophy of the ambiguous.

philosophically and, given the present state of world affairs, increasingly dangerous practically. When the existentialist says that the world is absurd, the term is a pejorative one only for those who need to think that there are definitive answers to human questions. The world makes sense, but not in the way orthodox philosophy supposes that it does. Existentialism does not offer to modify classical thought, it denies the validity of its premises—hence the accusations of the traditionalists whose impatience with existentialism is due not to being contradicted, but to having been left out of the debate. Existentialism, being a revolution, does not propose new answers, it asks new questions; and they are questions with which western thought as we know it was not designed to deal. There is consequently no common ground.

If existentialism resists a too rapid definition because it seems to make thought conform to life, for the same reason, the great majority of the critics who have attempted one have been either hostile, incompetent or both. For if it is true that to think effectively implies the necessity of living effectively, if *to be* is to become identical with *to act,* then our intellectuals, our professors of philosophy,[3] who suppose themselves to have an existence independent of their action, are as much in conflict with existentialism as are the absolutists of left and right. The existentialist offends *everyone.* An English professor of political science once complained to us that a continental colleague with whom he was collaborating tended to be "too political," and a professor of philosophy expressed the fear that the great tradition of continental philosophy might disappear altogether if the existentialists continued to squander their patrimony on literature and politics. These two men, consciously or not, were expressing the opinion that it is sufficient for the True and the Good to exist to prevail, and indeed they prevail precisely to the extent to which we

[3] Like Mathieu Delarue of Sartre's *Les Chemins de la Liberté.* ". . . The true idea," writes Sartre, "is an effective action . . ." ("Réponse à Lefort," *Les Temps Modernes,* April 1953.)

allow them to be, without interference on our part.[4] The immemorial "essentialist" tradition of occidental philosophy has so imposed itself that it never strikes us as odd that Evil should be considered not to exist apart from its manifestations, while the Good is always there whether we see it or not. Thus it is sufficient for our "clergy of intellectuals," as Malraux calls them, to "think" the Good in order to be it, whereas he who devotes himself to Evil is obliged to work for his substance.[5] Much of the extraordinary indifference to be found among intellectuals toward the immense cultural upheaval of existentialism is to be traced to the fact that the new philosophy is not the "love of wisdom" but the love of its utilization; that *L'Etre et le Néant* is not a "contribution to knowledge" but the basis of an ethic of action. Existentialism does not propose itself to our "appreciation," it suggests the possibility of an action *for the first time authentic* in that it refuses to be deflected from its immediate purpose by consideration for a nonexistent Absolute.

To be sure, Sartre is not the first thinker to have had enough of philosophy as contemplation of the Good. There is Marx; or for that matter Saint Francis. But, for Sartre, to act ". . . is to change the *face* of the world . . ."[6] and if he insists on the word "face," it is because he believes that the visage of the world was not preordained, that man is free to mould one that suits him, and to abandon it as soon as it ceases to suit him. However, the world of both the

---

[4] Speaking of Anglo-Saxon empiricism, Sartre writes: ". . . It believes, without admitting it, in the existence of a natural order which imposes itself on the world and on the mind. . . . In other words, the passivity of contemplation necessitates the activity of the object contemplated." "Réponse à Lefort," *Les Temps Modernes*, April 1953.) A good recent example of what Sartre means here is provided by E. R. Dodds's *The Greeks and the Irrational* (University of California Press, 1951). After arguing convincingly that Greek rationalism came to an end because men were unable to bear the spiritual freedom it had engendered, and after pointing out that this seems equally true of our own time, Dodds goes on to hope that thanks to our greatly superior knowledge of psychology, the fear of freedom will not drive us, in our turn, back into irrationality. In other words, the activity of the "contemplated object" (in this case the principles of psychology) excuses the passivity of the intellectual.
[5] A striking example of this is, of course, the Hitler régime, over which people refused to alarm themselves until it had proved itself in action.
[6] *L'Etre et le Néant*, NRF, 1949, p. 508.

marxist and the believer *is* preordained, so that the marxist acts only to produce the inevitable (as did the protestant who believed in predestination), while the acts of the believer can ultimately result in nothing that was not fore-seen, if not in this life then in the other. In brief, the only genuine philosophy of action is at the same time neces-sarily a philosophy of the absurd, for only in a world not scientifically or divinely pre-established is man's action free to select its own goals depending upon the exigencies of a given historical context. Action of this kind is an uncertain, arduous and never-ending business, compared to which the action of the marxist or clerical militant is a form of repose in which only the body suffers, the spirit resting in the lap of the Absolute.

Existentialism, therefore, rejects the centre and both extremes as forms of evasion. We may reasonably wonder what remains. An action which refuses to wait for the "ob-jective" to impose itself and which denies the existence of eternally fixed goals would seem to be more an agitation than an action. If thought is to conform to life, how can it at the same time direct it? One of the purposes of this study is to answer that question.

But what has all this to do with literature?

Our definition of existentialism is at the same time that of good creative writing. No great novel is written for the purpose of demonstrating an idea whether of the left or right, and, on the other hand, it is never objective in the sense of refusing to involve itself in what is of deepest concern to the society from which it issues. That, however, is the least important aspect of the matter.

The fear of the traditionalist that the existentialist heresy may eventually lead to the disappearance of philosophy as a separate discipline is perhaps ill-founded, but the very essence of philosophy may well be transformed. For if truth is part of existence itself and not the distillation of some complex scientific or logical apparatus, then it is accessible to all of us; it becomes, *par excellence,* the domain of literature.

We have said that existentialism is not an idea, but a movement. If this is true, there must be evidence of it everywhere in the thought and art most characteristic of our age, and as we shall see this is the case.[7] In this matter of the present-day fusion of literature and philosophy, we are too often content to note simply that Sartre, Simone de Beauvoir, Gabriel Marcel, Brice Parain, etc., are novelists or playwrights as well as philosophers. It is more important to recognize that there exists a literature, of which no one speaks in connection with existentialism, which, nevertheless, is existentialist in that it is *literature as philosophy*, its authors being as much philosophers as the above-mentioned philosophers are novelists and playwrights.

Philosophy has always exercised a strong, where not determining, influence upon literature, to such an extent that the latter is often a sort of practical demonstration of the principles of the former. The seventeenth century is that of Descartes; we find that Corneille is a Cartesian, but it would not occur to us to look for an influence of the French classics upon seventeenth-century philosophy. In the eighteenth century, literature all but ceases to lead an independent existence in order to undertake the work of universal enlightenment. Need we speak of the indebtedness of realism and naturalism to science, of Barrès to Taine, Péguy and Proust to Bergson, a host of authors to Freud and in general, of the way in which for over a century, science, or perhaps more exactly "scienticism" has dominated western culture.[8] Literature remains necessarily under the tutelage of philosophy for as long as it is believed that Truth or Reality is a hidden quantity accessible, like the North Pole, only to those with special equipment and training.

The existentialist movement constitutes an unprecedented reorientation of human thought in that it denies

---

[7] It is for this reason that the present work can be no more than the merest introduction.

[8] Who can fail to recognize in, for example, Thomas Hardy's sinister God (and in how much more contemporary despair of a similar kind?) the influence of determinism?

existence to everything of which we are not immediately and indubitably aware. To philosophize will no longer be to deduce or to analyse, but simply to *describe what exists*, and that not in view of establishing an eventual synthesis or hierarchy but to enable us to distinguish what really is from what, through the centuries, human ingenuity has created to explain the nature of the universe and to justify man's presence in it. Existentialism reduces life from what we would like it to be, to what it is; and the instrument employed is not this or that method, but lucidity. The writer who refuses to allow a faith, a hope or a theory to interfere with his work, who has the courage to confront existence itself, is also a metaphysician, because existence *is* Reality and not merely its outward form.

Three such writers are Gide, Malraux and Saint-Exupéry. Their thought is "metaphysical" to such an extent that we shall be able to see in *L'Etre et le Néant* a translation of it into philosophical terms. There is, of course, no question of an influence of any decisive nature; on the contrary, the point is that literature and philosophy should have arrived at the same conclusions almost independently of one another—that literature should *be* philosophy. At the same time, cultural phenomena that occur together, or almost so, can never be said to be independent of one another inasmuch as they are necessarily the offspring of a climate of opinion produced at a given juncture of human history. Consequently, before talking about the three authors just mentioned and about Sartre, it will be well to try to organize into some intellectually digestible form the *Zeitgeist* which each manifests in his own way.

It appeared to us that the best way to do this would be to try to show how much of contemporary French thought, in art as well as in literature and existentialism, has been a progressive *return to things in themselves,* which implies among much else, on the one hand the absurd, and on the other the disappearance of the Self. We must start with a brief account of the phenomenology of the German philosopher Husserl; for the movement which we are about to study is, needless to say, no more exclusively French than was romanticism, although it is in France that it has reached its fullest or perhaps its widest development.

Two remarks in conclusion:

First of all, we cannot insist too strongly upon the fact that we are not about to embark upon the elaboration of a system to which each writer and thinker we discuss must be considered as having contributed. Phenomenology is a "method," and existentialism will be hardly even that. The "irrationality," "despair," and so forth, of modern thought reside precisely in its refusal to believe in the possibility of system.[9]

Furthermore, the reader has probably assumed that the delicate business of bringing literature and philosophy to cohabit harmoniously in the same volume has been accomplished by limiting the discussion of Sartre to what may be gathered from his novels and plays. For several reasons this has not been done. Two very competent books dealing with the philosophical interpretation of Sartre's creative writing already exist,[10] and our use of it (with the exception of *La Nausée*) has been limited to an occasional remark. If, as we are to try to prove, authors like Gide, Malraux and Saint-Exupéry have, in the language of literature, been saying very much what Sartre has said in the language of philosophy, then it was indispensable to define that philosophy with as much precision as possible. Consequently, our final section is largely devoted to an analysis of the "heart" of *L'Etre et le Néant*: i.e. the chapter entitled *Les Structures Immédiates du Pour-Soi*. We have long since come to understand that the "objectivity" of classical rationalism was in reality the subjectivity of an epoch—the

9 The "absurd" in one form or another has become a popular subject for learned dissertation. See Camus's *L'Homme Revolté; The Open Society and its Enemies* by Karl Popper; *The Tarner Lectures* given by Gilbert Ryle at Cambridge (1953); *The Disinherited Mind* by E. Heller, etc.

10 *Sartre, Romantic Rationalist,* by Iris Murdoch, Cambridge, 1953; *Jean-Paul Sartre, ou une littérature philosophique,* by Robert Campbell, éditions Pierre Ardent, 1945.

work of the philosopher is as much a product of the times, as that of the painter. The break in continuity, therefore, between the second and third parts of what follows is more apparent than real, for the best introduction to *L'Etre et le Néant* is an understanding of the cultural revolution of our time.

PART ONE

Chapter 1

Husserl

Wir wollen auf die "sachen selbst" zurückgehen.
HUSSERL

THE WORK of Edmund Husserl (1859–1938) is very rich. Large parts of it have not yet been published, and the precise meaning of many of his ideas is much disputed. Of one thing we may be sure however—the fecundity of a thought without which the work of neither Heidegger nor Sartre would have been possible. Without Husserl, existentializing philosophies would have remained the activity of "visionaries" like Kierkegaard. Kierkegaard maintained that subjectivity is truth, an assertion which orthodox philosophy could not have been expected to take seriously, but one for which Husserl provides a philosophical foundation. The importance of Husserl is to have opened up the possibility of retaining the comprehensibility of the exterior world while abandoning the absolute by which individuals, in themselves meaningless, allegedly become susceptible to organization. He was able to do this thanks largely to his theory of "intentionality." Intentionality is by no means the whole of phenomenology, but it is a vital part of it, especially for us, since this is the aspect of phenomenology of which Sartre has made the most extensive use. Up to the present, the writings of Husserl have been less important in themselves than as a philosophical quarry. Even when a more solid understanding as to what he really intended is arrived at, this may continue to be so. In any case, our interest is less the thought of Husserl himself than that which his French interpreters considered to be his; furthermore our requirements are not such as to take us far below the surface of phenomenology where agreement is widest.

Every philosophy requires a starting point, a premise, and it is in the nature of these premises to be beyond verification. We must accept a philosopher's basic assumption just as we must accept Lear's inexplicable conduct at the beginning of the play. Intentionality is taken for granted in all existentialist thought. It is here that we must begin, therefore, if existentialism is to make sense.

Intentionality is a hypothesis conceived to explain how knowledge of the exterior world is possible for the mind; it is therefore a theory concerning epistemology—a word we use with some hesitation, for phenomenology, like all great revolutions in philosophy, does not "solve" the problems of its predecessors, it declares them badly posed or non-existent, as Husserl declares epistemology to be a needlessly invented complication. If we are to know what the dispute is all about, however, we should bear in mind a few of the basic ideas of this "false problem" that is epistemology, or the theory of knowledge.

For the ancients and the scholastics, who worked on the principle *adaequatio rei et intellectus,* there was no difficulty, since they believed in accord with common sense, that, given proper precautions, intelligence and perception may be relied upon to communicate to us things as they are. Up to the time of Kant's refutation of the ontological argument (to which we shall return shortly), although the question had become much more complex, philosophers were able to believe in the "adequation" of mind and matter. Their separation, however, which was to render matter ever more inaccessible to the mind, and eventually to suppress it altogether in the idealism of the last century, begins with Galileo's assertion that certain qualities previously believed to form part of objects really depend for their existence upon human perception.

If we are to appreciate why this issue suddenly became so important for seventeenth-century philosophers,[1] we must remember that the philosophers of that time were

[1] It had been known, in various forms, to Greek philosophy.

also in many cases men whose main interest was science, and if science was to make any progress, the exterior world had to be stripped of subjective elements. So natural has it become for us to think of the world as being divided into the objective and the subjective that it is difficult for us to imagine a mentality in which this distinction is not made. Yet we must suppose that when Galileo argued that since a feather tickles us in some places but not in others, the tickling must be in us and not in the feather, his argument met with as much incomprehension as does phenomenology today in asserting just the opposite. There was no division, before the Renaissance, into the "natural" and "scientific" attitudes toward matter. Aristotle's four elements, earth, air, fire and water, were identified by qualities we now consider to be in us: hot, cold, wet and dry, qualities which for pre-scientific philosophy belonged to the object.[2] But the matter need not be discussed so technically. Nothing is more common than the attribution of what is human to the non-human. Colours may be "warm" or "cold," a musical note "sharp," or a landscape "melancholy." This projection of the subjective into the objective was at one time the only way in which men could explain the functioning of nature. Mythology was the "science" of the ancients. Galileo's theory which is one of the cornerstones of modern physics, according to which an object once in motion will remain eternally in motion unless interfered with by another body, could not very well have occurred to a Greek or mediaeval mind for which an object in motion will stop unless "pushed." We still speak of the "virtues" of some substances, which reminds us that for the scholastics objects had virtues. "A key's virtue of opening, a hook's virtue of pulling,"[3] writes Pascal—though probably in ridicule. Da Vinci thought of force as being born of "constraint" and dying of "liberty."

[2] See S. C. Northrop, "The Implications of Traditional Modern Physics for Modern Philosophy" in *Revue Internationale de la Philosophie*, Tome III, 1949.
[3] *Pensées*, No. 55, Brunschvicg edition.

With Descartes the attempt to disengage matter from its centuries of animistic accretions makes decisive progress. For a long while after mediaeval art had lost its inspiration, mediaeval philosophy continued to form man's view of the world about him: ". . . If men," writes Etienne Gilson, "were abruptly to cease thinking of bodies as heavy, light, hot, cold, dry or wet . . . their thinking had to have the distinction rendered convincing by the verification constantly supplied to it by physics."[4] The distinction referred to is that between mind and body, one towards which Descartes, whose education had been scholastic, worked his way slowly, relying for assistance mainly upon mathematics. It was the exactitude, the infallibility of mathematics,[5] the achievements of which contrasted so strikingly with those of scholastic science, which led Descartes to believe that the understanding should replace the five senses as our chief means of acceding to what lies beyond appearances. The senses cause men to be divided in their opinions, the understanding unites them; we should therefore try to discover some quality of objects independent of the senses, some quality, that is, which would appear to all men with the self-evidence of an axiom of geometry. Descartes believed that "extension" was such a quality; whatever changes, for example, we cause a piece of wax to undergo, it will always retain the quality of extension. Consequently we may assume that its qualities of colour and consistency, being variable, are in the perceiving subject, while extension belongs to the object.

With the division of qualities into the subjective and the objective begins the disastrous influence that enthusiasm for science was to have upon philosophy. The creation of two separate entities, mind and body, which has had such

[4] *Etudes sur le rôle de la Pensée Médiévale dans la Formation du Système Cartésien*, Vrin, 1930, p. 168.
[5] "I delighted above all in mathematics, on account of the certainty and self-evident character of its reasoning: but I still had not the least idea of its right use and, thinking it served only the mechanical arts, I was astonished that, given such firm and solid foundations, nothing more advanced has been constructed thereon." Descartes, *Discours de la Méthode*, Vrin, 1946, p. 48.

happy consequences for the development of the physical sciences, left to philosophy the problem, with which it has struggled miserably ever since, of reuniting them. Descartes could be more casual about the matter than many of his successors because he believed in God, and so had a means of guaranteeing a liaison between inner and outer worlds; but for men of less faith the problem proved an embarrassing one.

It is to Locke that we owe the conventional terminology, "primary" qualities being those inherent in the object, "secondary" those contributed by the mind. Locke, furthermore, in an attempt to do away with supernatural interference, which is a necessary element of the Cartesian system, abolished the "innate ideas" of Descartes in order to present the mind as being, at birth, a *tabula rasa* upon which objects enregister the "simple ideas," of which thought is composed. It will not be necessary to concern ourselves further with Locke, he is important to us only for having rendered more irremediable still the isolation of mind from matter, thereby provoking the idealism of Berkeley and the scepticism of Hume.

Berkeley stands somewhat aside from the main course of philosophical evolution which passes from Locke to Hume to Kant, but he gives us a foretaste of the bizarre possibilities latent in the situation as Locke left it. Berkeley could see no valid reason for distinguishing primary from secondary qualities. Extension, for example, is conveyed to the mind by the senses of sight and touch just as are the secondary qualities of colour and hardness. The reality of extension, independent of mind, is therefore every bit as much open to question as is that of the secondary qualities. All that we can be sure of is sensation itself, and we have no right to infer the existence of an objective world corresponding to it.

We must devote somewhat more attention to Hume, for an important part of Kant's philosophy was conceived to answer some of the problems raised by Hume's meditations on the theory of knowledge. The philosophers we have mentioned up to the present looked upon the exterior world as an autonomous and mysterious realm that the mind had begun to explore with the aid of new scientifically approved instruments and methods. (It should not be supposed that Berkeley's world was any the less real for depending upon the mind than that of Locke. Not only did God assure its survival when no human was perceiving it, but Berkeley had simply transferred objects and their materiality from the outside to the inside of the mind.) Hume, however, suggested the disconcerting possibility that mind, in its investigations, might be discovering in the exterior world things such as the law of causality that cannot be logically justified. We say that one event causes another, but since there can be no causality *in* the mind—perceptions are contingent and not necessary—there can be none outside it, if we accept Locke's idea that whatever is in the mind came to it from without. Hume did not attempt to deny the existence of causality. He was concerned with giving it a firm logical foundation, but could go no further than to declare that what we call causality is simply the occurring-together of certain events.

Kant refused to be satisfied with this result, and the whole purpose of his *Critique of Pure Reason* was to find out how objects could possibly correspond to our purely subjective concepts. This occurs presumably when, for instance, the *a priori* science of geometry is utilized to measure distances or to construct a building. How is one to explain the existence of propositions like those of mathematics which extend our knowledge of nature and yet are not based upon experience? Kant called them "synthetic *a priori*" propositions and decided that the order they reveal to us is that of the mind and not that of the universe. Thus causality is that part of the mind whose function it is to arrange phenomena in an orderly sequence of cause and effect. It will be noticed that Kant does not, as did Berkeley, altogether suppress the exterior world, for there are the "phenomena," an incoherent mass which the mind, thanks to its "categories" is able to make comprehensible.[6]

Kant, nevertheless, delivered a much more telling blow to man's confidence in the reality of matter than had Berkeley for whom, as we have already remarked, objects retain their properties and therefore, in a sense, their independence; they have simply been moved from the outer world into the mind. Furthermore, it is not easy for most of us to accept a philosophy however well reasoned which refuses exterior reality to all we see, hear and touch about us. It is such philosophy that gives point to Valéry's *boutade:* "Philosophy pretends not to know what we do know," and he adds, "science to know what we don't know." Kant, on the other hand, more insidiously, has left us an exterior world, but one about which we can know nothing except that it exists. Before the system proposed in the *Critique of Pure Reason* could be shown to be necessary, Kant would have to destroy the age-old belief in ontology, the belief that things have "essences," in short, the belief that matter is in itself rational. Before mind could be given the rôle that Kant envisaged for it, the importance of the physical world would have to be diminished in proportion. This was one of the purposes of an essay entitled: *The only possible Ground of Proof for the Existence of God.* The ontological argument for the existence of God states that because God is a perfect being he necessarily exists, since non-existence would be incompatible with perfection. Kant replies that existence is never an attribute, that it cannot be considered as adding anything to a concept. It is pointless to talk of the existence of an object when all we can ever know of it is its "qualities," the thing-in-itself being inaccessible.

For as long as his influence lasted, and it was strong

6 This is accurate enough for our purposes; a more thorough treatment would require certain nuances; see Bréhier, *Histoire de la Philosophie*, Alcan, Vol. II (1), p. 530.

through most of the nineteenth century, Kant had made impossible the rational demonstration of an objective existence.

This very brief outline of the origins of modern epistemology might almost serve for modern philosophy in its entirety. It is indeed striking the extent to which, since the Renaissance, philosophers have allowed their thought to lose itself in the verbal labyrinths of the theory of knowledge. "The difference between ancients and moderns," Whitehead has written, "is that the ancients ask what have we experienced and the moderns ask what can we experience."[7] The "difference" is due no doubt to the gradual adoption by philosophy of a scientific attitude. The scientist accepts nothing which has not been verified by experience; but this scepticism before the undemonstrated which has been so rewarding in science has resulted in the practical elimination of philosophy from the contemporary scene. It is meaningless to speak of progress in philosophy as one speaks of progress in aeronautics.[8] Most philosophers would probably agree to this, but it is difficult to see on what other grounds philosophy's abandonment of the market-place for the universities is to be justified. The descent of the intellectuals into the arena is not in itself a bad thing, as Julien Benda would have us believe; the tragedy lies in the fact that other and better intellectuals are never there to receive them. Truth, being something sought almost exclusively in laboratories, it is not surprising that the public place should be given over to demagogues. Philosophy requires a "given," yet for a century or so its great preoccupation has generally been, in emulation of science, to be dissatisfied with them all. It has pre-

7 A. N. Whitehead, *Adventures of Ideas*, p. 288. Quoted by Dewey, "The Objectivism-Subjectivism of Modern Philosophy," *Journal of Philosophy*, Vol. XXXVIII, No. 20.
8 "The fundamental defect of philosophy is this. It is something purely personal, and that is the last thing it wants to be. It wants, like science, to constitute a capital investment that can be handed down and will grow. Hence the systems that claim to belong to nobody in particular." Valéry, *Introduction à la Méthode de Léonard de Vinci*, Œuvres Completes, NRF, 1939, Vol. VIII, p. 75.

ferred to wait for science to discover some final truth. Kant thought that the law of gravitation was one such, but we are able to see now that his philosophy was compromised by having been too much inspired by a science destined to be greatly modified. By taking absolutely nothing for granted, and restricting themselves to finding out "what can we experience," many philosophers seem to have concluded that we cannot be sure of experiencing anything at all except possibly our own sense impressions—and they came to be troubled by the curious spectre of solipsism.

The "given" of ancient and mediaeval philosophy was the *adaequatio rei et intellectus* which, seriously menaced when thinkers began to enrich subjectivity at the expense of matter, finally perished at the hands of Kant who had declared the "thing-in-itself" to be inaccessible to us.[9] It seemed that man had freed himself from the non-human; but in reality what had been given with one hand was taken back with the other, since limitations once imposed by things are now imposed by mind itself. This peculiar contradiction between total freedom (since it is human subjectivity which determines the shape of the world) and total enslavement (since that subjectivity is imposed and inalterable) runs through the entire nineteenth century. One of the most troublesome problems of theology, the reconciliation of divine omniscience with human freedom, comes to the fore again in the latter part of the century in the form of a conflict (which, however, does not seem to have particularly troubled the philosophers) between scientific determinism and confidence in human "perfectibility." It is a period at the same time classical and romantic, rational and mystic, democratic and fascist. Liberty is loved less for itself, than for the refuge from doubt and turmoil to which it is believed to lead. It is as though humanity, being no longer in secure communication with things, had set out on a wild, directionless hunt for some absolute to which

9 For a very instructive article on the subject of Kant's rôle in contemporary thought, see Hannah Arendt, "La Philosophie de l'Existence," in *Deucalion*, No. 2, p. 217.

it could cling. Universal suffrage is regarded more as a panacea, than as a political instrument. Intuition is made to give access to nothing less than the "life force"; and as for the symbolists: "I know what I am talking about," writes Valéry, "when I say that at that period we felt the possibility of the birth of a new religion, with poetic emotion as its essential quality."[10] Men are impatient as they never had been before, because it is essential not only to destroy the old order, but to give up the freedom so employed in the founding of a perfect society where it will no longer be necessary. It is a century of revolutions, but also of utopias; nothing goes unquestioned, but it is for the purpose of finding those answers which will abolish questioning forever. There is little difference fundamentally between the political aspirations of the rationalists of the time, and the peculiar religiosity of the romantics and the mystics. The goal in each case is a lost paradise, whether it be the dictatorship of the proletariat, or the "I am he who will be God" of Rimbaud.[11]

The pristine state of innocence, the One with which the romantics in particular yearned to be reunited, might it not be the world as it had once been—penetrable to the senses, comprehensible to the intelligence, ruled over by man? Romanticism is many different things, but surely it is above all this nostalgia.

Ils reviendront, ces Dieux que tu pleures toujours,
Le temps va ramener l'ordre des anciens jours. . . .[12]

The point of view we have adopted, which is rooted in the general philosophical reaction against the idealism of half a century ago, that of considering the "problems" of epistemology (that is, modern philosophy almost in its entirety) artificial and mischievous, has perhaps enabled

10 *Existence du Symbolisme,* Stols (Maestricht), 1939, p. 23.
11 What Albert Béguin has written about Balzac might have been applied to almost every writer and thinker of the century: ". . . He is possessed of the desire for eternity, of the need to seize upon an unchanging truth." (Quoted by Maurice Nadeau, *Littérature Présente,* Corrêa, 1952, p. 53.)
12 Gérard de Nerval, *Daphné.*

us to discover a common factor in the violent moral and political dislocations of the last century. It is less the amassing of detail with the passing of time that gives us our perspectives of the past, than the subsiding of a flood of detail that gradually reveals the unsuspected unity of a landscape. It is now clear that empiricism, and the idealism that grew out of it, are not, as traditionally supposed, fundamentally antithetical, but doctrines cut out of the same cloth. For the idealist the world is a deceptive appearance, but the empiricism of Locke leads to the same conclusion. Berkeley had shown that the process of distinguishing primary from secondary qualities could not be stopped short of the complete annihilation of the object. As we have seen, Berkeley, like Descartes before him, called upon divine intervention to save philosophy from the impasse into which it had thrown itself. Such a recourse was denied later empiricists who are left with nothing but sense data themselves which may or may not be in some way related to an exterior world which may or may not exist. And so both empiricism and idealism bequeath us this singularly disappointing conception of a universe in appearance so inexhaustible, in reality, partly or entirely, shut up within the mind.[13]

We have interpreted the political and intellectual temper of the last century as an attempt, stretching from Rousseau's "state of nature" to Bergson's "life force," to return to some lost security. But no such return can possibly be effected for as long as philosophy holds mind to be the principal reality. No truth not relative to the mind can logically exist. Again, empiricism, if we do not allow ourselves to be mislead by what the word popularly implies, is

[13] If it is considered that we are being unfair to empiricism in this particular instance, it can hardly be denied that, in any case, the empirical attitude leads to a particularly uninspiring conception of the world. After a visit to the botanical gardens at Padua, Goethe wrote: "As I find myself face to face afresh with the manifold, this thought grows ever more vivid—one might perhaps be able to develop all plant forms out of *one*." (Italienische Reise, Inselverlag, Leipzig, 1920, p. 64.) Such is the ambition of empiricism, or, for that matter, practically all of occidental thought up to the present—to reduce everything to *one*. Hence the necessity, toward the beginning of the century, for a "liberation"—but it came from Husserl, not Bergson.

very close to idealism; for the empiricist argues: "My perception of everything I perceive is dependent upon immediate data: immediate data are relative; therefore, everything I perceive is relative."[14] This relativism fitted well into the intellectual cast of a century whose most important accomplishments were in the fields of history and biology. Movement, or "becoming," everywhere replaces fixity, and where it does not, everything depends upon *moment, race* and *milieu*. Just as the nature of the exterior world is relative to the structure of the mind, or to sense data, so men and institutions are to be judged relatively to their degree of evolution, or to their physical and cultural environment. It was nevertheless assumed that science would eventually reveal the ultimate principle upon which relativity itself depends. Nineteenth-century thought did not presuppose an absolute relativity, and it spent itself in impotent attempts to find a point of orientation. A striking example of this was the refusal to recognize that religion was no longer such a point. Free thinking was almost always coupled with a desire to conserve Christian ethics. It is not until existentialism that we have ". . . an attempt to draw all the logical consequences of taking up a coherent atheist position."[15]

Toward the end of the century, relativism assumed a particularly acute form known as "psychologism," a theory according to which all intellectual pursuits, since they involve the mind, are based in the last analysis, upon psychology.[16] This view was widely held when Husserl began his career, and it is in reaction against it that phenomenology finds its point of departure. Husserl's first publication, *The Philosophy of Arithmetic* (1891), shows traces of the prevailing psychologism. The second volume, however, never appeared, for in his meditations on arithmetic,

14 John Wild, "The Concept of the Given," *Philosophical and Phenomenological Research,* Vol. I, 1940–1, p. 77.
15 Sartre, *L'Existentialisme est un Humanisme,* Nagel, p. 94.
16 See Chapter I of Marvin Farber's *The Foundation of Phenomenology,* Harvard University Press, 1943.

Husserl found increasingly intolerable the thought that arithmetic and science should be relative to subjectivity.[17]

> Scientific knowledge is based throughout upon the possibility of being expressed by means of merely symbolic or otherwise inadequate thought. But how is insight thus possible; how does one come in such a way to empirically correct results? . . . In view of the analogous doubts which concern all science and natural thinking, Husserl asks whether we ought to proceed from Hume's scepticism, and extend it to mathematics and all *a priori* science.[18]

In other words, Husserl is confronted by the very problem that interested Kant most deeply, that of the existence of synthetic *a priori* propositions. Husserl's proposed solution, however, will be diametrically opposed to that of Kant.

We will not go into the details of Husserl's arguments against psychologism, but content ourselves with formulating their underlying principle. It is briefly this: no thinking could take place, nothing in the world would be comprehensible to us, unless there existed truths, or ideal meanings on which the mind could base its functioning. Truth is not arrived at (contrary to scientific belief) by analysis and dissection; for example, the idea of a sphere is not derived from that of a semicircle revolved around its diameter; on the contrary, it is because the essence "sphere" is accessible to the mind, that any thought about spheres is at all possible; or, in the words of Merleau-Ponty, ". . . we need to know what we are looking for, otherwise we should not be looking for it. . . ."[19] What movement there was in the universe of Kant and his con-

---

[17] Just as Sartre, the moralist, will find it intolerable that (as in Proust) the qualities of a woman should be considered the insubstantial products of a lover's imagination.

[18] Marvin Farber, *The Foundation of Phenomenology*, pp. 93, 94.

[19] *La Phénoménologie de la Perception*, NRF, 1945, p. 36.

temporaries, was strictly regulated by natural law, and always fulfilled a purpose. It is the universe of Voltaire's "Clock-Maker" God and of the "Great Chain of Being." Kant could therefore be free to regard the mind as a thing with certain unchangeable characteristics. However, if man evolves, it is to be presumed that the nature of mind changes, and it becomes possible to speculate that the mind of a primitive is not simply that of a civilized man totally without instruction but an instrument of a different nature. This is psychologism, and Husserl would have none of it. Nevertheless, the mind is no longer, as in the time of Kant, a safe repository for the principles that make knowledge possible. Husserl will have to place his essences or ideal meanings *outside the mind*, free from all taint of subjectivity, something solid and independent at last to construct upon.[20] Science has lost the authority it enjoyed a generation or two ago. We have come to appreciate the full importance of Hume's philosophical criticism of science, and Berkeley, in remaining unenthusiastic about Newton's law, appears to us less whimsical. Of course, the judgment of Berkeley and Hume was not muddled by the incredible transformation of life and environment that science was to bring about; but now somewhat recovered from the shock, philosophers are beginning again to object to science's ignorance of the postulates upon which it is based; an ignorance that leads it to over-estimate the solidity of its foundations and therefore to presume upon its metaphysical reliability. Again, it will not be necessary for us to review in detail the philosophical criticism of science that has been in progress for half a century. It is essential to note, however, the importance of the question for phenomenology, which Merleau-Ponty describes as being "first of all the disavowal of science."[21] This "disavowal of science," even apart from phenomenology, does not

---

20 Husserl's "essences" are of course not those of classical philosophy, as we shall have occasion to remark later.
21 *La Phénoménologie de la Perception*, Avant-Propos, II.

reduce itself to the proclamation that it is no longer compulsory to believe in determinism (which in any case is not altogether accurate). The books of Emile Meyerson contain what is probably the most impressive contemporary exposé of the contradictions which underlie scientific interpretations of nature. We shall consider just one of them. Meyerson looks upon science as continuing Greek philosophy's attempt to discover beneath the bewildering variety and movement of matter, constants or essences with the aid of which man might hope to distinguish appearance from reality. "All the great [scientific] theories are directed to the same end. All aim . . . at designating an unchanging, self-identical *something* in which, it is believed, the ultimate essence of reality can be shown to reside."[22] Consequently in the interests of identity, science must attempt to abolish change. Such is the object of the laws of conservation of energy and matter. The weight of elementary matter is the same after as before the event, and energy is conserved, that is to say, nothing has happened. But since phenomena (unlike the basic identity which is the goal of scientific enquiry) are nothing but change, the extent to which we have "explained" matter is the extent to which it has been caused to disappear. "Every part of a phenomenon explained is a part denied."[23] The criticism of science, pursued far enough, leads directly to the formulation of a number of problems to which phenomenology is attempting to find the answers. As a result of this criticism we are forced to recognize "the failure of the theories that have tried to replace the universe we approach through our senses by a universe without quality, consisting theoretically of nothing but number and extent."[24] Descartes' substitution of the understanding for the senses is reversed—we are back to the point at which science induced philosophy to take an imprudent

22 R. Johan "Raison et Irrationnel chez M. Meyerson," *Recherches Philosophiques*, I, 1931–2, p. 145.
23 Emile Meyerson, *Identité et Réalité*, Alcan, 1908, p. 207.
24 R. Johan, *op. cit.*, p. 158.

turn.[25] It was not, of course, possible for Husserl to simply ignore almost three centuries of philosophy during which questions of ontology were allowed to languish, awaiting some definitive pronouncement from science. A return to "things-in-themselves" will have to be preceded by the clearing away of epistemology and of the psychology which has grown out of it. This is the task of intentionality to which we may now turn.

As a philosophical revolutionary, Husserl recalls in a number of ways that other revolutionary, Descartes. They both lived at times of crisis for philosophy, when new questions revealed the narrowness of old answers. Descartes rejected scholasticism for mathematics; Husserl, mathematics for "essences"; and both begin with subjectivity as the first certitude. The work of Descartes cleared the way for the development of the physical sciences; it seems likely that phenomenology is going to render the same service to the mental sciences.

The difficulty of explaining to the layman the latest developments in physics is the difficulty of conveying notions no longer susceptible of translation into diagrammatic or pictorial equivalents. Similarly, if we are to understand intentionality we must cease imagining the mind as some sort of physical entity containing other physical entities usually called "ideas." We must rid ourselves, as Sartre says, ". . . of our almost incorrigible habit of constructing all modes of existence after the type of physical existence."[26] Again idealism and empiricism, ostensibly opposed to one another, are seen to possess important affinities. Both schools imagine only one sort of existence, that of matter. Whether we set consciousness apart from the physical world or resolve the physical world into an

25 We may judge the extent to which the "spiritual vacuum" of our times, of which so many complain, is due to the loss of confidence in science, by remarking that when Meyerson says that there exists an "irremediable contradiction between our intelligence and nature" (*Identité et Réalité*, Alcan, 1908, p. 338), he reduces to a neat formula a good part of Camus's *Le Mythe de Sisyphe*.

26 Sartre, *L'Imagination*, Alcan, 1936, p. 3.

ingredient of consciousness—in either case consciousness
and the physical world are there in nature, with an identical mode of appearing and existing."[27] It could not very
well be otherwise, for once mind is separated from its
object, hope of re-establishing a communication depends
on their being of the same stuff. The traditional conception of how mentality functions is familiar to everyone;
according to it, the mind is a "mere passive admission
of the impressions through the organs of sensation."[28]
Thought takes place thanks to the "association of ideas";
a new impression usually recalls to us some previous one,
and so the system is set into motion. The way in which all
the faculties of the mind are based upon sense impressions
is well illustrated in Condillac's *Traité des Sensations.* Let
us imagine that we are aware of the odor of a rose; if we
suddenly become aware of a different odor, the persisting
sensation of the first is what we call memory. If now we
turn our attention simultaneously to both sensations, we
have comparison; if, as a result we perceive resemblances
and differences, the judgment comes into play. If comparison and judgment are several times repeated, we have
reflection, etc. The association of ideas, however, is of
secondary interest for us; what we must remember is the
fact that the mind is considered as containing things similar in nature to the objects of the exterior world to which
they correspond. It was for the purpose of showing that
this idea underlies the work of philosophers and psychologists from Descartes to the present and to indicate the
serious objections to which it is exposed that Sartre wrote
his first important work, *L'Imagination,* published in 1936
while he was still professor of philosophy in a *lycée* at Le
Havre. His thesis is briefly this: if the thing in the mind,
the "image" as Sartre calls it, corresponds perfectly (as
the traditional theory believes it does) to what it represents
in the exterior world, there can be no possible means of

[27] Emmanuel Levinas, *La Théorie de l'intuition dans la Phénoménologie de Husserl,* Alcan, 1930, p. 32.
[28] David Hume—quoted by A. N. Whitehead, *Symbolism, its Meaning and Effect,* p. 37.

distinguishing an image from an object. ". . . If, to begin with, . . . we assert that two objects are essentially identical, that assertion, by its very nature, removes from us the possibility of subsequently distinguishing between them."[29] And yet we all know very well whether what is present to our mind is an object or simply a subjective image of one;[30] there is consequently a difference of nature between an image and its object. We have here the inception of a train of thought which will culminate in *L'Etre et le Néant,* where the image, or mind, has become not only different from the object, the in-itself (*en-soi*), but its opposite, nothingness (*le Néant*).

But for the moment we must return to the beginning of the century—to Husserl who was the first to decide that consciousness must no longer be conceived as a kind of matter. The real nature of consciousness is intentionality; that is, the mind is nothing more than an "intention," not intention as the word is usually understood, but intention as a sort of "turning toward" or, as Gurvitch calls it, ". . . a sheaf of luminous rays."[31] If mind is simply that, it can "contain" nothing, such as the judgment (as it is ordinarily understood) or secondary qualities, etc.; therefore it must be in contact with reality. *Appearance must be reality.* In order to elucidate these crucial ideas we shall discuss the transformation they involve of orthodox attitudes toward matter, mind and their connection; remembering, however, that phenomenology disapproves of such divisions, which nevertheless must be retained if an entire new philosophical vocabulary is not to be invented. Let us begin with matter.

For the first time, with such application, philosophers are proposing that everything be considered as known. The world is exactly what it appears to us to be. Appearance instead of being an unreliable subjective flux, is truth

29 *L'Imagination,* p. 109.
30 Sartre's second work, *L'Imaginaire,* will be a detailed treatment of this question. Sartre maintains that even in dreams and hallucinations the image is never mistaken for a perception.
31 George Gurvitch, *Les Tendances actuelles de la Philosophie Allemande,* Vrin, 1930, p. 25.

itself; or, as Husserl says, "It would be absurd to deny value to 'I see it' when the question at issue is 'Why?'."[32] It is difficult for us not to think of Reality, Being, Truth, or whatever term we prefer, as the product of painstaking investigation, if we consider it accessible at all—in actual fact it is the very stuff of life. "The world is not what I think, but what I live."[33] In what concerns our knowledge of matter, reason leads us astray. For example, there is no intellection involved in my perception of a brown house; there is no joining together of two "things" in the mind, brown and house, to produce brown house. I can, if I wish, make the colour brown of the house the object of a particular perception, but ordinarily what I perceive is a brown house, and not a colour to be added subjectively to the perception of a house. Primary and secondary qualities are derived notions, they have no place in everyday perception, because objects *are* their appearance and not an aggregate of qualities assembled in the mind. It will be objected that objects often appear to be what they are not and that it is the business of judgment to distinguish. When this is the case, the object has been artificially isolated from its surroundings and made the subject of a special perception, just as it is possible for us to abstract a colour from its surface. Let us suppose that there is a piece of white paper lying on a desk. Depending upon the way in which the room is illuminated the colour of the paper will appear to change, yet there is never any doubt in our mind that the paper is white. We will be deceived only if the paper alone is visible to us; if, for example, we were to look at it through a tube which cut off our vision of everything else.[34] Again, people we see at a distance we see at their actual size; it is possible that we say to ourselves: "how small they seem," but we know that their real size is that

32 Quoted by Levinas, *La Théorie de l'intuition dans la Phénoménologie de Husserl*, p. 135.
33 Merleau-Ponty, *La Phénoménologie de la Perception*, Avant-Propos, XII. This idea introduces prematurely an element of existentialism into phenomenology. We shall return in a moment to the question of the transition from one to the other.
34 The example is borrowed from *La Phénoménologie de la Perception*, p. 261.

of our unreflecting first view. Furthermore we do not "reason" a confused vision into clarity. The shadowy form we see in the distance does not suddenly become a man thanks to the intensity of our attention; we either see a man, or nothing at all; there exists either the perception of a man, or no perception. "It is not our business to analyse the act of attention as a transition from confusion to clarity, because confusion is non-existent."[35] Of course, it is always possible that I take the man for a tree-trunk, but nevertheless ". . . right vision and illusory vision cannot be distinguished as can adequate thinking and inadequate thinking."[36] The mistake was due not to an error of perception but to the natural limitations of perception. Men have long assumed that nature contains deep within her a principle of order, which is to be reached by a constant process of simplification called analysis. One of the most important objectives of phenomenology is to put back together again what philosophy has analysed into incomprehensibility. An object cannot be "simplified." Colour contains within itself the object in its entirety, as do all the qualities of a given object. ". . . The yellowness of the lemon," writes Sartre, "is not a subjective mode of apprehending the lemon. It *is* the lemon . . . if I dip my finger into a jar of jam, the jam's cold stickiness is what reveals its sweet taste to my fingers."[37] Not only have we analysed object into qualities, but each quality has been assigned to a particular sense organ; while in reality we "hear" colours and "see" hardness. "We *see* the elasticity of steel, the ductility of red-hot steel, the hardness of the blade in a plane, the softness of shavings."[38] An examination of some primitive languages would seem to prove that mental habits formed in a culture strongly coloured by science are responsible for our apparent insensitivity to the real nature of what philosophers coldly term sense data. Ancient Arabic, for example, con-

[35] Merleau-Ponty, *La Phénoménologie de la Perception*, p. 35.
[36] *Ibid.*
[37] *L'Etre et le Néant*, pp. 235, 236.
[38] Merleau-Ponty, *La Phénoménologie de la Perception*, p. 265.

tained five hundred words for "camel." What to us would appear a simple difference of colour, the Arabs considered a difference of nature, sufficiently important to call for a different term.[39] Poets have never been whole-hearted about adopting an analytic attitude toward nature. There is no reason to suppose that Rimbaud is being facetious in his sonnet *Voyelles.*

We have not yet restored to the exterior world everything of which epistemology deprives it. If subjectivity is to be nothing but a "turning toward," then such reactions as those of fear, pleasure, dislike, etc., must reveal to us aspects of objects and not of ourselves. "The predicates of value, the affective predicates, etc., belong therefore to the existence of the world—and the world is not an 'indifferent' milieu of pure representation."[40] No object is, of course, totally indifferent to us. But just as we have been taught that two camels are of the same species and therefore are to be distinguished not from one another but from other animals, so we have learned that a chair and a book are both material, inanimate objects. And yet our awareness of a chair and that of a book obviously involves far more than our taking-in of sense data. It is said, however, that if such is the case, then the reason lies in the "associations" that a given chair or book has for us; that there will be as many emotional reactions to an object as there are people and that the cause of such reactions must therefore reside not in the object but in the persons concerned. The phenomenologists argue, on the contrary, that emotions are provoked by qualities of objects themselves, to which the mind makes no contribution. It is not subjectivity which is infinitely varied, but the object; for the material world is "inexhaustible."[41] The observations to be made upon an object, the points of view to be adopted in

39 "The Maoris have 3,000 names for colours, not because they perceive that many but, on the contrary, because they do not identify them when they belong to objects of different structure." Merleau-Ponty, *op. cit.,* p. 352.
40 Levinas, *La Théorie de l'intuition* . . . , p. 75.
41 Sartre, *L'Imaginaire,* NRF, 1940, p. 18; also: "The real lays itself open to infinite exploration; it is inexhaustible," Merleau-Ponty, *La Phénoménologie de la Perception,* p. 374.

relation to it, are practically infinite in number and so, consequently, are the meanings it may have for us. But we cannot profitably continue with this argument without looking further into the phenomenological conception of mind.

We might stop for a moment, however, to insist upon the distinction to be drawn between what has just been said and a genuinely irrational approach to philosophical questions. It is one thing to argue, as do the phenomenologists (and the existentialists), that perception of reality takes place entirely without the aid of reason, and quite another to make our knowledge of Being dependent upon some faculty other than reason, such as intuition. Bergson remains well within the tradition of occidental philosophy in trying to go beyond appearances to what presumably they hide. Phenomenology maintains, in contrast, that we require no instruments to understand the world about us; things are exactly what they appear to us to be, nothing more. Science is not a search after truth, since we already possess it, but a voyage of discovery. Matter being "inexhaustible," science need never come to the end of what it uncovers to our contemplation. "Rational" and "irrational" are no longer terms relevant to the act of perception but to what perception reveals to us.

What is the place of mind in a universe where it is sufficient to look to understand? If appearance is reality, then everything that appears exists, and the antique question of existence or non-existence has lost its meaning. As long as appearances are taken to be deceptive, we can never be sure that they represent anything real, and a great deal of philosophical ingenuity will be expended in barren attempts to decide what exists and what does not. If, on the other hand, everything that appears to us exists, then the whole orientation of philosophical enquiry changes from existence or non-existence to *mode of existence;* from whether or not a thing appears to the *manner* in which it appears.

Once we find being itself [writes Levinas] . . . we need no longer ask ourselves—as we would do with a pure and simple theory of knowledge—by what means, or in consequence of what events, we attain knowledge of the object, or whether the object we know is being—our problem is the very meaning of being in each one of the special cases involved.[42]

The question is no longer whether "universals" exist or not, since everything appearing in consciousness exists (we will enlarge upon this point in a moment), but the way in which they present themselves to consciousness. For example, an ideal object, or general idea, does not first exist *then* characterize itself by an indifference to space and time; indifference to space and time is the way in which it exists—"its mode of presenting itself in consciousness, of *constituting* itself there. . . ."[43] The reader will have guessed that mind is simply the way in which things exist, the way in which things express their particular kind of existence. It is no longer a sort of calculating machine into which one inserts a piece of paper called a perception to be processed by the machinery of association and immediately returned marked "ship at sea" or "sound of music"; nor must the mind be imagined as the interior of a camera to which the eye or lens transmits images of the exterior world, for the image itself would have to be known, and that would be possible only with the aid of another image, and so on to infinity.[44]

How does Husserl avoid this vicious circle in his concept of mind? It is one thing to call subjectivity the mode of existence of objects and another to explain how awareness of that very fact takes place. The matter is treated most simply in Levinas's study of the way in which Husserl modifies the *cogito* of Descartes.[45] In the *cogito ergo sum*, Descartes believed he had discovered something of whose existence he

42 Levinas, *La Théorie de l'intuition* . . . , p. 188.
43 *Op. cit.*, p. 153.
44 See *op. cit.*, p. 71.
45 *Op. cit.*, pp. 57–61.

could not reasonably doubt, and went on to extend the
certitude of his own existence to that of God and the exterior world. Descartes's preoccupation (and that of philosophy in general before phenomenology) is always with existence or non-existence. For Husserl, as we might expect:
"*Cogito* does not only offer a simple means of attaining
fundamental certainty from which to deduce the existence
of the world outside *cogito*. Interest turns to the mode of
existence of *cogito*, to the original type of existence that
characterizes it."[46] What is the "original type of existence"
of the mind? It is the fact that the mind does not have to
become the object of reflection to be aware of its own existence. Consciousness exists as an absolute. At all moments of our waking existence, we are not only aware of
what we are doing but we are aware of that awareness.
"Every conscious existence exists as consciousness of existing,"[47] as Sartre expresses the idea, of which he makes important use, and which he calls "the prereflexive *cogito*."

We said that we were going to discuss "matter, mind and
their connection," but it is clear now that there is no connection. Intentionality is the word used to express the fact
that between mind and matter there is no distance at all.
We have inherited three notions from modern epistemology
that make the concept of intentionality somewhat difficult
to grasp. First, it is not easy to overcome what Levinas
calls "naturalism," that is, the belief, not always clearly
formulated, that mind is some sort of material thing, not
necessarily palpable, any more than is air. But even air is a
form of matter, and however spiritual the substance of
which we constitute the mind, it remains a substance. Consciousness, however, is not a thing, it is "intention." (Or,
as it is expressed in the literature we are going to study,
"act.") Mind and matter are two "modes of existence"
which in no way resemble one another. "So there appears
as essential, a fundamental, difference between '*being as*

46 *Op. cit.*, p. 58.
47 Sartre, *L'Etre et le Néant*, p. 20.

consciousness' and '*being as thing.*' Thus emerges the difference of principle—nothing could be more important —in *modes of existence,* the difference between consciousness and reality."[48] The second obstacle to the understanding of intentionality is the reduction of our means of communication with the world to five senses, and of the five the three most important, sight, hearing and smell operate *at a distance.*[49] This mysterious ability of the senses to do without direct contact is perhaps not without importance in our representation of the mind as something "above" matter, and the complementary notion that the place of the intellectual is properly one "above" the strife of his time. There appears to be in man a strong reluctance to consider himself organically and inseparably joined to mere matter. This constant aspiration to ethereality has, at one of its extremes, mysticism, at the other, the immemorial stigma attached to all forms of manual labour. The senses, as ordinarily thought of, serve as much to keep matter at a distance as to unite us to it; not only for the reasons suggested but also because the function of mind is to "pierce through appearances," and this can only be done from a vantage point, just as we seek high ground from which to view a landscape. To these ancient and anthropomorphic habits of thought, phenomenology (and that of Merleau-Ponty in particular) opposes a conception of man "immersed" in the world about him as a body is immersed in a liquid. It is not only by the five senses that we are alive to our environment, the entire body participates in giving a meaning to the universe. However, we must guard here against supposing that phenomenology simply extends the functions of the sense organs to the rest of the body; the term "sense organ" means for most of us an instrument serving as intermediary between the mind and the outer

[48] Husserl, quoted by Levinas, *La Théorie de l'intuition* . . . , p. 52.
[49] In *Adventures of Ideas,* p. 169, Whitehead criticizes as an error: ". . . the assumption of a few definite avenues of communication with the external world, the five sense organs. This leads to the pre-supposition that the search for data is to be narrowed to the question, what data are directly provided by the activity of the sense organs. . . ."

world, but no intermediary is necessary because there is no separation.

> So [we read in *La Phénoménologie de la Perception*], ... we do not reduce the meaning of the perceived to a total of "corporeal sensations." We say that the body, in virtue of having "behaviour," is that queer object that uses its own parts as a general symbolism for the world and by whose aid we are in consequence able to "frequent" the said world, to "understand" it and to find a meaning for it.[50]

The third of the entrenched ideas with which intentionality must contend is that of a mind existing in a closed chamber, half independent of the exterior world which it uses as raw material for the creation of worlds of its own. The name of Proust immediately occurs in this connection as the most distinguished example of the literary utilization of a psychology whose genesis in Renaissance philosophy we have briefly traced. The form in which Sartre most frequently expresses intentionality is: "All consciousness is consciousness *of* something,"[51] by which means he emphasizes the fact that consciousness is always consciousness of something that is not itself. When we hate we hate *something,* when we love we love *something.* The love of Swann for Odette, and of Marcel for Albertine have not for their object, as Proust would have us believe, the subjectively created figures of the two women, but certain qualities which they really possessed and to which Swann and Marcel responded with their love. For the issue of the *Nouvelle Revue Française,* which appeared on the first of January 1939, Sartre wrote a very short article on intentionality, valuable perhaps less for the light it throws upon the subject than for the curiously unacademic *élan* which animates it. For example: "And now, quite suddenly, these celebrated 'subjective' reactions—hate, love, fear, sympathy

50 pp. 273, 274.
51 *L'Etre et le Néant,* p. 17.

—which were wallowing in the stinking brine of the spirit, wrench themselves free. They are no more than ways of discovering the world." One easily imagines many of Sartre's colleagues deploring the lack of "objectivity" of such language. There is in this article a cheerful enthusiasm that we never associate with existentialism. Between 1939 and its post-war vogue there had occurred events which gave to most existentialist thinking the sombre colours since arbitrarily extended to the entire philosophy. There remains in existentialism, if not the cheerfulness, at least the revolutionary enthusiasm of the pre-war years; the hope of constructing a philosophy at last that, instead of leading a parasite's existence in the shadow of science, will be a new way of life. Ethics play a conspicuously subordinate rôle in modern philosophy; it would hardly be an exaggeration to say that in existentialism everything is subordinated to ethics. But to return to more immediate concerns, Sartre, in the article under discussion, presents intentionality as being above all a liberation from subjectivity, from the "stinking brine" which has in the past involved so much futile soul-searching and perhaps, especially, so much flight from the undistinguished and unaesthetic realities of social responsibility. The mind can no longer serve as a refuge; for, and we are still quoting from Sartre's article, it is:

> clean as a great wind, it [consciousness] consists of nothing but a movement of self-escape, a slipping out of itself. If, *per impossibile,* you were to penetrate "within" a consciousness, you would be picked up by a whirlwind and ejected, to be deposited in the dust at the foot of the tree. You see, consciousness has no "within."

A few general observations may help to clarify what has so far been established. Of all the assertions we have been making in the name of intentionality, that most apt to have excited the scepticism of the reader is the objectivity of emotion; that is, objects are "gay" or "fearful" just as they are yellow or hard. The phenomenologists contend that when we are afraid, we are afraid of *something,* for when that something is removed, our fear ceases. Psychologists, in accordance with time-honoured theories, study fear as something "in the mind," apart from the things that provoke it.[52] Again, the objection to the interpretation of emotion as intention is the feeling that since the same object causes fear or joy in one and not in another, emotion has got to be "in" the individual. The fact is that "Emotion is a certain way of apprehending the world";[53] it is an "act," an "intention" to conduct ourselves in a certain way given certain objective circumstances. Emotions are not, as commonly supposed, something we experience passively, our activity being limited to attempts to moderate their intensity. An emotion is an act undertaken in view of achieving a certain result. For example, a defenceless man attacked by a wild animal faints. He is not, as one might think, the "victim" of a fainting fit, but has adopted that course of action as the only issue. Being unable to effectively influence events in his favour, he attempts to deny them; he attempts to escape from an impossible situation by suppressing it altogether in the blackout of consciousness. This is what Sartre calls a "piece of magical behaviour."

> Thus the true meaning of fear becomes clear to us. It is a form of consciousness that, by means of a piece of magical behaviour, aims at denying the existence of an object in the exterior world, and will go to the length of reducing itself to nothing for the sake of doing the same to the object as well.[54]

Our emotive life in general is of this sort. A fit of rage is an attempt to alter by "magic," circumstances we are in-

---

52 See Sartre's *Esquisse d'une Théorie des Emotions,* Hermann, 1948, p. 29. On the other hand, there is a considerable amount of agreement on the point we are discussing (as well as on several others) between phenomenology and *Gestalt* psychology—see K. Koffka, *Principles of Gestalt Psychology,* New York, 1935, pp. 356–61, 391–3.

53 *Esquisse d'une Théorie des Emotions,* p. 30.

54 *Op. cit.,* p. 36.

capable of altering in any other way. Emotions depend strictly upon the exterior world, they have no life of their own, they are "behaviour" assumed in the face of objects whose modes of appearing are inexhaustible.[55]

The changed signification of the word "existence" is a point worth insisting upon. Existence is not uniquely material existence. Everything that encounters consciousness exists, whether it be a stone or a memory. Consciousness is always consciousness of something, otherwise it would not exist, for there is nothing "in" consciousness. It is somewhat difficult for us to see how the object of a mental image could be "outside" the mind. Nevertheless, whether we actually see a chair or only imagine one, the chair is not "in" the mind. What happens is that we "aim at," we "intend" the *same* object in two different ways. In a perception the object itself is encountered, in a mental image it is not. Perceptions and images are two different "modes of existence" of objects either one of which the consciousness is free to "intend," but in each case the *same* object is involved, and in each case the same object exists independently of mind.

> . . . Whether I perceive this chair [writes Sartre], or imagine it, the object of my perception and the object of my mental image are identical. Each is the straw-bottomed chair that I am sitting on. Consciousness simply has *reference* to the same chair in two different ways. In either case it regards the chair in its concrete individuality, in its corporeality. But in the one case the chair is "encountered" by consciousness, whereas in the other it is not. Nevertheless the chair is not in consciousness. Not even as an image.[56]

In the same way, a feeling of pleasure or of dislike is not in consciousness; it exists as much as does a chair, and indeed

55 Sartre's ideas on the nature of emotion are very largely shared by Alain. See Alain's "Lettre sur le Sujet du Cœur et de l'Esprit," published in the back of Henri Mondor's book *Alain*, NRF, 1953.
56 *L'Imaginaire*, p. 17.

may be one of the many ways in which a chair can exist, one of the many ways in which it can be "aimed at" by consciousness.

One point remains to be dealt with. How and why did phenomenology, which Husserl intended to be a method for the discovery of the principles or "essences" upon which human knowledge is based, evolve so quickly into the philosophies of existence?

We have already remarked that Husserl's approach to the problem of synthetic *a priori* knowledge was just the reverse of that of Kant, that the mysterious interaction between subjectivity and the exterior world was not to be explained according to Husserl by the suppression of matter but rather by the objective existence of essences. Essences that are not, however, those of any previous essentialist philosophy, for phenomenology is a return to things in themselves, and essences as formerly understood were general ideas upon which our knowledge of individual things is based; for example, we know what an individual horse is because the "essence" horse exists containing in itself all individual variations. This practice of sacrificing the particular to the general, of seeing in the particular a mutilated copy of a perfect original has been of incalculable importance in Western thought since the earliest times. Here, perhaps, is one of the sources of man's seemingly incurable habit of "alienating" himself, of placing the responsibility for the conditions under which he lives in the hands of a caste, priests or intellectuals, especially trained to seek out the truth, always imagined as hidden and inaccessible to the uninitiated. The common man too often considers it natural that he be left to pit himself against the particular, that is against *existence*, against Evil, alone and unaided. The first concern of both religion and philosophy has usually been not to attack evil but either to explain it away, or to encourage us to turn our backs upon it. Etienne Gilson has been able to write: "From Plato's day to our

own, you would think, from the way things went, that the
fear of existence was the beginning of wisdom."[57] Existence
might almost be defined as intercourse with the particular.
We live in a particular house and wear particular clothes;
but particular things are precisely what philosophy will
have nothing to do with, because they are inexplicable. It
might be possible to say why trees exist, impossible to say
why this particular one exists. Individual things cannot be
forced into the categories that reason prepares for them,
just as the individual molecule seems to defy determinism,
while aggregates of them remain obedient to natural law.
And yet it is of particular things that existence is made up.
One is a man, not mankind; what is said about life and
death, cannot be applicable to *my* life or to *my* death.

It is thanks to Husserl that the particular has at last become an object of philosophical speculation. An individual
object is knowable not because we are able to refer it to the
appropriate essence but because it is its own essence. "The
essence of the object . . . is its necessary structure—that
which makes it what it is, that which, preceding any empirical characteristic of the object, renders such a characteristic possible and comprehensible: in short, its principle."[58] The philosophical prestige once enjoyed by abstracts
has been given to the concrete. No quality (as has been
already remarked) can be removed from its object, since
every quality *is* the object. Consequently the abstract "red-
ness," for example, instead of being a general idea from
which all particular shades of red are derived is an inferior
entity which we form by comparing a number of red objects. Thus the classical conception is reversed. No individual is subordinated to an abstract; on the contrary,
abstracts are dependent upon concrete objects.[59]

Having reached this point, the next step is to decide
what means will enable us to discover these essences. Since,

57 "Limites Existentielles de la Philosophie," in *L'Existence*, NRF, 1945, p. 72.
58 Levinas, *La Théorie de l'intuition* . . . , p. 159.
59 For further details, see Gurvitch, *Les Tendances actuelles de la Philosophie
Allemande*, pp. 40–3.

according to the theory of intentionality, there is no "distance" between mind and things, the problem is not to reveal what is hidden from us, but to "draw back" from matter sufficiently to be able to perceive what is so taken for granted as to pass unremarked. Such is the function of the "phenomenological reduction." It is by "reducing" the "flux of the lived," or, as it is most frequently expressed, "putting the world in parentheses," that we can throw into clearer relief the essences which make knowing possible. An engine about which we know nothing has to be stopped before we can find out what makes it run. In the same way, perception has to be "suspended" if we are to learn what makes it possible. But if consciousness is to be defined as intentionality, that is, if consciousness is always consciousness of something not itself, then our every feeling, our *existence,* in brief, is significant, meaningful; and therefore there can be no point to "suspending" it, since it reveals reality. Existentialism came into being when it was seen that Husserl had tried to retain a *representative* consciousness after intentionality had rendered it obsolete.[60] It will be recalled that phenomenology introduced the notion that existence is not necessarily material existence; consciousness being the most important example of non-material existence. Phenomenology becomes existentialism when emphasis rather than being placed upon the material objects "intended" by consciousness is placed upon the *existence* of consciousness itself. Since consciousness is always consciousness of something, since consciousness cannot turn itself toward what does not exist, our every feeling signifies something, it reveals some part of truth.[61] Understanding is no longer necessarily representation of an object; every "subjective" state is a means of understanding.

---

[60] This is a simplification because Husserl's ideas about the reduction evolved considerably in the course of his life; (see, for example, Alphonse de Waelhens, *Une Philosophie de l'Ambiguité: l'existentialisme de Maurice Merleau-Ponty,* pp. 89–93); all of which is in no way prejudicial to our account of the origin of existentialism as a deviation from phenomenology.

[61] "The horrible consists precisely in being a substantial quality, in there being a supply of it in the world . . . emotion is torn from itself . . . it is not a commonplace episode of our daily life, it is intuition of the absolute." (Sartre, *Esquisse d'une Théorie des Emotions,* Hermann, 1948, p. 44.)

The universality of the notion of meaning in the structure of the subject [writes Levinas], has both opened the way to existential philosophy and also caused it to diverge profoundly from the philosophy of Husserl. The multiplicity of structures that this meaning can present, and the impossibility of reducing it to the thought of the object, has enabled the philosophers of existence to find a meaning inherent in existence itself.[62]

Just as we should no longer consider truth as being "hidden" behind appearances, we should no longer think of existence as being something that underlies the feelings we experience, as a screen underlies the pictures projected upon it. Jealousy is not something that happens to us, we *are* jealousy, our existence *is* jealousy, and therefore there is a "meaning inherent in existence itself." There is no distance between consciousness and the table it perceives; in a sense, consciousness *is* the table; in the same way, consciousness *is* jealousy, and that sentiment exists on an equal footing with material objects. As always, the idea itself is quite simple, but the terminology we are obliged to make use of betrays us. We speak of consciousness and of jealousy and the reader supposes that two entities are involved; but there is only one—consciousness *is* jealousy.[63]

Many of our feelings correspond to material things—we hate somebody or something; but many of them do not, and the question arises, how are we to interpret the existence of, for example, the "anguish" of Heidegger, the "nausea" of Sartre, or the feeling of absurdity and of solitude in Malraux? Certain facets of what exists (and perhaps the most important) reveal themselves only to sentiment, just as vision is the appropriate means of distinguishing colour. "All comprehension takes place in a disposition that is affective."[64] The only truth is a felt truth,

62 *En Decouvrant l'Existence avec Husserl et Heidegger,* Vrin, 1949, p. 51.
63 When our eyes cause us pain ". . . the pain *is precisely the eyes* inasmuch as consciousness 'exists them.' " (Sartre, *L'Etre et le Néant,* p. 398.)
64 Levinas, *En Decouvrant l'Existence . . . ,* p. 73.

not a demonstrated one.[65] We are related to the objects around us chiefly by means of a greater or lesser affectivity; many of them are, for example, utensils, and the only way to "understand" a utensil is to use it. "The purely contemplative gaze, however penetrating, could never, while directed at the outward appearance of this thing or that, discover in it a utensil."[66]

Husserl's thought is Janus-like, as is no doubt that of all great innovators. In his very concern for replacing old theories of knowledge by intentionality, he identifies himself with the main current of Western philosophy since the Renaissance. His attitude toward the world remains essentially a "contemplative" one: "Before we can behave towards things, we have to understand them."[67] For the existentialists, however, our conduct in the world *is* our understanding of it; one is inseparable from the other. By preferring to remain a "method" for the identification of essences, phenomenology made the existentialist dissidence inevitable. Husserl's cure for epistemology may well have been so radical as to have killed the patient, but rather than the phenomenologists, the existentialists would appear to be the real inheritors. Seeing that they were no longer bound to answer the questions "what can we know," "how can we know," etc., they went on to ask: "What is the meaning of what we know"; their efforts are directed less toward explaining how appearance can be reality, than toward exploring the consequences of the fact.

Nietzsche described modern philosophy as one that: ". . . never gets beyond the threshold, and rigorously *denies* itself the right to enter—that is philosophy in its last throes, an end, an agony, something that awakens pity."[68] The existentialists have crossed the threshold.

[65] "Everything is simple when we do not search for reasons. Usually it is the explanation which gives cause to reflect." Jacques Chardonne, *Claire*, Grasset, p. 23.
[66] Heidegger, *Sein und Zeit*, p. 69. Quoted by Levinas, *En Decouvrant l'Existence . . .* , p. 62.
[67] Levinas, *op. cit.*, p. 50.
[68] *Beyond Good and Evil*, Foulis, 1911, p. 136.

The nineteenth century was one of feverish unrest because it had nothing to believe in. Never had there been such a succession of schemes to set the world aright; some involved going back beyond the Revolution or even further; others, on the contrary, were based on the certitude that no wrong turn had been taken, and that the promised land might be nearer than anyone suspected. No prophet, however, succeeded in gathering about him a decisive number of followers; no doctrine went long enough uncontested to enable the historians to label the century and shelve it along with the Age of Faith, the Enlightenment, and so on. It is a period of spiritual tragedy because the universal yearning to believe is thwarted by a general impotence to believe. What Sartre writes of Baudelaire we might apply to the times in which he lived. "There is no time to lose . . . before the second glance that will spoil everything."[69]

If the nineteenth century strikes us as being "between two worlds, one dead, the other powerless to be born," it is largely because the Age of Reason had destroyed a great deal for which it neglected to find a workable substitute. Kantian idealism, in one form or another, dominated nineteenth-century philosophy; but the relativism to which it gave rise, for example the psychologism which Husserl could not accept, was but one instance of a habit of thought common since the end of the seventeenth century. It was then that Europe began to drift away from the political and religious dogmatisms to which she had always been moored, and thanks to which a certain number of beliefs enjoyed the confidence of even the most enterprising thinkers. The Renaissance had broken the hegemony of the Church, but left religion itself and the state untouched. By the time of Bayle and Fénelon, however, Europe had

[69] *Baudelaire*, NRF, 1947, p. 118. Benjamin Constant is admirably representative of his time. He tells us in *Cécile* (NRF, 1951) that his unhappiness was the result of ". . . the continual effort I had made to direct myself alone" (p. 124), and he attempts a solution by a return to faith: "I am making a total sacrifice of every faculty, of all knowledge, all reason, all judgment" (p. 125).

awakened to the existence of cultures not her own, systems
of government and worship that seemed to function perfectly in blithe ignorance of the "eternal truths." Montaigne
and Pascal had toyed with the problem of the relativity of
truth; a problem which by the eighteenth century had
ceased to be one since it was generally agreed that ". . . a
meridian of longitude determines truth. . . ."[70] Reason
alone survives the general taking of stock.

To the relativity of place, the nineteenth century added
those of history and evolution. Right was simply what historical and biological processes had produced. But the matter did not stand there, of course; in the last century a
postulate of determinism will usually be offset by one of
freedom; Hegel is followed by Marx, according to whom
". . . history is nothing but the activity of man pursuing
his ends";[71] Balzac and Taine are counterbalanced by
Stendhal and Nietzsche.

Combine this idea of the relativity of value with that of
human freedom, and there is no longer any reason why
man should not create his own values, why God should not
be replaced by man. We are here at the very heart of our
modern dilemma. Can a civilization survive the extinction
of its beliefs; must man believe in something beyond himself, or will he prove capable of creating and respecting his
own laws? For such, certainly, is the way to a "higher
ledge," to borrow Professor Toynbee's simile; all other
paths lead backward and downward. Unfortunately, men
are prepared to go to curious extremes to satisfy their
longing for definitive answers in their struggles to avoid the
consequences of their own lucidity. Hugo's spiritualist se-
ances, complete with moving tables and conversations with
the departed, were but the *reductio ad absurdum* of an interest in occultism stretching from Swedenborg to Yeats
and which included Balzac and Rimbaud, to mention a
few. Mysticism, nevertheless, was perhaps the least objectionable of the refuges; we have probably not yet seen the

---

[70] Pascal, *Pensées*, No. 294.
[71] Quoted by Merleau-Ponty, *Humanisme et Terreur*, NRF, 1945, p. 19.

end of the catastrophes for which nationalism is so largely responsible, and as for science—there are those who hail in Eddington's cosmical number the discovery, at last, of an "eternal truth." It is not easy to face up to a universe which refuses to make sense; the nineteenth century spent itself in trying not to, the twentieth has the choice of doing the same or placing itself ". . . on the far side of despair,"[72] where a new departure will become possible.

Apart from the despised bourgeois following Guizot's advice to get rich and defined by Flaubert as that which "thinks basely," the century is neo-platonic; men aspire to immateriality, and are not on good terms with things. When nature is not actually hostile, as de Vigny, Hardy and often Baudelaire and Hugo consider it to be, it is esteemed less for itself than as a "mirror" of some romantic ego; or, later in the century, for what it "symbolizes." The period 1850–90 is, in philosophy, according to Bréhier, one of "indifference to the object";[73] actually, the entire century is characterized by that indifference. Flaubert has all the romantic's loathing for the real, but believed that artistic integrity required that he find a place for it in his work. Naturalism was a utopic attempt to suppress the real by bringing it to public attention.[74] However, the only way to affect the real is to *act;* and naturalism, being the literature of determinism is also in a sense one of impotence—Maupassant ended in madness, Zola and Huysmans in religion.

The combined action of the followers of Saint-Simon, of the positivists and of Marx [writes Sartre], brought into being around 1848 the dream of an *anti-nature*

72 Sartre, *Les Mouches*, Act III, Scene II.
73 *Histoire de la Philosophie*, Vol. II (2), p. 910.
74 Albert Thibaudet, in his *Histoire de la Littérature Française*, Stock 1936, p. 377, remarks upon ". . . the horror the naturalists had for reality." See also Roland Barthes's *Le Degré Zero de l'Ecriture*, Editions du Seuil, 1953, pp. 46–9. In support of Bréhier's remark which we have just quoted, consider this from Ravaisson's *Le Philosophie en France au XIX Siècle:* "It is towards an Absolute in possession of moral perfection that, in the final analysis, tend the speculations of Comte, Herbert Spencer, Taine, Renan and Renouvier." (Hachette, 1868, p. 111.)

. . . it was a question of instituting a human order directly opposed to the errors, to the injustices and to the blind mechanisms of the natural world.[75]

The "natural world" is the natural enemy, and, to enlarge upon Sartre's idea, the "human order" established itself at nature's expense. Immense energy is devoted to cutting the world down to man's size, oceans are joined, railroads open remote areas, cities spring up like armed men and two generations are sufficient to subdue entire continents.

Humility was not a nineteenth-century virtue. While the vulgar were re-creating the world after their own image, the intelligentsia were communicating with eternity. No one wished to look upon himself as being so tightly bound up with the world as never to be able to assume the point of view of God. Such a state of affairs could not be prolonged indefinitely; the instability and uncertainty fostered by relativist thinking, with its consequent repeated attempts to discover an absolute, ended in the "return to things," in the reintegration of man with his environment, the philosophical phase of which we have already considered.

If this movement, both of reconciliation and of renunciation, has the importance we attribute to it, it cannot be restricted to philosophy. Every historical period has its own "personality" which none of its products or activities fails in retrospect to impress upon us. We feel the Middle Ages as much in an illuminated manuscript as we do at Chartres. The contemporary rediscovery of the concrete is as notable in literature and art as it is in philosophy.

[75] *Baudelaire,* p. 118.

Chapter 2

From Baudelaire to Sartre

> *Nathanaël, nous irons vers les choses.*
> GIDE

I

WHAT WE mean exactly by a "return to the concrete" in literature may be illustrated quite simply. In the course of one of his excursions in the environs of Balbec, Proust's Marcel has a semi-mystical experience of which another was the episode of the *madeleine* and the tisane. This time it is a group of trees along the roadside which seem suddenly to reflect the presence of a kind of continuity, of a spiritual substratum in which inhere the apparently chaotic events of human existence and which guarantees that our life shall be something more than a "tale told by an idiot." Objects suggest, but at the same time shield from us things more real than themselves; we are still, like the people of Plato's cave, seated with our backs to the light, watching shadows on the wall. Turning from *A la Recherche du Temps Perdu* to a book like Gide's *Amyntas,* we pass from one century to another, from the inner to the outer world. *Amyntas* tells us about the desert, not about what it "symbolizes," what it "means," or what it "hides," but about the desert itself. Nor do we see the desert through Gide, as we see America through Chateaubriand, or Venice filtered through the self-conscious posturing of Barrès; on the contrary, Gide inaugurates an ideal (to which he adheres in all his creative writing) of the total anonymity of the author—an ideal which will lead eventually to Sartre's definition of the novel as being a mirror through which the reader jumps.[1] Here is a typical passage from *Amyntas:*

[1] *Situations I,* p. 14. We will return to this point in our chapter on Gide where we compare Gidean anonymity with that of the realists.

. . . Bordj—a vast courtyard, and how convey its dreariness? Everything is lacking. It is vast without effort. Nothing is cheaper than space here.

Once you are out of the bordj, the night seems so vast that within it the bordj seems tiny. Never had I seen so many stars. In every quarter of the sky they spring up like flowers before your eyes. Dogs barking . . . an indefinable pain takes hold of you—we are defenceless against the emptiness—everywhere the desert's surrender can be felt.[2]

Gide has a single purpose here—to evoke the desert night with the greatest possible *immediacy;* and in order to do so he has accepted to efface himself completely. *Everyone* is seized by an "indefinable anguish," and we are *all* poorly defended against the emptiness. Gide's art is a consummate one, but it does not feed upon itself—there was no greater enemy of "art for art" than he. His skill is comparable to that of an actor whose efforts are bent towards identifying himself with the person portrayed.

Before a return to things in themselves can be realized, two conditions must be fulfilled: the exterior world must not be considered as affording access to some metaphysical, "higher" reality; and the traditional conception of the ego, or self, must not be allowed to interpose itself between things and our perception of them. We shall be returning constantly to these ideas.

Gide, of course, like Husserl, is a transition figure. Like Husserl, Gide's work, at least during his early years, is "contemplative." It will be almost half a century before anyone sees clearly that the renunciation of absolutes must be counterbalanced by what has come to be called *engagement* (for which the same word in English is the only convenient, but very unsatisfactory, translation). "It is no longer even a question of culture, but simply of existence,"[3]

2 NRF, 1947, p. 80.
3 *Ibid.,* p. 104.

writes Gide in *Amyntas*. Not until Malraux will it be recognized among writers that if culture is to survive it must no longer be separated from existence. "Being human is difficult. But it is no more difficult to become so by deepening what one has in common than by cultivating one's points of difference. . . ."[4]

Gide needless to say is not without his predecessors. Most of them are poets, for it is as natural for the poet (and the artist) to be interested in the uniqueness, in the singleness of things, as it is for the scientist to be indifferent to that quality. Baudelaire was the first great poet to use his art not to describe, not to narrate, but to *evoke*. He seems to have been aware, in part at least, of what he was doing; as when he refers to poetry as an "evocative spell" (*une sorcellerie évocatrice*—article on Gautier) or when he writes, in *Le Balcon:*

> Je sais l'art d'evoquer les minutes heureuses.

His poetry is full of phrases which do not make "sense"; or, for that matter, entire poems, like *Harmonie du Soir,* may convey no particular meaning. Critics like Faguet and Brunetière were unable to appreciate Baudelaire, because they supposed that poetry could not dispense with "ideas."[5] An idea is the expression of a *relation* and Baudelaire, being interested in the evocation of the *thing itself,* had no need of ideas. He does not tell us about his childhood or about Paris, he renders them present—and he does so by freeing himself from the arbitrary coercion of rationality.

"Perfumes, colours and sounds answer one another"— we make no difficulty about accepting that, yet nothing more "irrational."

> Cheveux bleus, pavillon de ténèbres tendues,
> Vous me rendez l'azur du ciel immense et rond. . . .

4 Malraux, *Le Temps du Mépris,* NRF, 1935, p. 12.
5 See Gide's article in *Nouveaux Prétextes,* entitled "Baudelaire et M. Faguet."

We know that hair is not blue and that the sky is not round —they only *look* that way; and if we were to accept the evidence of our senses, if we were to believe that it is sufficient to look to know, and that things measured and related are not more "true" than things in themselves, then we would have to renounce making any sense of the universe. This is precisely what is happening.

Baudelaire is not only a great poet, he is the harbinger of an age. In its highest reaches, poetry, like painting is not content simply to evoke for us with greater force things already known, it moulds our vision of them, it is creative in the sense that it reveals aspects of things whose existence we did not suspect. Familiar poetry is poetry about familiar things. Baudelaire was not understood until people had had time to familiarize themselves with what his poetry had revealed—ennui, eroticism, the modern city, etc.; all of which already existed, to be sure, but dormant like the human form in the Middle Ages, before its rediscovery by the Renaissance. Baudelaire was the first of a number of French "metaphysical poets." Philosophy having been entirely swallowed up by science, it was the poets (and as we shall see in a moment, the artists) who undertook its work, which is to protest. It is poetry and art which introduce the absurd into European thought. That is the secret of the extraordinary favour enjoyed by Baudelaire, who is one of the very few French poets to be widely appreciated outside his own country. Hugo is perhaps a greater poet but Baudelaire fascinates us, because we find in him more than aesthetic enjoyment, we find an anticipation of the age we live in.

Rimbaud is the despair of the critics, for he refuses classification. He has therefore been seized upon by all the sects. Catholic, atheist, *communard,* mystic, surrealist, etc., he has been called all of these and although we intend to annex him in our turn, it is not for the purpose of reducing him to the size of a doctrine or a school, but of seeing in him the most important representative between Baudelaire and Valéry of the _Zeitgeist_ we are attempting to isolate.

The world is impoverished by Kantism and by empiricism. The former reduces it to a system of principles employed by reason in its construction of science and morality, the latter sacrifices it to the natural laws which "explain" it. But is life possible apart from one or the other, apart from both the withdrawal of idealism (Hegel considered that the Prussian State could not be improved upon) and the feverish activity of the political pseudo-scientists hastening the advent of the millennium? For Rimbaud, it does not seem to have been. Although Baudelaire felt:

> Wounded by mystery and absurdity[6]

by retaining a belief in good and evil he went less far than Rimbaud who killed himself with work at Harrar.

It is the thesis that Etiemble and Gauclère expose in their _Rimbaud_ that we have adopted here. Whatever reserves one may entertain towards it, we must grant it the singular merit of not attempting to make of Rimbaud anything more or less than he was—a poet. A poet whose peculiar genius is not that of a "prophet" or a "mystic," but simply that of a man whose extraordinary delicacy of instinct enabled him to sense, before the philosophers and scientists, that European rationalism had run its course. In so doing, he was but fulfilling the rôle of the poet as we like to conceive it, that of a person who seems possessed of a faculty more incisive than intelligence which makes his "criticism of life" more probing than that of other men. Unfortunately, the poet's message is often difficult of interpretation, for it is never explicit. That Rimbaud should have written: "our pallid reason hides infinity from us" is of little importance. The idea had become a commonplace since romanticism. But it is one thing to repeat an idea,

6 _Les Sept Vieillards._

another to live it; and the significance of Rimbaud's poetry is that it was perhaps the first great attempt to act upon the belief that reason rather than helping us to accede to an ever more comprehensive knowledge of matter, blinds us to its real nature which is to be infinite, "inexhaustible." Rimbaud, the *voyant*, was seeking nothing more esoteric than nature herself, but a nature as she exists before our concepts and our laws have reduced her to the insipid and colourless fabric we call "reality." The source of the poetic genius of Rimbaud was his conviction that the real world was the infinite one of his senses and not the pedestrian one of his understanding. Etiemble and Gauclère are worth quoting at length here, because the attitude they attribute to Rimbaud is so conspicuously that of contemporary philosophy:

> Reduced to normal existence, we experience nothing with intensity; we have so to speak "made our hole" in the real; . . . all things revolve about us, defined, constructed, analysed, interpreted for us; . . . but what Rimbaud demands . . . are the rights of matter, or more broadly the rights of "un-thought" reality. He is fundamentally anti-idealist; and he is such by instinct, not by doctrine. . . . In his imagination he restores each thing in its integrity, gives it the absolute existence it was unable to attain, but for which it was made. He protests against the enslavement of the world and of men to concepts. . . .[7]

Kant had declared the thing-in-itself inaccessible, the positivists were not interested in it; but Rimbaud ". . . reconstituted a metaphysic of the concrete—he *saw* things in themselves; followers in themselves."[8] Rimbaud was not so far in advance of his times as to be content with that. He wanted to substitute his poetry for his life. The purpose of this new vision was to help him to escape from a world no

---

[7] *Rimbaud*, NRF, 1936, pp. 141, 142.
[8] *Ibid.*, p. 234.

longer illuminated either by God or reason. In this he re-
sembled the symbolists.

There are symbolist poets, but probably no such thing
as symbolism considered as a doctrine. Furthermore, what
is vital here is not the practice of making one thing stand
for another as Baudelaire uses the Albatross as a symbol
of the poet. What happens is that the best poetry ceases to
produce emotion by "persuasion"; that is, by making *comprehension* a necessary preliminary to the enjoyment of
poetry. An attempt is made to by-pass the intelligence and,
as in music, to present not a description or analysis of emotion, but a "symbol" of the emotion in the form of a thing.
When we said, therefore, that Baudelaire was interested in
the "evocation of the *thing itself*" we meant the thing itself
as an "emotional equivalent." But if, except on the level of
philosophy (as we shall see), the return to things must
remain more or less imperfect, we must not forget that the
operation is conducted on two fronts—being *and* nothingness (*L'Etre et le Néant*) and to regard comprehension as
having been replaced by the immediate impact of emotion
embodied in a thing is to have dispensed with "interiority."
This is precisely what constituted Stendhal's originality. He
describes in general not the *emotions* of his heroes, but the
acts to which they led; here act has replaced romanticism's
lush subjectivity just as the object was to replace it in
poetry.

This "submission to the object" of which Marcel Raymond speaks[9] can take a quite different form. The poem
as a whole may be considered to be not a medium for conveying a given impression or emotion, but an object in its
own right, just as cubist paintings are often to be regarded
as autonomous objects and not as representations. The
poem may be an object in the sense that, as in the case of
material things, we may "go around it" and adopt in respect to it whatever "point of view" best suits us. This is
the attitude that Valéry encourages us to take toward his
poetry, as when he writes: "My verse has the meaning one

[9] *De Baudelaire au Surréalisme*, Corti, 1947, p. 42.

gives it"[10] and goes on to say that nothing is more destructive of poetry than the supposition that it must have a definite single meaning; that it is reducible to prose; that poetry is an accident of the substance prose. But we will have to look more carefully into the work of Paul Valéry for it is of great importance to our argument.

We have seen how important a place a form of the Cartesian *Cogito* occupies in Husserl's philosophy, and how, at the same time, Husserl postulates the independent existence of things. Paradoxically, a searching enough examination of subjectivity throws us back to the exterior world. ". . . The inwardness," writes Bréhier, "the deepening, of the self in itself does not issue in the self, but in a reality that leaves it behind. . . ."[11] We have already called upon Sartre to testify: "If, *per impossibile,* you were to penetrate 'within' a consciousness, you would be picked up by a whirlwind and ejected. . . ."[12] Romanticism appears to have made the same discovery, at least in the case of Novalis, who causes Albert Béguin to write: ". . . the way of subjectivism, pursued to the utmost possible limit, results in a rediscovery of the exterior world. . . ."[13] Marcel Raymond has been able to write à *propos* of Valéry: "What is a thought, a particular feeling, this or that prolonged sensation, or a certain desire; what are all phenomena of *interior* life, in the contemplation of the mind, if not *exterior* things."[14] (It will be remarked that this is precisely what is meant by intentionality.) The symbolists might themselves be symbolized by the myth of Narcissus for which they had a predilection; but self contemplation, as we have seen, leads back to the exterior world, and conspicuously in the case of Valéry for whom nature exists on an equal footing with consciousness. In the poetry of Valéry, symbolism comes down from the oxygenless heights where

10 *Charmes,* commentés par Alain, NRF, 1952 (Avant-Propos).
11 *Transformation de la Philosophie Française,* Flammarion, 1950, p. 118.
12 *Situations I,* p. 33.
13 *Le Rêve chez les Romantiques Allemands,* Cahiers du Sud, 1937, Vol. II, p. 109.
14 *De Baudelaire au Surréalisme,* p. 153.

Mallarmé conducted his experiments, to the point where Valéry could define poetry as being:

> . . . The attempt to represent, or to restore, by means of articulate language *those things* or *that thing* which cries, tears, caresses, kisses, sighs, etc. attempt obscurely to express, and which *objects seem to seek to express* in what they possess of appearance of life or of supposed purpose.[15]

Long before Gabriel Marcel and other existentialists began to talk of a "broken world," Valéry had indirectly approached the subject in his *Introduction à la Méthode de Léonard de Vinci* (1894), before speaking of it explicitly in *Regards sur le Monde Actuel* and in *Idée Fixe*.[16] Science, according to the existentialists, has "broken" the world into fragments and offers no suggestions as to how we are to restore it. Scientists of different specialities are frequently able to help one another; but the interpenetration of sciences has been negligible if we bear in mind that, in theory, science was to lead progressively to an intellectually satisfying explanation of the universe. If science had not both been founded upon a metaphysics and given to expressing opinions of a metaphysical cast, our criticism would be unfair; as matters stand, however, we are justified in complaining that the discoveries of science, instead of converging toward a centre, appear rather to be spreading outward like the spokes of a wheel. And so if we gather together a physiologist, a physicist, a psychiatrist, a sociologist, etc., to pronounce upon the human body for instance, we shall have as many different accounts as there are scientists.

---

[15] *Tel Quel I*, NRF, 1941, p. 144.

[16] ". . . We are at present witnessing a sort of bankruptcy of the imagination and a decline of the understanding, incapable as we are of forming a homogeneous representation of the world which will cover all the data, old and new of experience." (*Regards sur le Monde Actuel, Œuvres de Paul Valéry*, NRF, 1938, p. 56.) See also *Idée Fixe*, same edition, p. 148—"There are too many facts. . . . We no longer know how to pick up all our winnings in the lottery of experience. All these results speak at once. . . ."

In a commentary which Valéry added in 1930 to *Note et Digression*, we read: ". . . The real that it [thought] seeks to attain can only be of an *infinite* complexity—inexhaustible; and on the other hand, it can fix upon anything, and use what it has fixed upon, only by giving it some *simple* form."[17] That word "inexhaustible" is becoming familiar, and if matter may be correctly so termed, then it can never be definitively organized, it is absurd. What Valéry is suggesting furthermore, is that if the real is infinite, then methods for hacking it into comprehensible portions (into "simple forms") must also be infinite. Since matter in its totality is beyond our comprehension, then no method, including that of science, can be the "good" one; and yet for the very reason that no method can ever answer our questions once and for all, it is the method itself and not its results that concerns Valéry. "What interests me is not the work of art, it is the recipe."[18] Hence his interest in Leonardo da Vinci, who seemed to possess a method applicable equally to science and to art.

The fundamental theme of Valéry's writings is the radical division of what exists into two incompatible parts—consciousness, and the rest of the universe. The whole drama of his thought, the intellectual tension which gives substance to his poetry, is the tragic awareness that consciousness, that "flaw" in the fullness of Being, is all that matters; and yet all attempts to draw closer to this divine flaw are thwarted by the interference of what is foreign to it, the exterior world. By accepting as irreducible the duality of mind and matter, which are nevertheless inseparable since we cannot turn to one without encountering the other, by admitting the basic ambiguity of human life and the futility of trying to reduce it in its entirety to a system, Valéry relates himself closely to important preoccupations of contemporary thought. As in the philosophy of Sartre, man, as Valéry conceives him, is a "useless passion." The struggle of consciousness, in Valéry, to tear itself from the incoherent and to live within itself recalls

[17] *Œuvres de Paul Valéry*, NRF, 1938, p. 24.
[18] Quoted by Gide in *Incidences*, NRF, 1924, p. 205.

the Sartrean for-itself (*pour-soi*) in its eternally fruitless attempts to coincide with itself. Also, both the *Cimetière Marin* and *La Nausée* are dominated by the awesome presence, the inescapable immensity of the non-human. In *Le Cimetière Marin* it is called a "great diamond," in *La Nausée* it is the in-itself (*en-soi*), menacing in its refusal to submit to any of the requirements of rationality. In Valéry's poem, consciousness is nothing but a "secret change"; in *L'Etre et le Néant,* it will, in one sense, be altogether suppressed. Here is the source of our modern sense of the tragic—the exterior world is overwhelming and absurd, but there is no refuge from it; for, as we have seen, subjectivity is nothing but the manner in which objects exist; we are "in the world" and ". . . we must try to live!"[19] The sentiment of the absurd, as we shall come more and more to appreciate, goes hand in hand with the rediscovery of the concrete. How does this occur in Valéry?

Habit influences our perception as it does other kinds of comportment. If we are awake to but an infinitesimal part of what the exterior world in its "inexhaustibility" has to offer, it is because three centuries of rationalism have imposed a view of things which few of us are capable of laying aside. Such is the function of the artist—in teaching us a more supple use of our faculties, he causes nature to imitate art. Before Bergson, Valéry had pointed out that people see as well as think by ready-made concepts. "Most people see through their intellect far more often than through their eyes. Instead of coloured spaces, they take note of concepts."[20] And he gives us an example: "Knowing the surface of still water to be horizontal, people fail to recognize that the sea is *upright* in the distance."[21]

---

[19] *Le Cimetière Marin.*
[20] *Les Divers Essais sur Léonard de Vinci,* NRF, 1938, p. 76.
[21] *Ibid.,* p. 77. It is interesting to compare this idea with the first two lines of *Le Cimetière Marin:*

> Ce Toit tranquille, où marchent des colombes,
> Entre les pins palpite, entre les tombes.

Etiemble and Gauclère remark that the sea for Rimbaud was ". . . the sea as one sees it, not as one knows it." *Rimbaud,* p. 139.

Obscuring our view of things, are the factitious systems by which we attempt to deny their ineluctable singleness. This is one of the most important themes of Merleau-Ponty's *La Phénoménologie de la Perception*. The two men exploit their discovery in different ways, however. Valéry is a poet, and his first reaction to the strange new country discovered on the other side of absurdity is one of delight. "Certain men, with a special delicacy of feeling, take a voluptuous pleasure in the *individuality* of objects. They show a delighted preference for that quality in a thing of being unique—a quality all things possess."[22] And in another passage he speaks of ". . . the emotion that the least of things real gives rise to . . ."[23] To return to things in themselves is to become aware of a new world, and that is why Merleau-Ponty can look upon "wonder in face of the world" as being the best way to describe the phenomenological reduction.[24] One of Husserl's students declared that as a result of her studies she had been given "new eyes."[25]

The difference between Merleau-Ponty and Valéry is the difference between what might loosely be termed the metaphysical and aesthetic return to the concrete—a difference which is the watershed of two generations. It would be possible to find in Valéry many sentences that we could suppose taken from Sartre or Malraux,[26] the first principles of both generations being much the same; but the inferences from those principles are very different. Valéry remained a *clerc*. Although more clairvoyant than most about the dangers that menaced France and the world, he did not seem to consider it any of his affair; or perhaps more accurately his attitude had been fashioned by the

[22] *Ibid.*, p. 83.
[23] *Les Divers Essais sur Léonard de Vinci*, p. 76.
[24] *La Phénoménologie de la Perception*, Avant-Propos, VIII.
[25] See Farber, *The Foundation of Phenomenology*, p. 216.
[26] In *Monsieur Teste:* "One is handsome, or extraordinary, only for others. They are devoured by others." Or: "What is a man capable of." In *L'Etre et le Néant*, Sartre describes consciousness as a "hollow always to come." The phrase is used for the same purpose in the eighth stanza of *Le Cimetière Marin*, etc.

prevailing philosophy, that of determinism, to a greater extent than he would have cared to admit. ("So don't cherish any illusions about yourself!" writes Jules Renard. "If you had been born twenty years earlier, you would have gone in for naturalism just like everybody else.")[27] In any case Valéry was not of this world. He was "A mystic without God," as he calls himself in *Monsieur Teste,* and even claims that his writings were but the débris of a profounder labour, the exploration of his "mental functioning."[28] A sharper contrast with the generation that was to include a Malraux and a Saint-Exupéry can hardly be imagined. And yet if we have correctly identified the basic inspiration of contemporary thought, there is no break between Valéry and Malraux any more than there was between Husserl and the existentialists. The point of departure is always the same—in one form or another, the belief in the absurd. There are two very different ways, however, to react to the absurd. Men have either thrown themselves into action and, in the fraternity of common danger, attempted to establish, however transiently, communities founded upon human values alone; or they have had recourse to art as a device adapted to force nature to conform to human standards of law and order. To the first group belong, for example, T. E. Lawrence, Malraux, Saint-Exupéry; to the second, Baudelaire, Rimbaud, Valéry, Sartre in the final pages of *La Nausée,* and now the Malraux of *Les Voix du Silence.*

There exists, however, another notion of the absurd which is not that of the men just mentioned. It is what we might call a "qualified" absurd; for although it, like the other, was made possible by the discrediting of science as a metaphysic, it makes less of the matter because it is able to fall back on a higher than earthly order—that of theology. Here also, it is a poet who points the way; as Valéry

27 *Journal,* 2 October, 1895.
28 See Valéry's letter which prefaces the book of Rideau, *Introduction à la pensée de Paul Valéry.*

preceded Merleau-Ponty, so Claudel precedes Gabriel
Marcel. In a letter written in 1903 to André Gide, Claudel
says:

> My great joy is to think that we are witnessing the
> twilight of nineteenth-century science. . . . What a de-
> liverance even for the scientist himself who will hence-
> forth have full freedom to give himself up to the con-
> templation of things, without having to support the
> nightmare of an "explanation."[29]

The "twilight" of nineteenth-century science delivered men
from the necessity of looking at the exterior world with
"ready-made eyes," fashioned by the empiricists.[30] Modern
poetry is the discovery that the "great diamond" has facets
infinite in number of which no two are alike. The following sentences are from Claudel's *L'Art Poétique,* but they
might easily have come from *L'Introduction à la Méthode
de Léonard de Vinci:* "It is stupid to think that any object
of knowledge can be exhausted,"[31] and again: "Each thing
springs forth as *new, to be explained by reference to itself
alone.*"[32] Although Catholics and atheists may conceive the
absurd in different ways, the result, at least in what concerns aesthetics, is the same—a return to things in themselves.

Before taking up what constitutes the second phase of
the return to the concrete—*engagement,* it will be necessary to point out that the first—the interest in the exterior
world in and for itself that we have discovered in Rimbaud,
Gide, Valéry, has become increasingly noticeable on the
contemporary French scene.

The most fascinating and elusive object of historical
study is the psychology of an epoch—those mental traits
so fundamental that their presence is everywhere sensed,

29 *Correspondance de Claudel et Gide,* NRF, 1949, p. 48.
30 See Sartre, *L'Homme Ligoté, Situations I,* p. 299.
31 *Mercure de France,* 1913, p. 26.
32 *Ibid.,* p. 28.

and yet which cannot be clearly defined. The people of whom they were characteristic took them for granted, if indeed they were ever aware of them at all; and consequently such traits never come to any very explicit formulation. Their simultaneous appearance in all fields of cultural activity is perhaps what is most striking about them. It might be possible to explain why two scientific discoveries should be made at the same time by men working in different parts of the world in total ignorance of one another, but why should there be an obvious consanguinity between the sonnets of Petrarch and the frescoes of Giotto—or between the art of Cézanne and the theories of Husserl?

For modern art since Cézanne, like literature since the symbolists, has been a return to things in themselves. As we contrasted Proust and Gide, so we might contrast the impressionists and Cézanne. Monet did a series of paintings of the cathedral at Rouen under varying conditions of light. What Monet painted was less the cathedral itself, than the cathedral as a many faceted reflector of light and colour. It is not the object that is of central concern here, but the sensations to which it gives rise; just as, in Proust's *La Prisonnière,* the reader's attention is drawn less to Albertine, than to the "sensation" of which she is the cause—that of jealousy. With Cézanne, we enter upon a new era during which art will strive in a number of ways to see objects in their full, non-human independence. Perception is not guided by the intelligence, it is warped by it. This is the insight upon which the vision of Cézanne is based. His whole endeavour is to capture objects before his intelligence has organized them into something quite different from what they really are; as Valéry discovered that the sea is upright like a steeply-pitched roof, rather than flat as the intelligence would have it. Cézanne draws dishes with several contours, because that is how they actually are before the intervention of the mind. ". . . The outline of objects," writes Merleau-Ponty in an article on Cézanne, "conceived as a line marking their boundaries, belongs not to the visible world, but to geometry."[33] Also Cézanne will paint a dish on a table which is almost at eye level in such a way that the inside of the dish is visible. Again, the perfect ellipse which a more orthodox artist would have drawn belongs to geometry and not to the totally naïve perception which acquaints us with things as they are rather than with things moulded to suit the exigencies of a rationality of which the non-human knows nothing. The exterior world does not, for example, submit itself to the laws of perspective; if it did, it would not have been necessary to invent them. A hill which we see to be very high, appears insignificant in a photograph; nevertheless, we saw the hill as it really was, distance had not diminished it; but the photograph, by placing the hill in perspective, had worked a distortion. In the same way, a moving picture of an approaching train, causes the train to appear to grow larger more quickly than would be the case in direct perception.[34] Delacroix had suspected these truths, for he notes that it is necessary to correct "that rigid perspective which (in actuality) distorts our view of objects by its very exactitude."[35] Not only is every object unique and not simply an aggregate of detachable qualities, but it is united in many subtle ways to all that surrounds it. If we are able to recognize a piece of paper on a desk as white even though the room is illuminated by a yellow light, it is because every object in the room has been equally affected; and therefore we can no more see an object as it really is by isolating it, than we can understand the poetic value of a verse by examining each of its words separately.[36] The mistake of the impressionists was to break down, to analyse away the "wholeness" of each perception. (Art criticism refers commonly to the "sci-

[33] "Le Doute de Cézanne," in *Sens et Non-Sens*, Nagel, 1948, p. 26.
[34] See *La Phénoménologie de la Perception*, p. 300. Furthermore, the investigations of William Stern, Charlotte Bühler, Heinz Werner, etc., seem to prove that the world as we know it does not exist for children, who must *learn* to look at things as do adults.
[35] Quoted by Camus, *L'Homme Révolté*, NRF, 1951, p. 332.
[36] "Scientific objectivity consists in considering structures separately, in isolating them from the whole: under these conditions they appear with other characteristics." (Sartre, *L'Etre et le Néant*, p. 375.)

ence" of the impressionists and post-impressionists.) In that way they were able to convince themselves of the paramount importance of light, which, in reality, does not alter objects in any fundamental way, it simply puts them in other "registers." The artist whose ambition it is to submit himself to the object must try to create a world within a world:

> . . . Every touch upon the canvas must satisfy an infinity of conditions, and that is why Cézanne would sometimes meditate for an hour before placing it. It must, as Bernard says, "contain the air, the light, the object, the distance, the character, the design, the style." Expressing what *exists* is an infinite task.[37]

The "infinite task" of expressing what exists was carried on by Cézanne's successors, the cubists.[38] The influence of the cubists which is everywhere apparent in fashion, architecture, furniture, etc. seems grotesquely out of proportion with the popular appeal of their work. May the reason be sought in the fact that the paintings of the cubists lead us further than any of their predecessors toward a clear vision of the chaos that is a world of things incommensurate with anything human. A hostile nature can only be so by partaking in some measure of the human—it is therefore less terrible than the massive indifference of the absurd.

Light, which is the substance of most impressionist pictures, forms no part of the preoccupations of the cubists who return to the basic concern of painting—the representation of depth on a flat surface. Since Cézanne, the

---

[37] "Le Doute de Cézanne," *Sens et Non-Sens*, p. 28. In one of his letters, Van Gogh wrote: "What is drawing? How does one achieve it? It is the act of forcing a passage through an invisible wall of iron which seems to be placed between what one feels and what one can do." (Quoted by Antonin Artaud in his *Van Gogh*, K. Editeur, 1947, p. 44.) Artaud remarks that ". . . reality is terribly superior to all history, all myths, all divinity, all 'surreality.' " (p. 29.)
[38] See Jean Paulhan's article entitled "La Peinture Cubiste," NNRF, April and May 1953. He writes that the first thing that strikes him about cubist painting is ". . . the almost obsessive position occupied in the picture by an apple, a packet of tobacco, a pack of cards, a bottle label, a table drawer."

classical solution, by perspective, had been discarded, and the cubists adopt the method of giving several views of the same object—a face, for example, seen both in full and in profile. Representation can go no further than this, unless it be to incorporate a bona fide object such as a piece of newspaper into the composition, and this is precisely what the cubists occasionally resorted to.

One of the purposes of this digression into the realm of art is to argue that, just as symbolism aspired to be music, so contemporary literature aspires to be painting. For the artist has a supreme recourse denied the writer. Instead of attempting to represent objects he is free to create objects of his own; and many cubist paintings are to be appreciated as objects in their own right and not as representations. It is in the power of the artist to eliminate the problem of the return to the concrete, and the history of literature, or at least of much literary theorizing, between the two wars shows that writers were groping for a similar solution.

The poet Ponge well illustrates the point under discussion. Merleau-Ponty speaks of Cézanne as trying to capture things as they were "before man."[39] Ponge is attempting the same thing. He wants to find out what objects were before they became obscured by the language of men, and by the uses to which they were put. Such an approach to things enables him to make some curious discoveries: "Man," he writes, "has no curiosity about, nor love for, his body or its parts. On the contrary, he shows a quite strange indifference towards them."[40] His definition of man is as convincing as the traditional and pretentious "thinking animal": "The idea of man is close to the idea of equilibrium."[41] The "scientific mind" will not take such observations on man very seriously, but science will find it increasingly difficult to pontificate, particularly about man himself. The key to man's real nature is not in some

[39] "Le Doute de Cézanne," in Sens et Non-Sens, p. 30.
[40] "Notes Premières de l'homme," Temps Modernes, No. 1, 1945.
[41] Ibid.

secret place where the patience of the anthropologists will eventually seek it out. The truth is there for everyone to see; man is, among other things, a feat of equilibrium. There is no "deeper" truth concerning him, but we have grown so accustomed to looking for one, that observations like those of Ponge strike us as ludicrous, or childish. And they are childish—in the sense of naïve. Ponge, like Cézanne and Valéry, has the gift of "unprejudiced" senses; he has been able to overcome his education. "Real education," according to Valéry, "consists in undoing one's initial education."[42]

Ponge is not alone. Guillevic's *Art Poétique* might serve as a manifesto for almost all of modern French poetry:

> Je ne parle pas pour moi,
> Je ne parle pas en mon nom,
> ce n'est pas de moi qu'il s'agit . . .

> Je parle pour tout ce qui est,
> Au nom de tout ce qui a forme et pas de forme.
> Il s'agit de tout ce qui pèse,
> De tout ce qui n'a pas de poids . . . .[43]

As an example of what he means, here is a "still life," quoted in its entirety:

> Un pot de terre,
> Un papier vague,
> Un verre à vin.

> Si tout se perd,
> Tout se revient.[44]

We are not concerned with the aesthetic value of such verse, but with the surprising extent to which it is typical. In his

42 Marginal note to *Introduction à la Méthode de Léonard de Vinci, Œuvres de Paul Valéry*, NRF, 1938, p. 77.
43 In *Gagner*, NRF, 1949, p. 271.
44 *Ibid.*, 1949, p. 23.

Panorama de la Nouvelle Littérature Française, Gaetan Picon writes of present-day French poetry: "The strength of poetry no longer comes from the isolation of a special diction, but from the world, from life itself—*from the attachment of an open consciousness to an inexhaustible world.*"[45] The poetry of Reverdy ". . . although it is a poetry that moves us, nevertheless places the object in the foreground . . .";[46] that of Eluard is ". . . *an enumeration of the world of the senses:* it consists in 'calling things by their names.' "[47] There is in Follain ". . . a profound sense of the mystery of existence, of the eternal order in which the most ordinary gestures and the humblest objects inhere. . . ."[48] Prévert's poetry is a ". . . Poetry of reality, a poetry of the real world and of the modern world. . . ."[49] And examples are not exhausted. Henri Michaux, like Camus and Malraux, is sensitive more to the absurd in our world of disintegrating absolutes than to the unexpected beauties of a world "before man." Occasionally, however, he seems to combine both attitudes:

> There was a time when I was a bundle of nerves. Now I am on a new track:
> I set an apple on the table. Then I set myself in the apple. What utter calm![50]

Michaux's peculiar sardonic whimsicality does not detract from the significance of such a passage.

Style has all but disappeared from modern painting which, to quote Albérès ". . . insists upon being a contemplation of objects submitted to other objects and not to human aesthetics; it [cubism] seeks to rid art of its humanity and of its arbitrary but inveterate habits, to penetrate into reality in the manner of the mystics. . . ."[51] Authors,

---

[45] p. 29.
[46] p. 133.
[47] p. 148.
[48] p. 167.
[49] p. 190.
[50] "Lointaine Intérieure," in *L'Espace du Dedans,* NRF, 1945, p. 205.
[51] *L'Aventure Intellectuelle du Vingtième Siècle,* p. 126.

however, unlike the cubists, cannot create objects of their own; if literature is to exist it must make use of words and therefore of a style, and the reader is necessarily twice removed from the object described. Discontent with this state of affairs led to what Jean Paulhan has called "terrorism" in literature, or a widespread mistrust of language for its alleged incapacity to express what is demanded of it. Words come to be regarded as serving more to betray thought than to convey it, and there is general regret that words, like cubist paintings, cannot be the things themselves. According to Paulhan, modern poetry seeks ". . . a sort of lost attachment of diction to the things of this world;"[52] and a certain Reich, refusing all compromise, created letters of his own which appear on the page in relief.[53] The alternative to Reich's material creation is silence, and Sartre attributes to Jules Renard the invention of a "literature of silence." Maurice Blanchot is its theorist. Much of *La Part du Feu* is a meditation upon the strange fact that the goal of language is its own suppression. The function of a word is to make superfluous the actual presence of the thing signified. Ideally, therefore, the language which fully accomplishes its mission, annihilates the universe. But having supplanted everything that exists, it no longer signifies anything—it becomes that silence which is ". . . the ultimate possibility of words."[54] It has already been remarked that Valéry considered what he wrote a by-product of more serious occupations; his poetry, at best, an "experiment." Though all of us have by intentionality immediate access to things, language necessarily introduces a separation which no amount of

---

[52] *Les Fleurs de Tarbes*, NRF, 1941, p. 35.
[53] *Ibid.*, p. 36.
[54] *La Part du Feu*, NRF, 1949, p. 41. This idea is less fanciful than our summary treatment makes it appear. Blanchot applies it very effectively in his studies on Kafka and Mallarmé. It is, incidentally, impossible not to be continually and forcibly reminded of *L'Imaginaire* or *L'Etre et le Néant*, in reading what Blanchot has to say about language. "The word gives me being, but it gives it to me deprived of being. It is the absence of being, its nothingness, that which remains of it when it has lost its being; that is, the single fact that it is not." (*La Part du Feu*, p. 325.) As we shall see, this sentence could be used, word for word, to describe, instead of language, the mental image as it is presented in *L'Imaginaire*.

literary ingenuity can overcome. "Terrorism," which is the refusal to accept such a limitation leads to silence. We may, with no inconvenience to ourselves, deny the existence of the exterior world, but it could be dangerous to convince oneself that language is no fit instrument of communication, that words are not in some way related to the things they represent. Such was the experience of Brice Parain, the philosopher of "terrorism," who, after a long revolt against language, hints at a reconciliation in these terms: "At the end of a long period of letting go, I have learned that powers of mediation are charged with the duty of forbidding man to depart outside himself: at his extreme limits they set in his way those barriers on the further side of which destruction threatens him."[55] Parain belongs to the generation which preceded that of Sartre, and his research on the inadequacies of language, while typical of a philosophical tradition which worried so inordinately about "what we can know," is, at the same time, part of the attempt to suppress the distance between man and what he perceives. Parain is motivated above all by "the obsession of intuitive knowledge; that is, knowledge without an intermediary."[56]

But what Sartre says of Parain is equally true of the most important movement in French letters between the two wars—surrealism. Blanchot is struck by the resemblance between many surrealist ideas and phenomenology;[57] and, indeed, "automatic writing" is a kind of "literary reduction," it being assumed that we are in immediate touch with reality, which ratiocination obscures instead of revealing. However, surrealism is not only confidence in the reality of appearance, in the certitude of the *cogito*, but confidence in the ability of language not to "express"

[55] *Retour à la France*, quoted by Sartre in "Aller et Retour," *Situations I*, p. 189.
[56] *Situations I*, p. 208. Similarly, Alphonse de Waelhens writes of Rilke: ". . . He sees the necessity of a reconciliation [of man and his world] which he is still incapable of conceiving." (*Phénoménologie et Vérité*, Presses Universitaires, 1953, pp. 82–3.)
[57] See *La Part du Feu*, NRF, 1949, p. 93.

that reality, but to *be* it. That is, words can be made to *exist* like things instead of simply *representing* things not present. Surrealism purported to be the answer to terrorism.

The mistake of surrealism was one of emphasis rather than principle. If we know the truth, then our first concern should be to utilize it and not to enshrine it. If we are going to abolish thought (in the classical sense) as superfluous, then only action remains to us. It is consciousness itself which is the truth, and not words which are simply, as Sartre says: "existence in the presence of others."[58] Surrealism, therefore, would appear to have fallen between two stools—it was a revolutionary philosophy (most of the surrealists became communists) seeking to be an aesthetic.

If Parain gave fullest expression to the terrorist dilemma, he also, at least in part, has pointed toward the solution. In his thesis, *Recherches sur la Nature et les Fonctions du Langage,* he tells us that words are ". . . not natural signs for communicating knowledge of things directly to us, nor yet conventional signs for logical thinking (perhaps unrelated to fact) alone to play upon, but seeds of being, the prime movers of all invention."[59] Language is one of the ways in which human freedom exercises itself. To name is, in a sense, to create; as, in *La Chartreuse de Parme,* all that is required for Fabrice and the Duchess to fall in love, is that one of them use the word. If words cannot be things, they can at least have an action upon things. Michel Leiris has declared that it was his intention in writing *L'Age d'Homme* to write a book that would be an act.[60] Blaise Cendrars dedicated *Rhum*: "To the young men of today who are tired of literature, to prove to them that a novel can also be an act." According to Sartre: "To speak is to act,"[61] and Maurice Blanchot has written:

[58] *Situations I,* p. 237.
[59] NRF, 1942, p. 58.
[60] Introduction to the new edition of *L'Age d'Homme,* NRF, 1946.
[61] *Situations II,* p. 72.

". . . Literature ought . . . to be free, that is to say, committed."[62] Maurice Nadeau is of the same opinion: ". . . For me a work of art . . . is . . . a means of acting."[63] In his *Theses on Feuerbach* of 1845, Marx wrote: "Up to now philosophers have merely interpreted the world in various ways. The time has come to transform it." It has taken literature almost a century to become conscious of similar potentialities within itself.

II

It is probable that *engagement*, in the elementary sense of making literature useful, has, with insignificant interruptions, always existed. The fact is obscured, however, because what is useful in one society is not in another. Up until very recently, literature was produced as a *distraction* by and for a small group of idle, cultivated people whose happiness was menaced by one thing only—ennui. This group, where it has not vanished altogether, no longer constitutes "society." The *malaise* of contemporary literature is largely the result of an attempt to go on producing for a market that no longer exists, and to justify itself by pointing to practically all of literary history during which writing was essentially a diversion, however noble a one, for both author and public. If literature is to continue to be a distraction in the traditional sense, then an author has the choice of writing for the reading public, that is, of producing trash, since his work will respond to no fundamental need, or of "dedicating himself to his art" and writing for a group whose place in contemporary society is no longer a functional one.

The romantics, however, introduced a different conception of literature (the latest manifestation of which was surrealism), according to which it is not the function of the artist to amuse, but to teach; for some, even, literature appeared to be not a part of life, but a way of life.

62 *La Part du Feu*, NRF, 1949, p. 104.
63 *Littérature Présente*, Corrêa, 1952, p. 17.

A noblewoman of Samuel Johnson's acquaintance believed that all men should be equal, but it was considered bad taste on Johnson's part to suggest that the lady's footman be invited to dine with them. The romantics had to dine with footmen. What rationalists had only *thought,* the romantics had to *live.* With the collapse of the *ancien régime,* the littérateur fell heir to a responsibility greater than he had ever known.[64] Poets and writers undertook to fulfil the functions of priest, seer and prophet for a society suddenly bereft of its channels of communication with the beyond—King and Church. The Promethean romantic is the remote ancestor of *l'homme absurde;* the difference is that one hundred and fifty years ago man could not yet endure a world without God and so made one of himself. It is true that to increasing ingratitude and incomprehension authors respond with increasing withdrawal, until the century which had seen Chateaubriand, Lamartine and Hugo engaged in politics is brought to a close by the symbolists, of whom Valéry has said that however they differed among themselves they had one trait in common—a contempt for the public.[65] All of which is in no way incompatible with the conviction that literature is of all the means at our disposal the most apt to lead us to the good life or even beyond. We read in *Les Fleurs de Tarbes:* "I do not know whether it is true that writers were once content to amuse respectable people. . . . The most modest among us expect a religion, an ethic and the meaning of life at last revealed."[66] Consider the example of I. A. Richards who looks upon poetry as being: ". . . capable of saving us; it is a perfectly possible means of overcoming chaos."[67] Claudel is insulted if we suggest that his work is "literature." Aragon uses his art as a weapon in the class war.

[64] A responsibility that many, of course, were glad to turn away from. There is much of romanticism, including its melancholy, in Joubert's remark: "The revolution has turned my mind away from the real world by making it too horrible for me." (*Pensées,* Perrin, 1922, p. 4.)
[65] See *Existence du Symbolisme,* Stols (Maestricht), 1939.
[66] Jean Paulhan, *Les Fleurs de Tarbes,* NRF, 1941, p. 15.
[67] *Science and Poetry,* Psyche Miniatures, 1926, p. 82.

In brief: "It seems that one cannot be an honest man of letters, unless one is disgusted with literature."[68]

Obviously *engagement* in a broad sense is not new. The question by now is not whether literature shall take upon itself the burden of the times, but *how* it shall do so.

Particularly in what concerns *engagement*, it is well not to forget that the Frenchman is separated from the Anglo-Saxon by certain differences of temperament and historical circumstance. When Gide writes: "I hate the family!", the Englishman is surprised to learn that for certain Frenchmen this is a provocation. Similarly, most English-speaking intellectuals would find existentialist political philosophy easy to accept; some of it may even seem platitudinous to them; and if it has provoked such an uproar in France, it is because the need for it, and consequently the opposition to it, is greater than in the Anglo-Saxon countries. French political thinking is "logical," hence the institutions which issue from it, or which it supports, tend to petrify. Thus French capitalism, by its irresponsibility, is twenty years behind even the American. In politics, only the two extremes are logical—to compromise is to be content with "muddling through." There are no solutions in government; but theoretically, logically, there are solutions, which are that much more passionately defended for having been "reasoned out." French politics is the history of a despised (if not always weak) "third force" leading a precarious existence between two powerful uncompromising extremes, and what many Frenchmen object to in *engagement* is its "illogical" refusal to belong to one of them.

When Lionel Trilling writes: ". . . to organize a new union between our political ideas and our imagination—in all our cultural purview there is no work more necessary,"[69] he has the unhesitating approval of most of his readers. Sartre is saying precisely the same thing in France, where his ideas are received with hostility and incompre-

68 *Les Fleurs de Tarbes*, p. 17.
69 "The Function of the Little Magazine," in *The Liberal Imagination*, p. 100.

hension—to begin with, that of Gide. What has happened is that on the one hand, writers who, like Gide, attach a vital importance to the survival of literature confuse *engagement* with partisanship which they rightly consider incompatible with literature; while on the other hand, writers who are prepared to sacrifice literature, the militants of the two extremes, see that *engagement* is *not* partisanship. Sartre is therefore attacked by one group for being a partisan, by the other for not being one. He has, as usual, everyone against him—an almost sure sign that whatever he is saying merits our closest attention.

The theory of *engagement* is not a crude one. The hasty or prejudiced reader overlooks the nuances which make all the difference, and the result is the total confusion just described. We have no intention of summarizing *Qu'est-ce que la Littérature?* and other essays bearing on the subject in hand; they are readily accessible to everyone. We will try simply to define *engagement* and to bring out a number of neglected points in respect to it, after which we will be able to consider it in a more strictly philosophical context.

Sartre has nowhere defined *engagement* in so many words, but in *Qu'est-ce que la Littérature?* appears the following remark which will serve as an excellent point of departure: "For us there is no question either of escaping into the eternal or of abdicating before . . . the 'historical process.' "[70] Let us begin with the first condition—there is to be no attempt to "escape into the eternal."

We have already discussed that characteristic of our culture which consists in looking upon reality as somehow concealed "behind" what we see and hear and that to reach it we must withdraw into a contemplation, the essence of which is a mistrust of the senses. The nature of the reality we seek with such persistence, and devotion, may change its name from century to century, from place to place, but it is always *eternal*. That is what makes it precious. Whether God is one or many, implacable or merciful, omnipotent or circumscribed, he is eternal and

that is why he is worshipped, for it is in his timelessness
that he differs most from what he creates. Religion, however, is but one of the many ways by which men try to
palliate their tragic awareness of their mortality. Literature
is another. Literary criticism is often an attempt to discover that common element of great books that causes
them to endure. The possessor of the secret will be able
to address himself to future generations and will not be
led to attaching an exaggerated importance to the ephem-
eral concerns of his own time. It is observed that a great
artist bestows immortality upon whatever he touches; it
therefore follows that genius resides in the manner of
treatment and not in the subject treated. The duty of the
artist is plainly to devote himself to his art and to hold in
contempt anything not directly related to it. The theory of
art for art is no longer asserted with such unqualified
directness, it has even become popular to denounce it; but
so closely is it woven into our thinking about aesthetics
that its influence remains enormous and is probably most
apparent in the familiar notion that no important creative
writer can afford to allow himself to be distracted by the
affairs of the day. "Valéry, Proust, Suarès, Claudel and
myself," writes Gide, ". . . if I search for that by which
we shall be recognized . . . as belonging to the same age
. . . I believe that it is the grand contempt we had for the
events of the day."[71]

Is it true that the subject matter of a work of art has
nothing to do with its value? Obviously our appreciation
of one of Rodin's statues is not affected by the fact that it
depicts an aged prostitute, and it is possible to prefer a still
life to *Le Radeau de la Méduse*. Fine verse may be written
on any subject. It is nevertheless by no means certain that
form can or should be separated from content; but whatever the truth may be in the plastic arts and poetry, it is
sure that prose must say something; and *what* is said can
rarely be imagined apart from *how* it is said. The value
of a prose style is inseparable from the value of what it

71 *Journal*, 19 January 1948.

says. Just as it is unthinkable that an inferior painter teach us through his art to look with "new eyes" upon the world around us, it is difficult to imagine a great literary craftsman whose work would not be a "criticism of life," whose work would have nothing important to tell us. It is for this reason that we must accept Sartre's statement: ". . . No one could suppose for a moment that a good novel could be written in praise of anti-semitism."[72] But we can go further. The message that every great style carries to its readers is a commentary upon some matter of immediate concern. It is a response to a need. The goal of great literature is not literature itself. The purpose of mediaeval sculpture was as much to teach as to decorate, and the original purpose of great literature is to teach as well as to "decorate." The pedant is he who mistakes literature for ornamentation. Consequently, as has often been observed, a great writer is invariably a perfect representative of his time, which he succeeds in transcending only by identifying himself with it. As in the case of the dramatist, no portrayal of a type which is not also that of a unique individual will convince us, no author is "universal" who does not share in the uniqueness of the period in which he lived. We remarked that literary criticism is often a search for the formula which permits certain authors to survive. In the case of the French classics, for example, it would be, in part, the fact that their subject is man himself, who, since the experience of centuries seems to teach him nothing, will always find himself faithfully portrayed in seventeenth-century literature. Such a judgment, however, overlooks the fact that La Bruyère in writing his

---

[72] "Qu'est-ce que la Littérature?", *Situations II*, p. 112. It is important to remember that throughout this passage, we refer exclusively to prose literature. There is as much difference between prose and poetry as between architecture and painting, so that literary criticism might benefit from having the term "literature" dropped from its vocabulary. Sartre distinguishes between prose which says something precise (or should) and poetry which need not necessarily. It will be objected that eighteenth-century poetry had something quite definite to say. But this is an "essentialist" objection, based upon faith in the possibility of defining poetry for all time. As a matter of fact, there is between a Dryden and a Rimbaud a difference of kind. The reader is referred to Roland Barthes's chapter on poetry in his admirable *Le Degré Zero de l'Ecriture*, Editions du Seuil, 1953.

Caractères in no way showed a "contempt for the events of the day" in order to be able to give his attention to the human heart which is mistakenly believed to be unchangeable. The news of the day at the Court of Louis XIV was the news of human relations. We forget that for the aristocrats who created French classicism, there were no economic or social problems; their one problem was their conduct toward one another, and as a result a book like *Les Caractères* may be considered a response to a social need—but one that has been since replaced by others of an infinitely greater urgency.[73] There was no danger that the thirty years war destroy European civilization; and since a social consciousness had not yet come into being, we can hardly reproach the authors of the day for being indifferent to the hardships of the peasantry.

We no longer live in the seventeenth century. Wars no longer serve the purpose of raising up or casting down the *gloire* of privileged individuals, they are universal catastrophes, and the writer who does not devote his talent to combating their menace, far from following the example of great predecessors, is turning away from it; far from protecting their heritage, he is helping to destroy it. No contemporary novelist has the right to cite as a precedent Jane Austen, who, living at the time of the Napoleonic Wars, does not make a single reference to them in all her books.

We have been arguing that literature, far from incurring a risk by mixing itself with what is of deepest concern for the Age that produces it, draws its very strength from such involvement. It is this that gives weight to the programme outlined by Sartre in his *Présentation des Temps Modernes:* ". . . In *littérature engagée,* the *engagement* must, in no circumstances, cause us to forget the literature, and . . . our preoccupation must be to serve literature by giving it

---

[73] Stendhal calls La Bruyère "empty" and "puerile," and gives as the reason: "As a fine peach lasts but a few days, a given mentality (*esprit*) has gone by in two hundred years, and much more quickly where there has been a revolution in the relations of classes within a society. . . ." (*Vie de Henry Brulard,* Divan, 1949, Vol. I, p. 457.)

a new meaning, quite as much as to serve the community by giving it the literature that suits it." We cannot determine what the questions of our time shall be, but we can determine that what we write shall be an answer. Whether or not our answers come to be considered "literature" is not the point, because in any case there will be no literature apart from them. However "universal" we attempt to make ourselves, it is not within our power to live in any century but our own, and if it is one which requires that literature give way before journalism, there is nothing we can do—except transform journalism. It was after all precisely in such a way that Milton's *Areopagitica* and Pascal's *Lettres Provinciales* came into being.

With that we have discussed but half the problem, and by far the easier half. Granted the principle of *engagement*, to the attainment of what ends is an author to exert his influence? The second part of our definition will help us here. There must be no submission to the "historical process."

It is often said that dialectical materialism and leftist political philosophy in general are the modern guardians of the rationalist tradition, while romanticism is responsible for recent outbreaks of irrationality, such as the philosophy of Bergson and fascism. If the nineteenth century, as we maintain, is to be interpreted as an attempt many times repeated to re-establish a spiritual anchorage amid the *Sturm und Drang* provoked by the collapse of fixed values, then the vital distinction is not to be made between marxism and romanticism, whose objective was the same, the recovery of a lost absolute, but between these two and some third intellectual movement seeking a solution in other directions, looking ahead rather than behind. It was science that enabled eighteenth century rationalism to survive the blow that romanticism had dealt it. But some of the greatest authors of the last century, in spite of the general enthusiasm for science, considered rationalism compromised beyond all hope of restoration. We cannot safeguard a political institution by the firm determination that it shall remain unchanged, but by accepting the modifications that the times impose. This is equally true of an intellectual institution like rationalism which survives, not in the thought of those who refuse its conclusions, but in the writings of men ready to accept them as a basis of further exploration. The rationalism of the *philosophes,* like that of the Greeks, ended, as perhaps every rationalism must, in scepticism, and the contemporary form of that scepticism is the belief that the universe is absurd. Existentialism carries rationalism forward in the sense that it refuses to take refuge from the absurd in either religion, "objectivity" or communism, but instead attempts to build a philosophy which will take it into account. That is why such writers as Baudelaire, Dostoievsky, Nietzsche and Stendhal seem so close to us; they realized that the search for an absolute was an anachronism, that rationalism had freed men who were persisting nevertheless in remaining enslaved to one final truth or another. Dialectical materialism is a curious survival of another age— it is rationalism in a fossilized state. It came into being in the days when science was a sort of theology, in the days of Taine, Renan and Berthelot, celebrated for the unhappy remark: "The world is now without mystery." For the marxist mind, the world is still "without mystery," everything is explained by the "historical process" to which men may confide themselves as the Christian confides himself to God.

Existentialism as a political philosophy is based on the belief that the first condition of a political action which aims at improving our lot is that it be a response to an *immediate* human need, and furthermore that it should not aim beyond the satisfaction of that need. Systems which aim at the definitive elimination of political problems are suspect, because when men attach themselves to absolutes, their purpose is less the reaching of their objective than it is the achievement of that mental tranquillity which comes with the possession of what is taken to be the Truth. For too many communists, marxism is no longer an action, but

a faith; no longer a remedy, but a religion. A political programme which does not alter from week to week according
to circumstance has solidified into a "concept" and can no
longer respond with maximum efficiency to a concrete situation. A programme, on the contrary, designed to satisfy
an obvious need cannot be a harmful one. Anti-semitism
in Germany before the war is an illustration of the viciousness of abstract thinking in these matters—the anti-semite
being an example, on the lowest level, of the way in which
the desire for final solutions supplants the more difficult
method of judging each event on its own merits, taking into
consideration the very large proportion of uniqueness it
inevitably contains. In politics, as in our contemplation of
the exterior world, we utilize perspectives which instead of
ordering reality distort it.[74] In politics as in philosophy we
need a return to the concrete, and that is why we read in
Sartre's *Présentation des Temps Modernes* ". . . we have no
political or social programme . . ."[75] On the political as on
the metaphysical level there must be no absolutes, for an
absolute is never an expedient, it is a resting place which
helps us to forget that man, since he has no "essence," has
to be reinvented each day.[76] It is in this way that we are
to interpret *Les Mains Sales.* Hugo, like a great many
young bourgeois, became a communist because communism simplifies things; life otherwise is "too difficult."[77]
Hoederer, on the other hand, has accepted the difficulty of
living without a formula that will embrace all possible con-
tingencies. Hugo comes gradually to suspect that Hoederer
is right, but rather than adapt himself to changed circumstances, he sacrifices his common sense to his "devotion to

[74] The sacrifice of immediacy to concept is not confined to politics, it manifests itself in innumerable ways. See for example Lionel Trilling's essay
"Reality in America" (in *The Liberal Imagination*), where he speaks of the
American critics' initial mistrust of Henry James because he was too far removed from the workshop; and, on the contrary, their friendliness toward the
"peasant" Dreiser.
[75] *Situations II*, p. 28. "People want to forget a problem whose existence
Europe has suspected ever since the Greeks: might not man's estate be such
that there is no good solution?" Merleau-Ponty, *Humanisme et Terreur*, NRF,
1947, Preface XXXIV.
[76] *Situations II*, p. 313.
[77] Deuxième Tableau, Scène trois.

the cause" and assassinates Hoederer, the one person in the world he admires. The very *raison d'être* of an absolute is to be inflexible.

Certainly it is no easy task to persuade people to give up their "certitudes" for it is by such means that they shield themselves from the absurd, and consequently from their own nothingness. It is difficult just to exist, and not to pretend that one's life is in some way justified. ". . . How happy one must be," writes Sartre in *La Nausée*, "to be only a Legion of Honor and a moustache while no one sees the rest. . . . He has the Legion of Honor, swine [*Salauds*] have a right to exist. . . . I have the right to exist, therefore I have the right not to think. . . ."[78] Goetz, in *Le Diable et le Bon Dieu*, for as long as he incarnated Evil or Good had the right "not to think," for he was something well defined, like someone who wears the ribbon of the Legion of Honor. Goetz as Evil or Goetz as a Saint did not have to think because, in doubt, he always did evil or always did good. He existed like a *thing*, like a tool with a definite function, like something which is justified. But to exist like a *man* is less easy:

> GOETZ: . . . I want to be a man among men.
> NASTY: Only that?
> GOETZ: I know: it's the hardest of all.[79]

Most French intellectuals are not at peace with themselves until they have adopted or worked out a set of principles which explain why conditions are what they are and what is to be done to correct them. This is as true of literature and art as of politics; French literary history is full of *cénacles*, schools, movements and manifestos to a degree unknown elsewhere. Also, a doctrine may be considered of such importance as to be applicable to the whole of life, to both literature and politics—the "classicism" of Maurras, and the "revolution" of the surrealists. A French

[78] *La Nausée*, NRF, 1938, p. 135.
[79] Onzième tableau, Scène deux.

author who belongs to no recognized group runs the risk of not being taken very seriously, and Gide maintains that if Dostoievsky was not, at first, well received or understood in France it was because he could be fitted into no known category. "If I consider," writes Marcel Arland, "those whom I esteem the most, I discover hardly any of them who are not the prisoners of an attitude, of a formula, worse still, of the need for a formula."[80]

With every French writer under constant pressure both from within and without to become a partisan, it is not surprising that partisanship be regarded as one of the greatest menaces to which French letters are exposed. Hence Gide's scandalized outcry against *engagement*, which he judged too hastily. He points to Barrès as a typical example of an *écrivain engagé*, but Gide himself has told us why Barrès cannot be considered as such: "Barrès appeals far less to reason than to principles; the principles are there in order that reason need not exert itself."[81] A writer who has "engaged" himself, in the sense that Sartre attaches to the word, has not done so in the hope of bringing about the triumph of a fixed principle, but because he sees that Europe is about to be ground to pieces between the upper and nether stones of two fixed principles—communism and property as a divine right. *La Condition Humaine* and not Barrès *Leurs Figures* is *littérature engagée*. Malraux was interested not in principles, but in what could be done to restore to the immense majority of men, their dignity as human beings; that is, their freedom. For reasons of expediency, it may frequently be necessary to join forces with the absolutists, as Malraux associated himself with the communists (without ever becoming a member of the party) between the two wars, because only communism held out some hope of stopping the spread of fascism. In Sartre's *Les Mains Sales*, Hoederer considers that the interests of the people would best be served by a temporary alliance with the fascists. In politics,

80 *Essais et Nouveaux Essais Critiques*, NRF, 1952, pp. 33, 34.
81 *Incidences*, NRF, 1924, p. 57.

if anything is to be accomplished at all, one must be prepared to have "dirty hands."

As we have seen, literature as an instrument rather than as an end is the rule, not the exception. In 1924, Jacques Rivière could write: "No age perhaps . . . has been so far removed as ours is from practising 'art for art's sake.' "[82] What is new is the invention of a provocative term and the suggestion that literature be made to serve comparatively "humble" ends. For most intellectuals, other members of the confraternity, including Sartre, are blockheads until proved innocent, and the word *engagement* whipped the critics into a frenzy of opposition. But, on the one hand, Sartre is as much opposed as are Rivière and Paulhan to "promethean" literature, to literature designed to serve, in the words of Rivière: "transcendental ends,"[83] and, on the other, an existentialist cannot be a partisan in the ordinary sense of the word. Consequently, it would hardly be an exaggeration to say that far from destroying literature, *engagement* is quite possibly its one chance of salvation. Between the "escape into the eternal" and submission to the "historical process," between the Yogi and the commissar, between the "promethean" and the partisan, *engagement* offers a middle course. For one hundred and fifty years, more or less, literature has not been content to be a simple "distraction." It is idle to wonder whether this has been the cause of a decline. The fact is that the world is no longer interpreted to the masses by the Church and Throne: and the newspapers that have taken their place are inevitably either tendentious or simple organs of propaganda. How is the truth to be made known if not by literature? In the face of increasingly efficient methods for the dissemination of lies, literature is one hope that they will not eventually swallow up the facts.

Most criticism of *engagement,* as we have explained, is irrelevant because it confuses *engagement* with partisan-

82 "La Crise du Concept de Littérature," NRF, 1 February 1924.
83 *Ibid.*

ship. There is, however, a better informed criticism,[84] which is based upon the feeling that no great book can be produced if its author allows his writing to be influenced in the slightest degree by considerations extraneous to it; that is, a work of art has its own exigencies, to which it is the duty of its creator to submit himself. What Gide tells us of Valéry's *La Pythie* is true in some measure of all art:

> Paul tells me . . . that *La Pythie* in its entirety grew out of a single line:
>
> Pâle, profondément mordue.
>
> He sought the rhyme, the rhymes. They dictated the form of the stanza, and the whole poem developed without his having known beforehand either what it would be like, or what he was going to say in it.[85]

It is this, no doubt, that makes aesthetic creation the most fascinating of human pursuits. A great writer is literally a creator; his work takes on life in the sense that it is never completely submissive to his will. A good novel is always a co-operative enterprise, with the characters portrayed taking an active and occasionally decisive part in their own formation. The novel which "proves" something, the novel which is refused all independence, rarely survives its own generation. The writer devoted to his art has for the *roman à thèse* an instinctive contempt. "A literary work containing theories," writes Proust in *Le Temps Retrouvé,* "is like an article with the price ticket left on it."

There are few subjects about which it is more dangerous to generalize than aesthetics; but among its few and uncertain principles, that which we have just exposed is one of the most solid, and in so far as *engagement* is prejudicial to it, it is probably destructive of literature. But, apart

---

[84] That of Marcel Arland, for example. See *Essais et Nouveaux Essais Critiques,* NRF, 1952, pp. 281–314.
[85] *Journal,* 2 January 1923.

from the novels of Sartre himself, Malraux has furnished us with proof enough that a *roman engagé* is not necessarily a *roman à thèse,* as have Forster's *A Passage to India* and Lionel Trilling's *The Middle of the Journey,* two good examples of *littérature engagée* as we have defined it; Forster's book exposing in masterly fashion the inevitable viciousness of the most "enlightened" colonialism, while the hero of *The Middle of the Journey* refuses to believe that there can be no middle way between communism ánd the Church. If it is true, as we have maintained, that great writing is inseparable from the deepest concerns of the epoch of which it is a part, and if the deepest concerns of our own age are political, then it is in this direction that an author might well seek his inspiration. That some eminent novelists of the past completely ignored politics in their work proves only that politics were not at that time the omnipresent, obsessive affair they have since become, and not that politics are unsuitable matter for literary treatment. It is difficult to be a good novelist, but no more so in "deepening what one has in common than by cultivating one's points of difference."[86]

It must nevertheless be admitted that in some cases the author's personality, or the nature of his gifts, could not be adapted, without that extra artistic constraint which is destructive of art, to the requirements of a *littérature engagée.* Gide is a case in point. His play, *Robert, ou l'intérêt général,*[87] written during the period of his interest in communism, is probably (even in its modified form) one of the worst things he ever wrote. There is no doubt but what Gide's art would have been irreconcilable with a too exacting social consciousness. Obviously, *engagement* demands that Gide as a novelist and literary critic be sacrificed to the author of *Souvenirs de la Cour d'Assises* and *Voyage au Congo.* Even those who have a clear understanding of what is meant by *engagement* may here part company with Sartre. If Sartre has not seen fit to try to

86 Malraux, *Le Temps du Mépris,* NRF, 1935, p. 12.
87 Published in *Littérature Engagée,* NRF, 1950.

appease some of his critics with a long essay demonstrating the compatibility of *engagement* and literature, it is because he wishes it to be clearly understood that first things must come first, the survival of our way of life is of greater concern than that of literature. "Our way of life *is* our literature," it will be answered; and we realize suddenly that we are in the presence of one of those irreducible oppositions of temperament such as that which divides the believer and the non-believer. It was not without reason that we spoke of religion in connection with our remarks on the "immortality" of literature.

The general public, and in many cases the critics, are not aware that the catchwords of existentialism—liberty, despair, anguish, responsibility, etc., are like what is visible of an iceberg—only a small part of a mass which extends to great depths beneath the surface. So it is with *engagement*.

As we have seen, phenomenology starts from the premise of intentionality, according to which consciousness is always consciousness of something that is not itself; that is to say that consciousness is in immediate contact with things in themselves, and that consequently understanding involves no reference to an absolute of which things would be the shifting and unreliable appearance. Husserl's main preoccupation was to discover, by means of the phenomenological reduction, how it is possible for things to be in themselves meaningful. Existentialism, on the other hand, was created by philosophers who placed greater importance upon the *fact* that everything encountered by consciousness exists, than upon the question of the structures which makes these things comprehensible to us. The existentialists saw that the life of consciousness is not primarily one that reveals material things; on the contrary, consciousness is fundamentally "emotive" or, as Levinas expresses it: "In face of the real, is our primary attitude one of theoretical contemplation? Does not the world present itself to us, in its very being, as a centre of action, as a field of activity or of *solicitude.* . . ."[88] The most common state of consciousness is one of "feeling"—joy, fear, boredom, etc. But since consciousness can reflect only what exists, since feeling exists equally with matter, then the entire *existence* of consciousness, what would formerly have been considered our "subjective" life, becomes a fit subject of philosophical enquiry. Anguish, for example, *exists,* as much as does a tree or a chair and therefore has all the significance of anything contained in the "objective" world. All this has already been discussed and our purpose in recalling it is to show that to confer an ontological status upon subjectivity, to recognize that material things have no essential primacy is at the same time to declare the uniqueness of every human existence.

Husserl set himself the task of explaining how every object could be absolutely unique and yet comprehensible. For an object is not simply an agglomeration of interchangeable qualities. No colour can be separated from its object; it *is* the object, and not merely the means by which we perceive the "real" object hidden from us. Enlarging upon this idea, the existentialists pointed out that human existence must also be unique. Just as the colour red is never twice the same because it is inseparable from its object, so no two existences can ever be identical. Existence is not a sort of secondary quality added to others to produce "man." Man *is* his existence. There is no universal essence "man" to which existence is "added" as philosophy once supposed that secondary qualities were added to the primary ones to produce objects. Existence, in other words, precedes essence. (An idea which Malraux expresses in the formula: "A man is the sum of his acts.") A human being cannot first be defined as a rational being, as a "featherless biped" or whatever definition we prefer and *then* called an Englishman of a certain profession living in a certain city at a certain date, for these qualifications are his *only* existence, apart from them he has none. The fact

88 Levinas, *La Théorie de l'Intuition dans la Phénoménologie de Husserl,* Alcan, 1930, p. 174.

that a man is a doctor and not a railroad worker is part of his being; just as, in phenomenology, a difference of colour is tantamount to a difference of kind. *232787*

This uniqueness of human existence, the existentialists express by saying that man is "situated" (*en situation*), i.e. he has an historical and physical *engagement,* which are his sole existence, and which preclude "fixed points" of time and space. No one would deny that our ways of thinking change greatly from century to century, that we are the products of our time as a plant is the product of a certain soil and climate. But it is also felt that there is a substratum called "human nature" that is unchanging. And yet if we accept that man has no definition, that he is nothing more than the events of his life, then there can be no human nature in the abstract. Love, as Proust for instance depicts it, is a sentiment to be found only under certain historical conditions;[89] it is not the universally applicable phenomenon that novelists of "eternity-through-human-nature" like to think. The spirit of analysis that our society has cultivated for four centuries leads us to believe that the proper approach to any problem is the division of wholes into parts. To understand is to analyse into component parts. We have not sufficiently considered the possibility that analysis, rather than reducing matter to a greater coherence simply reveals other aspects of it *ad infinitum.* In any case, human psychology is not susceptible to understanding by analytical methods. A personality is always more than the sum of its parts. There exists no stock of universal sentiments to be conferred or withheld so as to make up a given character. A man is born into a certain historical situation and thereby acquires a nature which differs in kind from that of men of other ages.

Here, as is so often the case, existentialism is but the logical development of ideas which have been common coin since the eighteenth century. It might almost be said that existentialism is but the organization at last of rationalism's "chaos of clear ideas." It was no doubt this that

[89] See Sartre, *Situations II*, p. 20.

Sartre had in mind when he defined existentialism as little more than "an effort to develop all the consequences of a coherent atheism";[90] and what, in part, Merleau-Ponty means when he writes: ". . . In reading Husserl or Heidegger, several of our contemporaries had far less the feeling of encountering a new philosophy than of recognizing what they were waiting for."[91] We may seek to define man in one of two ways; by his origin or by his destination. For the Christian, the nature of man derives from the fact of his creation by a benevolent God. Rationalism, finding the problem of origins unclear, sought to explain man in terms of an alleged progress toward human "perfectibility." Generally speaking, we have long since abandoned both these hypotheses, and yet we continue to think and act as though we had not. Since we are in ignorance as to where we came from and whither we are going, it is time to conclude that we have neither origin nor goal, or at least that such preoccupations are idle.

We said that there is a physical as well as an historical *engagement,* and we shall have to insist upon this conception of man as a being "in-the-world"; for while most of us are ready to admit that "progress" and "human nature" are ideas that cannot be satisfactorily defined owing to the impossibility of establishing a fixed point in the stream of time, it is far less generally understood that we are no more firmly anchored in space than we are in time. If only for the reason that science, like art and literature, forms part of the physiognomy of an era, we might suspect its "objectivity." The fixed sun of Newton's universe corresponded to an age of essences in philosophy and eternal values in religion. Einstein's relativity is the "science" of existentialism; the science that naturally accompanies a return to the concrete. The decision that the sun should no longer be considered as stationary was reached while Husserl was seeking a means to replace the "stationary" essences of traditional philosophy by the concrete essences of phenom-

90 *L'Existentialisme est un Humanisme,* Nagel, p. 94.
91 *La Phénoménologie de la Perception,* Avant-Propos, II.

enology. We can no longer rely upon the sun as a spatial absolute; as a result astronomical calculations are immensely complicated, being based no longer upon a fixed point, but upon a moving observer. Our moral universe has undergone a parallel complication, for in the absence of moral absolutes, the only possible point of orientation is the individual himself. Each of us has his own moral "calculation" to work out, and it must be done alone, because no one else's "position" can possibly be identical with ours. Our position in space as well as in time is unique. The simple fact of my being *there* (*Dasein* in the language of Heidegger) and not elsewhere is not, as we saw a moment ago, an indifferent qualification to be added to the "essence" man, but a fact that alters our very being. The nature of love differs not only from age to age and perhaps from one generation to another, but also from one social class to another.[92] No existence is conceivable apart from a given position or situation, and one philosopher defines existence as ". . . the primordial traffic that position maintains with things."[93]

Inasmuch as there are no longer any absolute ethical or historical positions, *our* situation in the world becomes the "point of view" in relation to which the universe orients itself. The Christian's every act and thought receives a value depending upon its approximation to or remoteness from the Christian conception of the Good; in the absence of such a point of orientation, the act *itself* becomes the supreme Good. The Christian can do good or evil as he sees fit, only he himself is involved since Good exists independently of him; but when moral absolutes are refused,

[92] "At that time people were quoting an exchange between two American novelists on the subject of the very rich. 'The very rich are different from us,' one novelist had said, and the other had replied, 'Yes, they have more money.' It was generally felt that the second novelist had disposed of the first who had shown himself to be a snob, but Kermit Simpson suggested that the very rich are indeed different, that they move at a different tempo, have a different density and intensity, that they have different nerves and, when they are innocent, as Kermit was, a different kind of innocence." Lionel Trilling, *The Middle of the Journey*, Secker and Warburg, London, 1948, p. 221.
[93] J. Gérard, "Existence et Position," in *Revue Internationale de Philosophie*, No. 9, July 1949.

then our every act concerns not only ourselves but everyone, since it is *creative* of good or evil. Our every act is the only good and consequently, a recommendation that others conduct themselves in the same way. Each of us is a legislator, and therefore our responsibility is limitless. ". . . In choosing what I shall be, I choose what man shall be."[94] If existence precedes essence, then it is through existence that man comes into being, and since there is no "absolute" existence, but only individual ones, every existence is responsible for what man is. Furthermore, the universe being inexhaustible, each of us has, so to speak, a sector for which he is responsible, a view of things which is nowhere duplicated, a facet of reality which can exist only through us. "It is through me," writes Sartre, "that one aspect of the world is revealed: it is to me that it is revealed. . . . I can say that I *bear witness* to it, in the sense in which Gide tells us that 'we ought always to bear witness.' "[95]

Philosophy, religion and perhaps art are the story of man's attempt to become God. The history of his effort to forget that, attached indissolubly to a given time and place, it is not in his power to attain to knowledge true in all places and for all time. The point of view, for instance that of the Platonic Ideas or of scientific law, from which the universe is visible as a whole, can only be that of God, that of a Being not subject to the limitations imposed by man's estate, which is to be "situated." One of the most inveterate traits of human thought is this ambition to "see itself from a distance," not to be compromised by the fragile clay with which it must enter into association. Existentialism, on the contrary, accepts that: ". . . I cannot judge the world, since my judgments are a part of it."[96]

This notion of man as a creature who is "in the world" and who is therefore incapable of contemplating it as a whole, from a distance, is at the heart of existentialist

94 Sartre, *L'Existentialisme est un Humanisme*, Nagel, 1946, p. 27.
95 *L'Etre et le Néant*, NRF, 1943, p. 666.
96 Sartre, *Situations I*, p. 136.

thought. Great revolutions in the way we think do not come about because we solve the problems of our forefathers, but because we discover them to be irrelevant. Francis Bacon did not resolve the disputes of the nominalists and realists; he denounced as futile the entire system of which they were a representation. In somewhat the same way, existentialism has placed itself above the disagreements of the schools by discovering that their arguments have a common factor with which it is not in sympathy. Unlike the Middle Ages, however, the struggle in modern times took place not between rival philosophical schools, but between philosophy and science on the one hand, and religion on the other. Existentialism has lost interest in the debate of faith versus reason which has been the main concern of so many generations, not because it thinks it has found a solution in atheism, but because both the believer and the free-thinker are attempting the impossible. Because they aspire to escape from time and space, religion and science are fundamentally the same.

The rationalist conceives truth as necessarily universal and impersonal, absolute and objective. The two terms complement one another, for if there is an absolute truth, then there must be some impersonal quality (reason according to the rationalists) that men have in common by which the absolute can be known equally to all. Deny, on the other hand, the existence of the absolute, and presumably one can dispense at the same time with the "transcendental Ego"; that is, with that portion of the self which "transcends" subjectivity. It is at this point that the existentialists categorically refuse to accompany Husserl. There is much disagreement about the phenomenological reduction, but no radical division. When Husserl, however, in his later work attempted to reintroduce a transcendental Ego after having eliminated it through intentionality, there was widespread disaffection among his followers. It appeared to them that Husserl had compromised one of phenomenology's greatest achievements—the conception of consciousness as absolutely "pure," "containing" nothing not exterior to itself. The question, of course, was of particular importance for Sartre, for if consciousness is to be a "nothingness," it must be left free of an Ego as well as of images, and the machinery of association. But we shall return to that later. For the moment, the point is that the existentialists have rejected the Ego along with the absolute. They have taken the Cartesian *cogito* and transferred the emphasis from the verbs to the pronoun—*I* think, therefore *I* am. That is to say: for the rationalist who believes in the existence of an objective "I," it makes no difference whatsoever *who* thinks, the result, under ideal conditions, will be the same. But we have just seen that thought apart from a given situation is inconceivable, there are no ideal conditions. *What* is thought depends upon *who* thinks. ". . . The meditating Ego," writes Merleau-Ponty, "can never abolish my inherence in an individual subject, whose knowledge of everything is acquired within a particular frame of reference."[97] Classical philosophy assumes the possibility of a thought unconditioned by time and space.

Rationalism confuses truth and objectivity. It observes that science has acquired a body of information which no one disputes. A scientific truth is *the* truth because it compels universal consent. However, universal consent is a no more effective means of identifying truth, than of proving the existence of God. Scientific investigation is concerned with those aspects of things which are *measurable* and which consequently involve universal agreement; but on what grounds does the rationalist identify that which is measurable in a thing with the thing itself? In what way is a table analysed into atoms and molecules more real or more "true" than the table considered as an object on which to write? If we had any reason to suppose that the discovery of the atomic structure of matter had brought us any closer to the discovery of some final principle which would once and for all "explain" matter, then we should have to accept scientific truth as the only one. However,

[97] *La Phénoménologie de la Perception*, p. 74.

in the total absence of any such reason, it is safe to assume with phenomenology that matter "conceals" nothing, it is what it appears to be; and it appears, not to a disincarnate Ego divorced from time and space, but to the *individual* consciousness which, furthermore, as we saw in our study of intentionality, can only be aware of what really exists. It will be recalled that Merleau-Ponty described phenomenology as being first of all a "disavowal of science";[98] but he also remarks that it is the ambition of phenomenology to become an "exact science."[99] Obviously he refers to two different kinds of science. Science, as ordinarily understood, is founded upon the identification of truth with objectivity, while the basic certitude of phenomenology is the *existence* of whatever is revealed by the *individual* consciousness. Since phenomenology does not admit the possibility of a truth existing independently of time and place, investigation is shifted from "objective" phenomena to existence itself. Consciousness is always consciousness of itself, we can therefore be certain of what it reveals to us. "Objective truths" are but an infinitesimal part of the life of subjectivity, *all* of which exists; and the object of phenomenology as a science will be not the aggrandizement of our stock of objective facts, but the description of what exists in subjectivity, because of that existence we are certain. Since nothing is "hidden" in phenomena, the customary scientific procedure by analysis, while expanding our knowledge of what exists (but only the "measurable" portion of what exists), in no way brings us any closer to "reality." Everything that consciousness reveals is equally real, and therefore the task of phenomenology as a science will be to *describe* what exists, to discover its significance, and not to analyse it.

We have a right to ask whether all this has translated itself into anything tangible. How can the "description" of subjectivity be of scientific value? Needless to say, phenomenology does not pretend to be of any assistance to

98 *Ibid.*, Avant-Propos, II.
99 *Ibid.*, I.

physics. Its rôle *vis-à-vis* the physical sciences is limited to denying that they can have any absolute validity. However, in the case of those sciences which have been trying without notable success to adapt to the study of man procedures which have proved successful in the investigation of matter, phenomenology is of decisive value. The difference between the scientific and phenomenological approach to the problems of psychology and related subjects, is to be found in these words "analysis" and "significance." A psychologist's study of, for example, emotion is undertaken in the same spirit as a physicist's study of a particle of matter; the object is analysed in order to discover exactly how it functions or what it consists of. However fruitful such a principle may be when applied to material things, it cannot be exercised on man himself because what occurs in human consciousness *signifies* something; it occurs not as a result of law, but as the result of intention. Intentionality is here, as always, the basic fact: ". . . Every consciousness exists precisely in so far as it is consciousness of existing."[100] An emotion like joy does not "happen" to someone as dissolution happens to salt when put in water; but we are joyful to the extent in which we are *conscious* of being joyful, to the extent in which we have "intended" joy. In other words, joy is something we have assumed; it is an "organized form of human existence."[101] Consequently, since emotion is something we have consciously assumed, we must have had a reason for so doing; that is, emotion must *signify* something in a way that a non-human event can never do. An emotion is not primarily *fact*, as psychologists would have it, it is first of all *significance*, and the facts of psychology will remain meaningless until the significances are decided upon.[102] Psychology's method of studying man is like that of someone who, never having seen a hammer before, upon being given one in order that

---

100 Sartre, *Esquisse d'une Théorie des Emotions*, Hermann, 1948, p. 8.
101 *Ibid.*, p. 11.
102 Valéry defines a fact as: ". . . that which does without signification." (*Tel Quel I*, NRF, 1941, p. 97.)

he may decide exactly what it is, begins by analysing the metal and wood. But until it is discovered what the hammer "signifies," until it is discovered that it is an instrument for driving nails, no amount of analysis will lead anywhere. Before we have decided what it signifies that human consciousness should be able to "intend" an emotion, there is no point whatever in analysing the fact of emotion. Modern science began when men realized that the appropriate question in what concerns natural phenomena is how and not why. Primitive peoples insist upon asking why rain falls instead of how, and therefore invent gods instead of science. Nevertheless, if we are to understand man, we must return to the question why—why is there such a thing as anger and not how does it occur. According to Sartre, emotion "signifies" ". . . the totality of the relations between human reality and the world. The transition to emotion is a total modification of 'being-in-the-world' in accordance with the very special laws of magic."[103]

We have already discussed what Sartre means by emotion being "magical conduct" and our present interest is not the conclusion of *Esquisse d'une Théorie des Emotions,* but its method. The essence of that method is to have replaced an analytical, objective procedure in psychology, by the investigation of the *individual* consciousness: "What will cause all research on man to differ from the other types of exact enquiry, is precisely the all-important fact that human reality is ourselves."[104] The fact that we assume our joy or our sorrow, that they do not just "happen" to a passive self, implies, on the part of the individual, an understanding of the realities of human existence. Such understanding may be obscure and inauthentic, but the fact remains that it is in oneself that it must be sought. "I can therefore question myself, and on the basis of this interrogation, successfully carry out an analysis of 'human reality,' which will serve as a foundation for an anthropology."[105] *L'Esquisse d'une Théorie des Emotions,* however, is hardly more than a statement of principle, and it will be possible to illustrate in more striking a manner what can be accomplished scientifically by abandoning the kind of objectivity which has always been supposed a *sine qua non* of science.

Psychology approaches its task in true scientific form by dividing the difficulty; it "analyses" man into two parts—mind and body. It is assumed that the body, being matter and "objective," can be explored and known as well, if not better, by an observer, as by the subjectivity to which it is attached. And yet my body is *for me* quite a different thing from my body as it is perceived by somebody else. I do not recognize my own voice heard in a recording; and occasionally even, for a fleeting moment, I fail to recognize as myself the person appearing in a mirror which I pass unexpectedly in the street. It is for this reason that the problem of "inverted vision" is a false one. If physiologists are puzzled by the fact that images on the retina of the eye are inverted, it is because they do not distinguish between body as it exists for the individual concerned and body as it exists for others; because, in other words ". . . an attempt has been made to link *my* consciousness of objects with the body of the other person."[106] Of course, I can watch my hand touch something as though it were the hand of somebody else; but I am, in this case, artificially assuming the attitude of another. I cannot simultaneously contemplate my hand as a *thing* (that is, take toward it the attitude of another) and as "my-hand-touching."[107] If bodies are not interchangeable like things, as their status as "matter" would lead us to suppose, it is because we are physically as well as socially and historically "situated." It is to *La Phénoménologie de la Perception* that we must turn for an understanding of how the conception of man

105 *Ibid.,* p. 9.
106 Sartre, *L'Etre et le Néant,* p. 367.
107 *Ibid.,* p. 366.

as a being who is physically a "part of the world" can be scientifically useful.

In speaking of the reasons for the existentialist deviation from phenomenology, we explained that existentialism considers man's relation to the exterior world as being an "emotive" and not a "contemplative" one. The word "emotive" is used for want of a better term and is to be taken in a very broad sense as meaning that we are able to comport ourselves in the world not because we "understand" the things which surround us but because we have a *physical solidarity* with them. If intentionality is possible, if there is no "distance" between consciousness and the thing in itself, it is because we are "in the world" to the extent of being a part of it, of being at one with it. We are accustomed to think of man as a "visitor" in the world, over which he rules in the manner of a *podestà,* or in which he fulfils God's purpose. We are here in a strange environment for a brief moment between two eternities and are only able to acclimate ourselves because we are thinking beings. The existentialist view is quite different. Man is in the world not as a stranger obliged to "reason" his way, but as a crustacean in its shell, which it "knows" not by a process of enquiry but because it is a part of itself. To pursue our analogy further, the shell would not exist without the animal that inhabits it, nor could the world exist deprived of that part of itself called man. According to science, the world was there before the first appearance of a human being. But the existence of a pre-human world forms part of *our* experience—it is inconceivable apart from such experience. This does not mean that consciousness "creates" the world, but simply that it is impossible to get "before consciousness," which is always already there.[108]

In his *Phénoménologie de la Perception,* Merleau-Ponty interprets phenomenologically some case studies of Gelb and Goldstein. A patient is unable to execute "abstract" movements; that is, he is unable to do anything which is

[108] See Merleau-Ponty, *La Phénoménologie de la Perception,* p. 494.

not functional, such as complying with an order to move his arm in a specified way. Artificial movements become possible only after a series of preparatory movements usually involving the entire body, the purpose of which is to enable the patient to "find" that part of his body he has been asked to move. And yet all the activities called for in normal daily existence are performed rapidly and accurately. For example, the patient immediately claps his hands to the spot where he has been stung by a mosquito, but is unable to touch the same spot when asked to do so. He is able to do what he is asked under experimental conditions only after reintroducing the movements into a living context. Asked to pretend to comb his hair, the patient also pretends to hold a mirror before his face; he can mimic the act of using a hammer only by simultaneously raising his free hand as though to hold a nail. Another patient is able to point to a given part of his body only if he is at the same time allowed to seize it. Why should anyone know where a given part of his body is when allowed to use it, and yet not know when asked simply to point to it? We find ourselves obliged to admit that knowledge of place (or of space) must exist in two forms. First, the objective, positional knowledge which classical psychology has borrowed from science, but which is clearly not relevant to the case just described. If place has only objective existence, that is, if it may be determined by us only *intellectually*, then we either know where a given place is or we do not know; it is inadmissible that a patient be intellectually ignorant of the whereabouts of a given part of his body while having no difficulty whatever in locating it when it is a question of accomplishing some normal activity. There must be, in addition to objective space, a subjective, or what Merleau-Ponty calls a "phenomenal" space within which the body moves in entire independence of intellect, just as the blind man moves about with complete assurance in a room long familiar to him and where sight, for the purpose of finding his way, is superfluous. When the patient claps his hand to the spot where he has been stung by an insect,

> the action takes place entirely in the order of the phenomenal, and does not traverse the objective world. Only the spectator, who lends to the subject of the movement his objective representation of the living body, can believe that the sting is felt and that the hand moves in objective space. Only he, consequently, can feel surprise at the same subject's failing in experiments of designation.[109]

However, we cannot stop there. The "phenomenal" space in which we move and which is not that of science, extends outward to the entire portion of the world present to our senses at a given moment. The patient referred to above, Schneider, is employed in a manufactory of wallets where he uses the tools and materials with almost the efficiency of a normal person. Consequently, if he is unable to represent to himself intellectually a part of his body, the same must apply to the instruments of his work, which he is nevertheless able to use because they form part of the "functional," or "intentional" system which unites him with the world. Our liaison with objects is effected by the body itself which has no need of "representation." ". . . My consciousness of the world is effected by means of my body."[110] An object is large or small, not by comparison to some objective standard, but depending upon its size relative to that of the body. It is by reference to the body that we say "over," "under," "on the side," etc. The body is more, however, than a point around which the world organizes itself, for it would seem to have the power of making material things "extensions" of itself.[111] Classical psychology is at a great disadvantage in trying to explain habit

109 *Ibid.*
110 See Merleau-Ponty, *La Phénoménologie de la Perception*, p. 97.
111 "I am an organism of which the aircraft is an extension." (Saint-Exupéry, *Pilote de Guerre*, Œuvres Complètes, NRF, 1950, p. 295.

in terms of intellectual syntheses, for the habit once acquired (typewriting for example) we obviously cease to respond to each individual stimulus, a system of response having developed which allows us to relax our attention. Evidently the body itself has much to do with the acquisition of habit, yet we must not suppose, as does Bergson, that habit is simply a kind of automatism stamped into the organism by an intellectual effort gradually discontinued. Habit is to be explained neither by intellect nor by the body considered as an object, but by the body imagined as a "mediator."

> Consciousness is being in a thing through the medium of the body. A movement is learned when the body has grasped it, that is, when the body has incorporated the movement into its "world." Moving the body is "aiming" by means of it at things: it is allowing the body to respond to their invitation, and this is exerted on the body without any representation.[112]

A woman able to keep a safe distance between the feathers in her hat and objects which might break them, has not developed her ability to do so through habit. She "feels" the ends of the feathers as we "feel" the tips of our fingers.[113] Again, the driver of a car knows whether the space before him is wide enough to permit his passage, he does not compare the width of his car with that of the opening. We "get used" to a cane in a matter of seconds, we know exactly what objects are within reach of it and which are not, the cane has become almost an extension of our sense of touch. To habituate oneself to a hat, a car, or a cane, ". . . is to settle into them or, to put it the other way round, to make them share in the extension in space of the body as such."[114] Should we still feel that all this is simply a matter of practice, however rapidly accomplished, there

112 See Merleau-Ponty, *La Phénoménologie de la Perception*, p. 161.
113 *Ibid.*, p. 167.
114 *Ibid.*, p. 168.

is the example of organists who, with an hour's preparation, are able to give concerts on instruments whose key-
boards and stops may be quite differently arranged from
those of the organ to which they are accustomed. It is unthinkable that in so short a time a whole new set of reflexes
could be formed. What has happened is that the body has
"dilated" itself to comprise the space occupied by the key-
boards; like the cane, the instrument becomes in a sense,
an extension of the body, it has been incorporated into the
organist's "living space"; a system has come into being in
which the body "mediates" between consciousness and
things.[115]

Two arguments have been proposed. There is no objectivity in the rationalist sense, and therefore no objective
Ego, its necessary counterpart. Each of us has an individual perspective which can in no way be surmounted.
Secondly, the fact of so complete an *engagement*, physical,
social and historical, far from condemning us to ignorance,
is the sole basis upon which a satisfactory view of the
world may be constructed. The only way to understand
the world is to renounce trying to persuade ourselves that
there exists somewhere an absolute principle of order with
an absolute "human nature" to take cognizance of it, and
to recognize that there is not one truth, but as many as
there are individual perspectives. An individual sentiment
or idea is not clear or unclear, existent or non-existent, by
reference to an ideal of absolute clarity which alone exists.
Every event of subjectivity is an event of the exterior world
and therefore exists in its own right. ". . . Cannot one
know," remarks Benjamin Fondane, "an unintelligible
thing, precisely *as being* unintelligible?"[116] For example,
the feeling of anguish (as distinguished from fear which is
a conduct assumed in the face of something real) does not
seem to be associated with any specific object, it comes

[115] Needless to say we have, in these brief paragraphs, done scant justice to
Merleau-Ponty's arguments.
[116] "Kafka et la Rationalité Absolue," in *Deucalion*, No. 2. "To be vaguely conscious of an image, is to be conscious of a vague image." (Sartre, *L'Imaginaire*,
NRF, 1940, pp. 27–8.)

upon us unexpectedly, *à propos* of nothing in particular; however instead of condemning it as "unintelligible," Heidegger takes anguish to be the experience of "nothingness."

But if we grant equal reality and truth to each individual perspective, have we not returned to the psychologism which intentionality was supposed to have supplanted? Or, to put the question more precisely, must we not attribute to such phenomena as dreams and hallucinations a reality equal to that of any other event of consciousness? Is the world of the dreamer and of the madman as real as any other? If whatever consciousness "intends" really exists, then dreams and hallucinations are in fact as real as perceptions. Such events cannot be understood if we attempt to deny their reality by comparing them to some objective absolute such as the geometric space of rationalism which the vision of the schizophrenic violates. We have the choice of agreeing that a person who sees something knows that he sees it, and in this case we must accept the word of the madman; or we may believe that no one is judge of what he sees, but in this case the rationalist absolute can be an illusion.[117] Nevertheless, although dreams and hallucinations are real, the dreamer and the schizophrenic do not mistake their vision for a real perception. According to orthodox psychology, an hallucination is not real, the patient is deceived; while for the existentialist, the hallucination is real, but the patient is not deceived. If the theory of intentionality is not to collapse, then consciousness must always be able to distinguish between a perception and what is only a mental image. Although everything that consciousness "contains" exists, whether an event of

---

117 See *La Phénoménologie de la Perception*, p. 335. The time has come for us to believe Gérard de Nerval when he writes in *Aurélia*: "Be that as it may, I believe that human imagination has invented nothing that is not true, in this world or in others, and I could not doubt what I had so distinctly *seen*." We might also cite Valéry in this connection: "The incoherence of what someone says depends on the listener. The mind appears to me to be made in such a way that it cannot be incoherent for itself." (*Monsieur Teste*, NRF, 1948, p. 27.)

consciousness is *materially* real or unreal is readily determined because the two appear in different ways.[118]

There exists a substantial world of perception from which even victims of mental disorders do not altogether escape. In spite of our being unable to transcend our individual perspectives, communication and understanding are possible; we therefore inhabit the same world. This world that men hold in common, which Sartre calls "the backdrop of the world" (*le fond de monde*) and which in the *Phénoménologie de la Perception* is called "the natural world" (*le monde naturel*), is none other than that of Baudelaire, Rimbaud, Valéry and Cézanne, which philosophers have taken up in an attempt to make it "thinkable." One cannot live the absurd; the mere statement that the absurd exists is creative of a sense. The task of phenomenology and of existentialism is to reconcile the absurd with the fact that human life is possible. "The innovations of phenomenology," writes Merleau-Ponty, "do not consist in denying the unity of experience, but in establishing it on a basis different from that of classical rationalism."[119] The existentialist believes that a kind of unity is conceivable without hypothesizing the complete intelligibility of the universe. Nature in its entirety is neither intelligible nor unintelligible; all we can affirm is that some sense can be made of it. That sense, or unity, is to be found "beneath" the operations of intelligence; it is the condition of their possibility. The "intelligibility" which it has been the aim of science and philosophy to discover, is what makes philosophical and scientific research possible.

The discovery that there were no stationary points upon which to base astronomical calculations did not ruin astronomy as a science. A calculation, although made in reference to a changing individual position, is yet uni-

versally valid. In the same way, the abandonment as un-
realizable of rationalist objectivity does not mean that each
of us is sealed up within his own subjectivity—and that for
two reasons. First, inasmuch as man has no essence, his
every act is creative of man. Secondly, events of subjectivity are in reality events of the exterior world. For an
absolute acknowledging neither time nor space and its corol-
lary, the transcendental Ego, has been substituted a world
which cannot be seized in its entirety and which offers as
many "points of view" as there are individuals. But if what
each of us must "manifest" is unique, it is also, as we have
just seen, universal—and that is what has made possible
one of the most striking characteristics of contemporary
European culture, the fusion of literature and philosophy.

There is a philosophy inherent in all literature. We must
have a certain number of unassailable convictions before
anything can be said at all. Our convictions will eventually
come to be considered naïve, mistaken or even vicious,
but unless they are replaced by others of which history will
be equally critical, there can be no creativity. Also, as we
have had several times occasion to remark, philosophers
have, since the Renaissance, been so mesmerized by science that philosophy as a guide through life and as a preparation for leaving it, has been given over increasingly to
literature. The trend reached its limit when, from Baudelaire onwards, poets became metaphysicians while philosophers devoted themselves to debates reminiscent of the
disputation by gesture of Rabelais's schoolmen.[120]

If philosophy is not to die of inanition, being as a science (particularly in the latter half of the last century)

[120] "Baudelaire, Mallarmé, Rimbaud . . . dreamed of 'surmounting man.' . . .
They all failed and one may think in connection with them of Icarus and
Prometheus. This is not the place to enquire into the circumstances which
have led . . . to such an exacerbation of the eternal metaphysical ambition—
at a time when the philosophers, on the contrary, were humbling themselves
before the exact sciences—and to ask why man should have taken it into his
head to look to poetry for an answer to the problem of his destiny." (Marcel
Raymond, De Baudelaire au Surréalisme, Corti, 1947, p. 45.)

misleading when not actually harmful, as the "philosophy of science" superfluous, and as an ethic non-existent, then it will have, in trying to revivify itself, to look to literature as well as to the history of philosophy. What is new in the current situation is not that literature has become philosophical—it has always been so—but that philosophy is seeking through literature to regain access to existence. However, such a recourse could only result in the gradual absorption of philosophy by literature, in the pulverization of philosophy into as many systems as there are authors, unless the particular could somehow be made universal. We have seen how this has been accomplished. At the same time, every attack on the part of writers themselves upon the rationalist principle of objectivity was a preparation for the establishment of literature and art as sources of truth inferior to none.

It is again in the extraordinarily prescient *Introduction à la Méthode de Léonard de Vinci,* and especially in an amplification of 1929 entitled *Léonard et les Philosophes,* that we find hints of what was to come. Valéry was one of the first to suspect that art is no more "subjective" than is philosophy, and that it is quite as valid a commentary upon the Real.

> Perhaps the philosopher thinks that an Ethic or a Monadology are more serious things than a suite in D minor? It is true that certain questions that the mind sets itself are more general and more natural [or "measurable"] than this or that artistic production. But there is nothing to prove that these questions are not naïve.[121]

The greatest obstacle to the understanding of what Valéry is saying, and which the work of Husserl was to remove, is the feeling that the particular is somehow of less consequence than the general.

[121] Valéry, *Œuvres de Paul Valéry,* NRF, 1938, Vol. VIII, p. 124.

What most manifestly separates philosophical aesthetics from the reflection of the artist, is that the former issues from a way of thinking that believes itself foreign to the arts and feels itself to be of an essence other than that of the poet's . . . in that . . . it misjudges itself. For it, works of art are accidents, particular cases, effects of an active and industrious sensibility blindly tending toward a principle of which Philosophy must possess the vision, or the idea pure and unmediated.[122]

In giving our attention to the particular, we fear the risk of fixing ourselves upon an exception to the rule; an apprehension whose only justification could be the existence of an ultimate truth imagined as being more or less distant depending upon the greater or lesser generality of our ideas. Art is by nature existential; it is concerned with particulars, while rationalism is interested only in their relationships. After science has analysed into parts or joined together by law we are no closer than we were before to this particular thing which then falls into the limitless domain of art where it will receive its only "explanation." In theory, therefore, contemporary philosophy restores to art a prestige it has not enjoyed since artists fashioned real gods out of stone or wood during the Ages before art became an "imitation of nature." Husserl, in the words of Sartre, ". . . has given back to us the world of the artists and the prophets. . . ."[123]

Artists themselves, to be sure, have not waited for the consecration of the philosophers to be persuaded of the reality of their particular "hallucination," whether that of Cézanne's "mad" perspectives or of Joyce's dream world. Nevertheless, it is conceivable that lesser artists allow themselves to be bullied by rationalism into believing that what is not measurable is subjective, that is, fanciful, and generally irrelevant to the serious business of the scientific pursuit of truth. This, according to Sartre, is what hap-

[122] *Ibid.*, pp. 132, 133.
[123] Article on Intentionality in the philosophy of Husserl, *Situations I*, p. 34.

pened to Jules Renard.[124] We may ask whether the phenomenon of "terrorism" in literature did not come as an aftermath of half a century of empiricism. Though it has now become possible for writers to believe that no system can exhaust what exists, Renard and his contemporaries accepted the scientific view of things as analysable syntheses of a certain number of knowable substances. The seeming infinite variety of things is produced by the great number of ways in which a finite number of substances may enter into association with one another. The only mystery is what we put there. Science, therefore, like Kantism, effectively blocks the path back to the particular, back to things-in-themselves. The terrorist is he who obscurely suspects the fundamental premise of contemporary philosophy, that it is to existence and not essence, to the particular and not the general, to life itself and not what "lies behind it" that we should devote our energies. However, the basic tenets of a philosophic and scientific tradition extending back to antiquity would have to be radically modified before such an undertaking could be anything but a mystification. It is not sufficient, as André Breton thinks, to call logic "the most hateful of prisons,"[125] something more than "automatic writing" has to be substituted for it. Such is the misfortune of the terrorist, a nostalgia for existence wed to a philosophy which denies it all importance. How to effect a "return to the concrete" since words were not made to render the absurd? But if the absurd cannot be written, it can be lived, and that was the solution, imposed partly by the pressure of events, of, among others, Malraux and Saint-Exupéry. The terrorist overcomes his paralysis in realizing that to write is to act. If literature, like philosophy, is not to die of inanition, it must renew its bonds with existence.

Science has slowly deprived philosophy of its fields of enquiry until there are now none left, at least for a philosophy which continues to accept scientific criteria of

124 See "L'Homme Ligoté," *Situations I.*
125 *Nadja,* NRF, 1928, p. 188.

truth. Classical philosophy is reduced to consoling itself with the thought that after science has "discovered everything," there will still be the problem of utilizing what has been discovered, there will remain the problem of conduct, and that is a philosophical one. However, nowhere more than in ethics has modern philosophy been so conspicuously sterile, and the reason is that the business of living has been turned over to "experts" for a pronouncement. From the utilitarians' pleasure-pain arithmetic, through the marxists' "scientific" study of history, to sociology and psychoanalysis, we have clung to the hope that existence, like an object, could be analysed, measured, formulated and finally "exhausted," so that our responsibility for it might be at an end, and our "uniqueness" proved a baseless fear. Literature as well as philosophy, though to a lesser extent, had the ground beneath its feet cut away by scientism's attempt to deny that the individual is comprehensible apart from the group. Hence the series of colossal literary (or, in the case of Balzac and Zola, "scientific") undertakings from *La Comédie Humaine* to *Les Hommes de Bonne Volonté*, whose purpose it was to depict not individuals but entire societies, or at the very least, family groups. The individual is "explainable" only in terms of the milieu; in terms, that is, only of the impersonal or objective. The result was the mania for documentation which obliged Flaubert to consult thousands of volumes in the preparation of his books. The document, like a measurement, is something which in theory compels universal agreement and so exorcizes the unwholesome spectre of subjectivity.

No one did more than Charles Péguy to expose the absurdities involved in studying men and their civilizations as though they were products like "sugar and vitriol" (to use the words of Taine) and the danger of the eventual complete absorption of the individual by the more easily "measurable" mass. Péguy's offensive against what he called "the intellectual party" has been so successful that already after less than half a century it is becoming hard to believe that the issue was a vital one and bitterly fought. Was it ever necessary to assert, as did Péguy, that "the fate of metaphysics is in no way linked with that of physics,"[126] that is to say, scientific progress is not moral progress? The answer is to be found in the pages of books like *La Fontaine et ses Fables* of Taine, or *L'Avenir de la Science* of Renan. Here is the opening sentence of *La Fontaine et ses Fables*: "One can look upon man as an animal of a superior species, who produces philosophies and poems almost as silk-worms make their cocoons."[127] In Renan's *Dialogues et Fragments Philosophiques*, we read: ". . . When scientific omnipotence is concentrated in the hands of a good and just being, that being will wish to resuscitate the past in order to redress its innumerable iniquities."[128] Now, at last, man was really to become God, with the power to resurrect the dead, and not merely to survive eternally after death. That period of history which prided itself most upon its objectivity, appears in retrospect the most subjective of all, for (it believed) science was the end point of human evolution, the systems that preceded it were now obsolete. Science (and to an alarming extent this is still true) was walled up within itself. As a result, the writings from which we have just quoted already seem more remote than many texts of the Middle Ages.

Western philosophy may very well have reached its nadir in the latter part of the last century. The grossest contradictions went unchallenged because of the general feeling that philosophical questions could be left in abeyance until science had found time to dispose of them once and for all. The necessity of reconciling divine omnipotence and human free will places the theologian in a philosophically impossible position from which he extricates

126 *Situations*, NRF, p. 119.
127 Quoted by Péguy in "Zangwill," one of a collection of Péguy's articles to be found in a volume entitled *De Jean Coste*, NRF.
128 *Ibid.*

himself only through faith. The same may be said of nine-teenth century scientific rationalism which, thanks to its faith in experimental methods did not trouble to explain how man could be determined, a product of his environ-ment, a thing, in brief, and at the same time able to know it, able to "perfect" himself, to bring about the resurrection of the dead or the cessation of history in the final triumph of the proletariat. Contemporary philosophy represents a return to rigour, or perhaps simply a return to common sense, by insisting that man can be neither wholly matter (empiricism) nor wholly mind (idealism). Consequently the philosophies of existentialism are philosophies of "am-biguity," because man, being at the same time "in the world" and (since he has consciousness of things not him-self) separate from it, he can neither achieve absolute clarity by "seeing himself from without" nor absolute "in-conscience" by becoming a thing. Human life makes its uncertain way through this limbo somewhere between the total vision of God and the blindness of the animal.

Péguy's refusal, therefore, to accept science's compe-tence to pronounce upon human affairs is in the spirit of present day recognition of the autonomy of consciousness, of its absolute incommensurateness with matter, alone amenable to scientific investigation. Raymond Aron's *In-troduction à la Philosophie de l'Histoire* is a good example of the utilization of this principle. His purpose is to decide what limits must be set upon the objective study of history, and limits there must be because there is no common measure between man and the rest of creation. The mys-tery of the origin of consciousness must remain impene-trable; its insertion in an evolutionary process is no ex-planation: ". . . for we shall never explain consciousness by what is not conscious, nor reason by non-reason. The impossibility of deducing consciousness is evident, for such a deduction involves consciousness itself."[129] Aron has applied to the study of history two concepts (which are in

---

[129] Raymond Aron, *Introduction à la Philosophie de l'Histoire*, NRF, 1938, p. 38.

reality one) by now quite familiar to us: the difference of nature between consciousness and the rest of what exists (or the absurd) and the impossibility on the part of consciousness to "see itself" (or the non-existence of the Absolute). These ideas are but aspects of one more fundamental still, one which we have been developing, in one form or another, throughout these pages—the particular cannot be reduced to the general—human existence (the particular) may not be reduced to an essence (the general).

We remarked that every literature springs from a more or less clearly formulated metaphysic; while, on the contrary, it has always been the pretension of philosophy to impose upon, rather than to allow itself to be influenced by, literature. This is no longer true, and the remainder of our work will be devoted to examining the process by which many of the ideas of the authors we have chosen to discuss have been inserted into an existentialist context.

Contemporary French literature seeks, in the words of Gaetan Picon, to make of itself ". . . an instrument of metaphysical consciousness."[130] If literature is now mingled with existence and preoccupied with metaphysical questions it is because Valéry, Péguy and of course a host of others, scientists and philosophers as well as poets, saw the arbitrariness of sacrificing the particular to the general, the individual to the mass, existence to essence. Literature could not overcome "terrorism," or the feeling that it was not "biting into reality" until the metaphysics of science could be discredited, until the particular could be made significant; and this was accomplished (apart from phenomenology) mainly on the one hand by asserting, as had Péguy, that the secrets of human life are not accessible to science, and on the other by casting into doubt, as had Valéry, the very principle of objectivity.

But literature has not become "an instrument of metaphysical consciousness" for the first time. No writer of

130 *Malraux*, p. 64.

today is more "metaphysical" or more "political" than was
a Nerval or a Shelley. Nevertheless, however many paral-
lels one may discover between the literature of today and
that of the past, a divergence exists which makes of these
rapprochements mere historical curiosities. The gulf we
found separating Proust and Gide is the same which separates existentialism from the whole nineteenth century, it
is the difference between *The Quest for the Absolute* and
the return to the particular. The nineteenth century could
be satisfied with nothing less than definitive solutions,
mystico-religious for the Nervals, political for the Shelleys.

As long as men continued to believe in the existence
of a religious or political absolute, it was as natural for
writers to turn to philosophy for guidance, as it is for a
citizen to turn to a lawyer for information about the law.
But if there is no law except what the citizen himself
creates, then the lawyer must consult the citizen, and
the philosopher the writer. "Metaphysical consciousness,"
writes Merleau-Ponty, "has no other object but daily experience."[181] Or, in other words, "true philosophy is re-
learning to look upon the world; and in this sense, a simple
story can reveal the world with as much 'profundity' as
can a philosophical treatise."[182] And so Merleau-Ponty rejoins Valéry who, even before the turn of the century, has
denied that Kant or Spinoza are any more "true" than
Leonardo or Montaigne.

There took place, at Paris, in January 1935, a public
meeting at which André Gide defended his philosophy
against a number of his Catholic or rightist adversaries,
among whom was Henri Massis. Massis remarked, referring to the "Gidean I," ". . . it lacks . . . a certain notion
of man which would serve as an ideal toward which it
could tend." To which Ramon Fernandez replied, "If you
assume an *a priori* notion of man, you falsify the search,"
and Gide, "That is the whole question."[133]

[181] *Sens et Non-Sens*, Nagel, 1948, p. 188.
[132] Merleau-Ponty, *La Phénoménologie de la Perception*, Avant-Propos, XVI.
[133] *André Gide et Notre Temps*, NRF, 1935, p. 34.

We are going to examine the ideas of three men, Gide, Malraux and Saint-Exupéry, who hold this supremely important conviction in common: there is no *a priori* definition of man, he is *self-creative*. There will consequently be no need for these authors to seek in religion, science, politics or philosophy a definition or an absolute which they know does not exist. They know that the "point of view" they have adopted is as legitimate as any other, that *because* it is absolutely individual, it is also absolutely universal. If philosophy, however, has little to teach them, they have much to teach philosophy.

PART TWO

Ils ont cherché à recommander non leur dire, mais leur faire.
MONTAIGNE

Chapter 1

Gide

> *Il arrivera peut-être, plus tard, que tel lecteur ... à propos de certaines déclarations ... "existentialistes" ... s'étonne et proteste: "mais Gide l'avait dit avant lui."*
>
> GIDE

HOWEVER UNORTHODOX Gide's ideas became, there was always a segment of opinion he could never alienate—that of the literary aesthete, of the person whose pride it is to be able to despise what is said in order to savour how it is said. Gide the "master of French prose" has consequently come to occupy a place out of all proportion with his real importance.

It is possible to study the Gide who was a theorist of the novel, or the Gide who was a literary critic, or Gide as a creative writer, but to do so is like studying a battle divorced from its historical context. Such investigations can be of interest only to the specialist or the *amateur,* and Gide wrote for neither one nor the other. His work was not intended to amuse, but to disturb; it is more a series of interrogations in the form of plays and stories than a sequence of works of art which incidentally pose disquieting questions about some of our most cherished convictions. The pertinence of these questions was such as to attract two philosophers as eminent as Gabriel Marcel and Jacques Maritain to the public debate of which we spoke at the end of the last chapter. Strange times, in which philosophers consider it worth their while to question artists—or was Gide in reality less an artist than a thinker? He was, of course, both; but because he was so important a thinker, it is a mistake to consider him primarily as a literary craftsman, and yet since he was so conscientious

129

an artist there is little point to studying Gide's thought apart from that of his time; for he has no "system," it is not the business of the work of art to "conclude."

Gide himself has done much to encourage the aesthetic approach to his work. He writes in his *Journal*: "To speak soundly of my work, it is the aesthetic attitude alone that must be adopted."[1] Or again: "It is from the point of view of art that what I write is properly to be judged."[2] This is very well, but what if Gide's ideas are of greater consequence than the way in which he expressed them? What if, as many believe, his *Journal* is his greatest accomplishment? Books like those of Jean Hytier written from the point of view recommended by Gide will be none the less "true," but they will, increasingly, leave the reader unsatisfied. Albert Guérard's work on Gide is a striking case in point. After demonstrating that Gide as a creative genius cannot be placed among the highest, and even that he cannot be considered the equal of Conrad or of Mann,[3] he is embarrassed to explain how Gide could be one of those who "helped fashion the twentieth-century mind."[4] In one of his letters to Guérard, Gide congratulates him in the warmest terms upon his critical depth of insight, but then goes on to say:

> The positive effect my books may have, the influence they seem to exercise today—these are evidently not due to a certain quality as novelist which I can well understand your refusing me, especially if you compare me to Thomas Hardy or to Conrad, and I certainly do not protest. But the profound perturbation of mind and heart has then been brought about by something else, and that is what it would have been interesting to show; that is what one hardly catches a glimpse of in the whole of what you have written.[5]

[1] 25 April 1918.
[2] 13 October 1918.
[3] Harvard, 1951, p. 182.
[4] *Ibid.*, p. 183.
[5] *Ibid.*, p. 241.

The difficulty was that Guérard had no clear idea of what exactly the "twentieth-century mind" is. Intellectual movements do not accept our chronology, and many ideas fathered by nineteenth-century mentalities are still very much with us. Freudism is one of these. By its symbolism, and by the determinism involved in the theory of a sub-consciousness, Freudism is far removed from what the twentieth-century mind really is—in one form or another, an existentialist mind. We cannot hope to understand the significance of Gide, if we think of him in terms of systems which he was instrumental in overthrowing. Guérard writes that Gide: ". . . dramatized the unending buried struggle between conscious intention and unconscious need, the forms which uncalculated self-destructiveness may take, the minute workings of repression and sublimation, the 'gratuitous acts' of unconscious identification."[6] If such language has any meaning at all, in reference to Gide it has none whatever. The immense importance of the conception of "gratuity" both in the work of Gide and in contemporary thought has been completely overlooked because an attempt has been made to judge twentieth-century ideas on the basis of a system derived from nineteenth-century confidence in the existence of "solutions." Certain details of *L'Immoraliste* are made clearer for us if we understand that Michel is a homosexual who does not yet realize that he is one. But to regard the latent sexual drama of *L'Immoraliste* as the "key" to the book's meaning (as Guérard seems to) is to find a "solution" which is not there and which singularly restricts the interest of the moral problem the story sets forth. Gide had no interest in Freudism or in any of the techniques to which it gave rise, indeed his thought was diametrically opposed to it. The constant attendance of a psychiatrist is of no help to Boris of *Les Faux Monnayeurs;* the only permanent cure will be

6 *Ibid.*, p. 180. The Freudian and totally erroneous interpretation of *l'acte gratuit* is all but universal. There is no basis whatever in Gide's writings for such an interpretation—a good example of the unfortunate cleverness to which Freudism has given rise in literary criticism.

one that *he himself* brings about, one that he sees fit to will.[7]

Freudism is the last of a long series of nineteenth century attempts to find a substitute for the Christian concept of man. If it can be demonstrated that man is simply this or that thing, if not a creature of God, then the victim of a subconsciousness—at any rate, dependent upon something foreign to himself—he is relieved of the responsibility (or of the "anguish") of making his way through life unaided and uncomforted, "condemned to be free."[8] There are few themes to which Gide returns with greater insistence than that of the "incompleteness" of man. Man is whatever he will eventually make of himself; his possibilities are limited only by his unfortunate eagerness to accept ready-made definitions which permit him to substitute contemplation for action. The expression "I know myself" invariably implies "therefore I cannot. . . ."[9] Life is not a possession; it is an experiment. No one knows whether he is courageous or cowardly until faced by danger; but even then, confronted by a different danger the result could well be different. Man, like things, is "inexhaustible." Since there is no "human nature" with the aid of which we could impose upon existence a meaning and a direction, it is existence itself which can be our only guide.

This is the fact of which we must not lose sight in thinking about Gide. No critic fails to remark that Gide's writings should not be separated from his life; it would be more exact to say that his writings *are* his life, that they contributed to the elaboration of his greatest work—an ex-

[7] Gide enjoyed satirizing psychoanalysis. See parts of *Œdipe,* and his "joke in one act," which he called *Le Treizième Arbre.* Also, one of the reasons for his interest in crime (see the preface to *L'Affaire Redureau*) was his conviction that psychology is far less informed about such matters than it imagines itself to be.
[8] See Sartre's *L'Enfance d'un Chef* in which the hero takes refuge in Freudism before finally discovering a haven in anti-semitism. ". . . A corrupt society invented psychiatry to defend itself against the investigations of certain people endowed with superior lucidity whose divinatory faculties were embarrassing it." (Antonin Artaud, *Van Gogh,* K. Editeur, 1947, p. 10.)
[9] Gide, *Journal,* 30 October 1935.

emplary existence. That he put his talent into his work, but his genius into his life, is far more true of Gide than of Wilde.

Few authors, it is true, have meditated more carefully upon the problems involved in creating literature that would endure. Gide repeatedly compares the hostility or indifference of the critics towards his books to the neglect which Baudelaire and Stendhal had suffered before him. He writes for future generations as much as for his contemporaries: "For a long time now I have not claimed to win my case except on appeal. I write only to be re-read."[10] One has the impression that Gide would have found it more difficult to emancipate himself from religion had he not been able to fall back upon another deity— the work of art. It is for this reason that his conversations with Valéry were often ordeals in which Gide did his best to defend the sacred places against intrusions of this sort: "Would a man of profound and merciless intelligence be able to interest himself in literature? In what connection? Where would he find a place for it in his mind?"[11] He had the alternative of finding either his literary activities or Valéry's ideas absurd.[12]

Gide thought, lived and wrote too much, and above all was too honest intellectually not to have contradicted himself on more than one occasion. We must not insist upon a given phrase, but be attentive to the tone and the context. To do so is to be struck by the difference which separates Gide from those authors who considered that art precedes life: Flaubert, the Goncourts, the symbolists, Proust, the surrealists, or the Balzac of "Let us get down to serious business. Let us talk about Eugénie Grandet." Gide has created no fictitious world which invites comparison with the real; one does not "withdraw" into his books which were written, if we are to believe his *Journal In-*

[10] *Journal des Faux Monnayeurs*, NRF, 1934, p. 53.
[11] Valéry, *Tel Quel I*, 1948, p. 182. ". . . The more one writes, the less one thinks." (*Monsieur Teste*, 1948, p. 105.)
[12] *Journal*, 9 February 1907.

time,[13] less for themselves than as an attempt to persuade his wife Madeleine to accompany him on the spiritual adventure that was his life. But in addressing himself to Madeleine, Gide was not unhopeful of attaining an infinitely wider audience which his books might serve to liberate from all allegiance except that which we owe to ourselves. Gide was a moralist endowed with an admirable prose style and a deep insight into the aesthetics of literary creation; as a result, he exposed the problems which occupied him not in treatises, but in novels and plays.[14] After meditating upon the relative importance of the individual and society, he concludes that such questions cannot be summarily treated—"Dialogue would be needed, a novel or a play."[15] Is it not here that we are to seek the reason for the too abrupt endings of, for example, *La Porte Etroite* and *La Symphonie Pastorale,* which surprise in the work of so accomplished a craftsman? Once the reader is in possession of whatever he need know to form an opinion, "All the rest is literature"; Gide is in haste to explore elsewhere. He was deeply conscious of the fact that there is no lasting art apart from perfection of form, and yet how often form is sacrificed to content, in *Robert,* in *Geneviève,* in the *Journal,* and in those books we have already mentioned where he seems impatient to have done.[16] However, in prose writings, perfection of form often condenses itself to the beauty and strength of language, as in the case of Montaigne and Pascal; and form, so understood, is, as we have already seen, abso-

13 "Until *Les Faux Monnayeurs* (the first book in writing which I tried to disregard her entirely) everything I wrote was written to convince her, to carry her along with me. The whole thing is nothing more nor less than one long piece of special pleading. No body of work has ever had more personal motives than mine. Failure to recognize that in it shows a distinct lack of perspicacity." (*Et Nunc Manet in Te, suivi de Journal Intime,* Ides et Calendes, 1951, p. 111.)
14 It is worth remarking that several of his early works, Gide called "treatises."
15 *Journal,* 27 June 1932. Also: "Perhaps even one gets closer to truth in the novel." (*Si le grain ne meurt,* NRF, 1949, p. 281.)
16 If we accept the following remark unconditionally it is of great importance in this connection. Referring to letters written to his wife over a long period of years and which she had one day destroyed, Gide wrote: "It was in them above all that I hoped to survive." (*Et Nunc Manet in Te,* Ides et Calendes, 1951, p. 91.)

lutely dependent upon the value of the ideas expressed.[17]
Here is the reason for Gide's devotion to his art—the art
of writing is, in the aesthetic of Gide, the art of the communication of ideas. "When the thought goes awry, so does
the style."[18] Art is not an end, but a means. "Certainly,"
he writes in his *Journal,* "I am no longer tormented by an
overmastering desire to write. The feeling that 'the most
important is yet to be said' no longer haunts me as once
it did."[19] The need to create is identical with the need to
convey an important message. What Gide says of his
Œdipe is equally true of everything he wrote: "My object
is not to make you shudder or weep, but to make you
think."[20] He hopes to make of *Les Faux Monnayeurs* "a
crossroads—a meeting-place of problems."[21] It is difficult to imagine Flaubert, whose only problems were technical, talking in such a way of one of his books. How un-
likely that the "artist" so many wish to make of Gide
would have written: *"Corydon* remains to my mind the
most important of my books. . . ."[22]

Had Gide's whole *raison d'être* been his art, his life
would have been comparable to that of his own Alissa.
Gide's art never abandoned him, to be sure, as completely
as Alissa's God abandoned her, but the confidence of his
old age is not that of his youth.

> Everything that still occupies our thinking may dis-
> appear [he writes], sink into the past, cease to hold, for
> the men of tomorrow, anything but an archaic signifi-
> cance. Other problems, unsuspected yesterday, may well
> trouble those who are to come after, and they will not
> even understand any more what it was that made up
> our justification for living. . . .

[17] "It is certainly difficult for me to believe that the soundest thought, the wisest and the most sensible, is not at the same time the one which, projected into writing, gives the most beautiful and the most harmonious phrases." (*Journal,* 5 October 1928.)
[18] *Ibid.,* 31 [sic] June 1923.
[19] *Ibid.,* 20 October 1930.
[20] *Ibid.,* 2 January 1933.
[21] *Ibid.,* 17 June 1923.
[22] *Ibid.,* 19 October 1942.

He adds in parenthesis, "I write this without really thinking it"[23] but he thought it sufficiently, both to write it and not to strike it out at the time of publication. A few years later there was even less hope that the culture to which Gide had contributed and with which he would survive or disappear might somehow be preserved. He permits himself no illusions on this score, for he writes *Ainsi soit-il* "in expectation of the cataclysm that will wipe everything out."[24]

If Gide is able to think such thoughts with reasonable equanimity, it is because his life had a meaning beyond that of art, it was its own meaning, it was an end in itself, and so he could write: "All things considered, I have won the game I played."[25] The only regrets of his later years are occasioned not by what he had left unwritten but by what he had left undone—the countries he had failed to visit, the temptations to which he had refused to yield. If it is the duty of man to "surpass himself," it is not toward a given goal, but simply toward the enrichment of existence itself, which is the only goal. "I feel the *duty* to be happy, higher and more imperious than the artificial duties of the artist."[26] Gide was profoundly attached to his wife, yet he always refused, or was unable, to give up his way of life for her sake. During the period of his interest in communism, however, he completely sacrificed his art to his political preoccupations. There is no better illustration of the relative places occupied in his esteem by his life and his art. *Thésée* was Gide's last creative effort; it is his artistic and philosophical testament and it ends with the sentence: "I have lived."

Whatever Gide's absorption in the problems of his art, or however high he placed it in the scale of human activities, it never determined his existence.

23 *Ibid.*, 10 April 1943.
24 NRF, 1952, p. 141.
25 *Ainsi soit-il*, NRF, 1952, p. 15.
26 *Journal*, 1889–1939, La Pléiade, 1948, p. 715. "It is a duty to make oneself happy." (*Ibid.*, p. 34.)

What rubbish all this literature is! [he writes]. Even
if I were to consider only the most successful writing,
what business have I, when life is here, with these reflec-
tions, these duplicates, of life? The only thing that matters to me is what can lead me to modify my way of
seeing and acting.[27]

Life is not derived from art as, for example, Mallarmé and
the *fin de siècle* aesthetic in general seemed to believe; art
is derived from life. The idea is innocuous in appearance
only, for it is one of the forms in which we may express
the principle which distinguishes modern thought from all
which preceded it—the particular is in itself meaningful;
or, if one prefers, existence precedes essence. Gide, by
sensing that truth is not to be attained by a "procedure"
whether artistic or intellectual, but that it is *immediately*
accessible to perception and sensation, turned his back
upon the past and associated himself closely with the literature and philosophy of the twentieth century. Let us take
up the story now in detail.

Gide's youthful adventures in North Africa revealed to
him not only the peculiarity of his sexual instincts, but the
exterior world as well, and the innumerable sensual delights to which it invites us. He began to doubt that human
life achieves its greatest plenitude in intellectual activity,
which indeed may even miss the essential. What struck
Gide most forcibly was the *evidence* of sensation, as opposed to the always contestable results of reasoning. ". . . I
spent three years of travel forgetting . . . what I had
learned with my head."[28] The sterile confusion of the
world of books is contrasted to the pressing reality of that
of the senses: "All sensation has an infinite *presence*."[29]
The only indubitable knowledge is that founded not upon

[27] *Ibid.*, November 1947.
[28] *Les Nourritures Terrestres*, NRF, 1944, p. 19.
[29] *Ibid.*, p. 24.

logic but upon sensation: "All knowledge not preceded by a sensation is useless to me."[30] There is no intellectual system, however solid in appearance, to which we cannot oppose another equally convincing; and the child is perhaps never more father of the man than when he replies simply: "because I saw it," or, "because I felt it." *Les Nourritures Terrestres* is the book of a man who, like Descartes, unconvinced by the "truths" his society had bequeathed him, rejected them all so as to start from the beginning with an unencumbered mind. Gide, in revolting against the values closest to European hearts was doing in literature what, at the same time, Husserl was attempting in philosophy. Both saw that rationalism had been mined out, that a radical new departure was necessary and that it was to be made by recognizing the immediate intelligibility of things which any attempt to "systematize" succeeds only in denaturing, distorting and impoverishing.

Les Nourritures Terrestres is a hymn of praise to those things which provoke in us the strongest physical sensations—the desert especially with its thirst and fatigue serving to make the shade, the fruits and the moisture of the oases that much more poignant. Gide's entire person becomes simply a means of access to things. "I sometimes used to keep the bread I took with me until I almost grew faint. Then, it seemed, it was less strangely redolent of nature and it entered more fully into my being. It was something flowing into me from without. At every open gate of sense, I welcomed its presence. . . ."[31] The object is never separated from the sensation it can be made to give us. ". . . There were merchants of aromatics. We bought different kinds of resins from them. Some were for sniffing. Others were for chewing. Yet others were burned."[32] The sense of touch is the most precious as being the most immediate. ". . . Sheer *being* grew for me into something hugely voluptuous. I could have wished to

[30] *Ibid.*, p. 35.
[31] *Ibid.*, p. 75.
[32] *Ibid.*, p. 162.

savour every form and condition of life—that of fish, that
of plants. Of all the joys of sense, I coveted most those of
touch."[33] Re-reading *Les Nourritures Terrestres* in later
years, Gide sees in it above all "a defence of 'dispossession'" (*dénuement*).[34] The mind is emptied of its concepts, the body stripped of its possessions, there is no
longer anything between us and things, one by one they
"penetrate" us, it is in us they exist. We may refuse their
solicitation if we wish, but there is no other certitude, no
"higher" truth.

The literature of the world is full of tributes to the
beauty of nature. *Les Nourritures Terrestres* is not one of
them; if it had been, it would not have exercised the influence it did, and we would not be speaking of it here. There
is no romanticism in Gide.[35] *Les Nourritures Terrestres*
is a joyful partaking of the fruits of the earth; the prevailing tone of romanticism is one of melancholy when it is
not one of despair. Romanticism is a quest, not a possession; and if the romantic's longing is inevitably an unhappy
one it is because what he is seeking does not exist. For
"Nature" does not exist any more than does the "Youth,"
"Maturity," "Death," etc., of which Sartre speaks in *La
Nausée.*[36] Only individual things exist, and it is to them
that general ideas owe their purely verbal existence. Much
of the impact of *Les Nourritures Terrestres* is to be attributed to its implicit revolutionary idea that things *in
themselves* hold forth, accessible to everyone, all that life
has to offer. Objects are neither "symbols" nor manifestations of "laws" more important than themselves, but independent entities that have successfully resisted all of man's
attempts to organize them into other things that can be
neither seen, heard nor touched.

This notion of the primacy of the particular was to ac-

[33] *Ibid.,* p. 114.
[34] *Ibid.,* p. 13.
[35] Except perhaps for the often ludicrous Ménalque, whose appearance in
L'Immoraliste is that book's most obvious defect.
[36] NRF, 1948, p. 157. We find the same idea in Valéry: "The universe exists
only on paper. There is no idea to present it, no sense to reveal it. It is
spoken of, and that is all." (*Monsieur Teste,* 1948, p. 107.)

quire great importance in Gide's thought. In a different form, he had already touched upon it in *Paludes*—in 1895 its originality was such that it could only be treated in a *Sotie* which no one would be obliged to take very seriously. He argues that normality in people is the absence of something that would permit them to be abnormal. Thus a sick person is a normal person plus his sickness and not a normal person lacking health. Just as individual things and not essences or generalities are creative of sensation, so only people who are not "representative" are instructive. The protagonists of Gide's books are all, in some way, very remarkable persons. Michel, Alissa, Lafcadio, a number of the personages of *Les Faux Monnayeurs,* and, of course, the heroes drawn from Greek mythology or the Bible. The "average" person is, in the work of Gide, usually marked out for ridicule or disapproval. Gide's admiration for *Armance* is due in part to the fact that Stendhal has portrayed in his central figure an impotent. If Stendhal seeks the rule, writes Gide in his preface to *Armance:* ". . . his point of departure is a unique and particular case"; and Gide reproaches the French classics for having concerned themselves not with individuals, but with "Man."

One often hears that Gide discredited realism in the novel. Traditional realism, yes. A realism whose ambition was less to eliminate the subjectivity of the author (an impossibility) than to eliminate the unusual so as to isolate the general which, so writers had learned from science, alone counts. The characters portrayed in realist literature are invariably "typical," the author in creating them has, like a mathematician, "taken an average." If realist novels are frequently brutal and sombre, it is because life is most commonly like that—wealth or good breeding being exceptions. And yet, in what sense is the exceptional person or event any less "real" than the average person or the commonplace event?[37] As a matter of fact, the "average person" does not exist, any more than does "Nature." It might therefore be argued that Gide, by introducing the

[37] "As though the frequent were more natural than the rare . . . lead more natural than gold!" (Preface to *Le Roi Candaule,* 1930, p. 13.)

"particular" into literature, has created a realism more genuine than the old. *Les Faux Monnayeurs* is, in many respects, more "real" than *Germinie Lacerteux*. It makes use of two actual happenings, an affair of counterfeiting and the suicide of a schoolboy at Clermont-Ferrand.[38] But above all, Gide has not allowed the requirements of his plot to hamper the development of his characters or the exploitation of a situation that particularly interested him. He obliged himself to draw the fullest possible substance from a given situation or character by refusing to profit from the momentum of his story. "Never profit from acquired momentum—such is the rule of the game I play,"[39] writes Gide in *Le Journal des Faux Monnayeurs;* but even more significantly: ". . . There would be superfluous characters, ineffective gestures, conversations that come to nothing, and the plot will not get under way."[40] Existence, or reality, we have already remarked, is commerce with the particular, and this is precisely what Gide has tried to capture in *Les Faux Monnayeurs*. Life is full of superfluous players, ineffective gestures, conversations that come to nothing, and above all there are no "plots." Life, unlike the stories told about it, has no beginning and no end, it contains no adventures,[41] only disconnected events; consequently *Les Faux Monnayeurs* will end abruptly, but ". . . not because of the exhaustion of subject matter, which must give the impression of the inexhaustible."[42]

Gide had few friends as close to him as was Roger Mar-

38 Gide's interest in the *fait divers* is further attested by his *La Sequestrée de Poitiers* and *L'Affaire Redureau*. The rumour concerning the abduction of the Pope, upon which *Les Caves du Vatican* is based, actually circulated.
39 NRF, 1934, p. 89.
40 *Ibid.*, p. 30.
41 See *La Nausée*, especially pp. 56–7. It is as though *Les Faux Monnayeurs* had been written in an attempt to bring the novel closer to what Sartre defines as "life" in contrast to literature.
42 *Journal des Faux Monnayeurs*, p. 109. Gide's return to existence in literature has been carried on by, for example, Louis Guilloux in his *Jeu de Patience*; and in the domain of language itself by Raymond Queneau who uses in his novels a "spoken" and not a "written" French. It is to be remarked in this connection that dialogue occupies a far more prominent place in novels than it once did. Compare Hemingway to James, Malraux to Proust, etc. Furthermore, a book like Faulkner's *The Sound and the Fury* is as disjointed as life itself. The author does not trouble himself to provide us, in their proper order, with certain details necessary to a complete understanding of what is taking place.

tin du Gard. The deep sympathy they had for one another
could serve to illustrate the fundamental compatibility between what is best in the rationalist tradition, and what in
Gide's thought will perhaps one day come to be called pre-
existentialist, as one now talks of pre-romanticism.[43] The
questions posed by Antoine Thibault are those with which
Gide was all his life preoccupied and to which Sartre will
eventually offer very precise answers. But if there is continuity, there is also a very decided divergence between the
two men, at least as novelists, and it takes place because in
his writings Martin du Gard has remained convinced of the
greater truth of the general. We read in Gide's *Journal:*

> Faced with any question whatever of psychology
> (even—or rather especially—in his capacity as a novel-
> ist) Roger readily drops anything to do with the excep-
> tional, even with the minority. What he is continually
> asking himself is—what, in these particular circum-
> stances, most usually happens?[44]

The relationship of the work of Gide to existentialist
thought offers an admirable example of the mysterious
process by which ideas hidden in the intuition of the artist
are brought to light and pushed to their logical conclusion
by subsequent generations. It does not really matter that
the artist may refuse, often with indignation, to acknowledge his progeny. "The work of art endures," Valéry remarks, "to the extent that it is capable of appearing quite
other than as its author created it."[45] And so it is that Gide
is repelled by the existentialist notion of the absurd, and
fails to see that it is latent in most of what he wrote. Again,
as in the case of *engagement,* it is the term itself that
frightens rather than what is meant. In a lecture given after
the war at Beirut, Gide criticizes a number of contempo-

[43] ". . . We are constantly of the same mind, Roger and I. Talk does not set
us at loggerheads. It instructs, informs and enlightens us." (*Journal,* 25
December 1939.)
[44] 2 October 1936.
[45] *Tel Quel I,* NRF, 1948, p. 168.

rary authors, including Sartre, for holding the opinion that "we live in an absurd world, where nothing tallies with anything else."[46] However, on 9 May 1940, in his *Journal*, Gide quotes Martin du Gard: "The more you think it over . . . the more you realize the obvious truth that it doesn't add up," and comments, "But what the devil would you have it add up to?" That is to say that Gide had succeeded so thoroughly in reconciling himself to the non-existence of inalterable principles (which is all the existentialists mean by the absurd) that he is unable (or feigns to be unable) to understand why people continue to waste their time looking for them or lamenting their lack of success. Furthermore, like the existentialists, Gide sees in the revelation of the absurd not a defeat but an opportunity: "Don't turn away in the cowardice of despair. Go through it. It is on the other side that you should look for a reason to hope. Go straight on. Don't be turned aside. At the other end of the tunnel you'll find light again."[47]

Modern science as well as literature, philosophy and art has been forced to acknowledge the absurd, and some of the sharpest insights of *Corydon* (to which opinion still refuses a number of signal merits) were made possible by Gide's hypothesis that there is no "purpose" in nature. "I wager that in less than twenty years such expressions as against nature, contrary to natural law, etc., will no longer be taken seriously."[48] It is taking somewhat longer, but Gide was right. To talk of what nature "intended" is to commit an anthropomorphism similar to those once universally held—"nature abhors a vacuum," etc. "It is *uselessly* that the poppy, etc. . . . *uselessly* that lucerne . . . there is a PRODIGALITY of *forms* in Nature, as there is prodigality of seed. The SUPERFLUOUS, that is what dis-

46 This lecture was published under the title *Souvenirs Littéraires et Problèmes actuels* by L'Ecole Supérieure des Lettres de Beyrouth, 1946, p. 53.
47 *Journal*, 1889–1939, La Pléiade, 1948, p. 902.
48 *Corydon*, NRF, 1929, p. 39. It is difficult even for the scientist to rid himself of the habit of seeing order or intention where there is none. Thus, in biology, the division of animals into species does not represent the discovery of a divine Plan, but the *invention* of a device; and one which has now outlived its scientific usefulness.

concerts, but that is what we must admit."[49] But to admit the superfluous, the useless, is to admit the absurd.

The sentiment of the absurd, which may take several different forms, is essentially a recognition of the absolute uniqueness of things, of their existence in and for themselves, of their *uselessness;* they are, as Sartre says, *"de trop";* they serve no *purpose.* This revelation of the independence of things would seem to be, depending upon whether one is an artist or a philosopher, exhilarating or terrible. It gratifies the senses but cows the intellect. *La Nausée* is the philosopher's reaction to the world of *Les Nourritures Terrestres.* The famous tree-root in the public garden at Bouville with the aid of which Antoine Roquentin comes to understand at last the meaning of his "nausea" is a thing that defies classification. It is not enough to explain what it does. "Function explained nothing: it made it possible to understand more or less what *a* root was, but not at all *this one here."*[50] Nor can it even be described. "Black? The root *was not* black: what was on this piece of wood was not blackness—it was . . . something else. Black, like the circle, did not exist. I looked at the root: was it *more than black* or nearly black?"[51] This uniqueness, "unjustifiability" or "contingence" as Satre calls it, of all particular things, is what man has unceasingly struggled to conjure away by placing between himself and the exterior world a protective screen of logic, whose function it is to discover the "inter-relationship" of things. To interest ourselves, therefore, in *individual* things, to proclaim that things are intelligible in themselves, is to be able to dispense with concepts. What is meant exactly by the existence of a thing must be *felt,* explanations are necessarily inadequate. "Existence is not something that may be thought of at a distance: it has to invade you abruptly, fix itself upon you, weigh heavily on your heart like a great unmoving beast. . . ."[52] All of which does not mean that

---

[49] *Journal,* 1889–1939, La Pléiade, 1948, p. 808.
[50] *La Nausée,* NRF, 1948, p. 169.
[51] *Ibid.,* p. 170.
[52] *La Nausée,* NRF, 1948, p. 172.

Antoine Roquentin's encounter with existence was a "subjective" experience of no general importance. "The feeling
of Nausea is not in me: I feel it *over there* on the wall.
. . ."[53] It is just that the barrier of logic has been broken
through revealing on the other side the chaos of which
Baudelaire, Rimbaud, Cézanne and Valéry have given us
a foretaste. Gide also, and particularly the Gide of *Les
Nourritures Terrestres,* hints at these things. Thought is an
impediment rather than a help in acceding to greater
awareness. ". . . We spend our time walking about, and
have ceased to think."[54] The dispossession of Gide involves the shuffling off of old habits of thought and perception as well as of material possessions. This means,
however, not only conventional attitudes toward morality,
but the very way in which we think and perceive. It will be
difficult for us to explain the extraordinary spiritual rever-
berations produced by *Les Nourritures Terrestres* for as
long as we continue to look upon it as a sort of contemporary *Rubáiyát.* It is an invitation to the discovery of another world, that of sensation, one which not only is not
"subjective" but far more real than the world reduced to
the limits of the intelligence. Gide makes this more clear
in the *Nouvelles Nourritures,* where he writes: ". . . I
have learned more in sensual delights than in books; . . . I
have found in books more obscurity than light."[55] The
learning to which he refers enters into no known category
of thought. ". . . Who will deliver my mind from the heavy
chains of logic? My sincerest emotion is rendered false as
soon as I express it."[56] He has more confidence in what he
feels than in what he thinks.

> The fear of stumbling causes our minds to cling to the
> hand-rail of logic. . . . There are those who reason and
> those who let others be right. . . . There are those who
> do without living and those who do without being right.

[53] *Ibid.,* p. 35.
[54] *Les Nourritures Terrestres,* NRF, 1944, p. 155.
[55] *Ibid.*
[56] *Ibid.,* p. 200.

. . . Ah, dearest and gayest of my thoughts! Why should I seek any longer to legitimate your birth?[57]

Although Gide was not in the least concerned to give a logical organization to his thought, it is not disjointed; it has a consistency, or harmony (with one exception which we shall discuss in a moment), which is that of an organism rather than of a philosophical demonstration. He senses, for example, that if reason is not capable of supplying us with a comprehensive view of reality it is because reason itself is part of that reality, that man is "in the world." He therefore believes "That matter is penetrable by the mind, pliable to it, adapted to it; that the mind is associated with matter to the point of losing itself in it . . ."[58] And also that ". . . our logic fashioned itself after nature and . . . we view nature after the manner of our brain. . . ."[59] Gide was an amateur naturalist of wide learning but one who looked upon nature from the point of view of the moralist and aesthete rather than from that of the scientist. The modern philosophico-scientific attitude toward the world may be compared to that of a person who, confronted by a painting of one of the masters, shows an interest exclusively in the tools and materials by which it was realized. However, the marvel is not how it came into existence, but that it exists at all. Wherever the philosopher sees a problem which is not one of value, he has deliberately or unconsciously ignored a solution. ". . . always and everywhere in nature," writes Gide, "the solution and the problem are one. Or better still: there is no problem; there are only solutions. Man's mind invents the problems afterwards. It sees problems everywhere."[60]

[57] *Ibid.*, p. 208.
[58] *Ibid.*, p. 236.
[59] *Journal*, 1889–1939, La Pléiade, 1948, p. 806. ". . . I've reached the point where I don't even distinguish the mind from the body. I cannot conceive one without the other." (*Ibid.*, 15 May 1949.)
[60] *Ibid.*, November 1947. "The whole world . . . is but answers to questions that, properly considered, it is not specially necessary nor even expedient to ask. Because the question can never come save as an afterthought." (*Ibid.*, 18 March 1929.)

Existentialism is drawing philosophy out of the quag-
mire of epistemology by persuading it to drop a great
number of false problems, notably those of perception.
"Problems of perception" exist only because philosophers
persist in seeking the principle which makes perception
possible; but once we admit the absurdity of there being
nothing "behind" the fact of perception and turn our attention to *perception itself* the problems become solutions.
Perception is a problem only for those looking for "laws"
or erecting systems; for others, it is a miraculous solution
to the problems of a creature both "angel and beast," both
mind and matter, obliged to make his uncertain way "in
the world." "The world," remarks Merleau-Ponty, "is not
what I think, but what I live. . . ."[61] Gide's world was a
"lived," and not an "explained" one, for he discovered
that once we have ceased to violate our common sense in
the search for reassuring absolutes, the world begins to
make sense.[62] The immediate, thanks to the undeniable
sensations associated with it, always makes sense; it is in
the organization of immediates, to which we insist upon
sacrificing all the rest, that uncertainty begins. "Emotion,"
we read in *Paludes,* "is never false; . . . error begins with
judgment."[63] "The wonder in face of the world" which, in
philosophy, is replacing the attempt to "explain" it, is very
characteristic of Gide: ". . . That there should be something, anything at all, how strange! It will never cease to
astonish me."[64] It is in this way that we prefer to interpret
the title, borrowed from the Bible which Gide gave to the
story of his childhood and youth—*Si le grain ne meurt.*
Until we die to our craving for metaphysical certitude (religious in the case of Gide) we cannot be reborn to a world
which, if we will accept the evidence of our senses, is its
own solution.

[61] *La Phénoménologie de la Perception,* NRF, 1945, Avant-Propos, XII.
[62] " 'Good sense' consists in not allowing oneself to be so far dazzled by a
sentiment or an idea, however excellent, as to lose sight of everything else."
(Gide, *Journal,* 16 October 1927.)
[63] NRF, 1936, p. 59.
[64] *Journal,* November 1947.

Few of us doubt that we possess an Ego or a Self, an entity somewhere inside us that gives a coherence known as character or personality to our acts. And yet if we look inside ourselves we discover no fixed unchanging thing we can call the Self, but only the aimless passage of memories, perceptions and emotions. Are we obliged to accept the existence of something of which we have no consciousness? On the contrary, if appearance is reality, it follows that what does not appear to consciousness does not exist. The Self exists no more than does the essence "horse," or "nature," or the "average man" or countless other generalities which men have imagined to support their contention that the universe is explainable.

The classical conception of mind as an organizer and classifier of sense data entering from the exterior world required the existence of an Ego. But the idea of the Ego is too deep rooted a one to have a merely philosophical origin. The Ego is in reality the soul, redesigned for philosophical purposes. A religion in which, like the Christian, reward and retribution, innocence and guilt, play such vital rôles, cannot do without the existence of a Self absolutely individual yet transcending change, which will be, according to its conduct, recompensed or punished. In more general terms, the soul, or Self, is a channel of communication with the absolute. Not only are we attained through it by the justice of God, but inversely, it is by the Self, or rather by the suppression of Self, that the mystic rejoins God and the romantic identifies himself with nature. If this is true, then a loss of confidence in the existence of absolutes should be accompanied by doubt as to the reality of the Self, at least as traditionally conceived. And this is what in fact occurred. There could be no grounds for fearing the absurd in the outer world if we could be sure that in us there was a piece of that world, solid and reassuring, a "thing" that could be labelled good or evil. Stendhal and Baudelaire are, as usual, precursors.[65] One of the reasons why Stendhal's novels met with so little appreciation at the

[65] And perhaps even more strikingly, Dostoievsky.

time of their publication was that readers were unable to "catalogue" a Julien Sorel. They resented not being sure whether they should approve or condemn a given personage—a problem that seldom arises with the characters of Balzac. And then, how to "explain" an event like the attempted assassination of Madame de Rênal, so little in accord with Julien's interests, which we had a right to assume he would place above everything else? "Gratuitous" acts were called to a brilliant future. This inability to calculate (i.e. to be a defined type) in Stendhal's heroes is perhaps a reflection of the fact that Stendhal was not very certain of what he himself was. ". . . I ought to write my autobiography. Then perhaps I should at last know . . . what I have really been—light-hearted or sad, a wit or a dullard, a brave man or a coward."[66] Or again: "But at bottom . . . I do not know what I am—good or bad, witty or dull."[67] The feeling that he was not one but many was a frequent source of consternation for Baudelaire. The firmest resolutions of the most conscientious of artists and of the affectionate son were continually thwarted by the lucidity of the thinker and the extravagance of the dandy. The absurd had installed itself in the centre of his being, and Baudelaire could not have said who or what he was. Such is perhaps the least fanciful interpretation of the mysterious remark: "From the vaporization and the centralization of the *Self*. Everything is there."[68] Were it not for the tendency of the Self to "vaporize" itself, we might succeed in giving our existence an orientation, or at least know what attitude to take toward it. To "centralize" the Self is to arm oneself against the absurd. Whatever interpretation one prefers,[69] however, the essential for us is that Baudelaire recognized the possibility of the disintegration of the Self. "In every man," he writes, "at every hour, there are two roads of desire—one towards God, the other

[66] *Henry Brulard*, Divan, 1949, p. 15.
[67] *Ibid.*, p. 317.
[68] "Mon Cœur mis à nu," *Œuvres de Baudelaire*, Vol. II, La Pléiade, 1941, p. 642.
[69] Albert Béguin has another; see *L'Ame Romantique et le Rêve*, Cahiers du Sud, 1937, Vol. II, p. 403.

towards the Devil."[70] As far as Sartre is concerned, the context of Rimbaud's "I, is another" proves that Rimbaud meant simply that consciousness does not spring from a Self, but that the Self is constituted subsequently, with the aid of reflexion.[71] An important part of the meditation of Valéry is devoted to the question. Valéry, like Gide, was reluctant to "conclude," but he suggests in a great number of his reflexions that the Self is a popular superstition. To restrict ourselves to the collection of observations contained in the first volume of Tel Quel, we remark, "In our best moments, as in our worst, we no longer strike ourselves as being ourselves. We squander, or submit to, some indefinable and improbable self."[72] "We know of ourselves only what circumstances have given us to know."[73] "The more a consciousness is 'conscious,' the more its individuality, its opinions, its acts, etc., appear to it strange—even foreign. It would tend therefore to use what is most its own and what is most personal to it as it would things exterior and accidental."[74] (Had Valéry consented to be a philosopher, his work would no doubt have been based, as is that of the existentialists, upon an "intentional" conception of consciousness.) "Every investigation of oneself, every accident that causes us to seize upon ourselves, every unaccustomed point of view, shows self in a light we did not know it under. It is not certain that knowing oneself makes sense. . . ."[75] "My innermost idea concerns my inability to be the person I am—I cannot recognize myself in a finite form. And MYSELF is forever fleeing my person, which, however, it sketches out or imprints even as it flees."[76] There are many other reflexions of a similar tenor which we might have chosen.

[70] "Mon Cœur mis à nu," Œuvres de Baudelaire, Vol. II, La Pléiade, 1941, p. 647.
[71] See Sartre's article "La Transcendance de l'Ego," in Recherches Philosophiques, Vol. VI, p. 119.
[72] NRF, 1948, p. 61.
[73] Ibid., p. 62.
[74] Ibid., p. 63.
[75] Ibid., p. 65.
[76] Tel Quel I, NRF, 1948, p. 187. As we shall see eventually, Valéry has here expressed a leit-motiv of L'Etre et le Néant.

Just before the war there appeared a novel, the hero of which was a man sufficiently honest (or "sincere" to employ the Gidean term) and courageous to refuse to believe in the existence of a subjective constant of which he had no personal experience. The novel is Camus's *L'Etranger.* Meursault is not only a "stranger" in the world because the world is absurd, but a stranger among men because he alone accepts to *live* the absurd; that is, accepts the suppression of the Self which must, if we are rigorous, follow the suppression of sense in the exterior world. Meursault has no subjectivity considered as a thing; his crime is therefore a "gratuitous act." The evolution that has taken place in less than half a century from Proust, who is still a Kantian,[77] to Camus, is almost startling. Duhamel's Salavin sought to "change his soul," a Maurice Sachs would have been content simply to possess one. Sachs passed his life aspiring *to be,* suspecting obscurely that no one ever succeeds.[78]

If we are to appreciate fully what is most original and influential in Gide's thought, this is the point of view from which it should be approached—that of the suppression of the Self. This is the theme that will enable us to perceive the cohesiveness of a philosophy that taken as a whole may appear diffuse and ineffectual.

We have maintained that Gide's art is a reverberation of his existence, an attempt to formulate and to explore some of the questions that his day to day experience suggested were important. Among such experiences none was more frequent, nor more rich with possibilities for his art and thought, than that of his inability to decide upon the

77 "The various sensations of pleasure or disgust depend less often on the nature of the exterior objects arousing them than on each individual's feeling of being moved by them to like or dislike." (Kant, *Beobachtungen über das Gefühl des Schönen und Erhabenen,* Inselverlag, Leipzig, 1924, p. 3.)

78 See in *Le Sabbat,* the episode of Sachs's attempt to become a country gentleman. In an article on Charles du Bos republished in *Littérature Présente* (Corrêa, 1952), Maurice Nadeau wonders whether the disintegration of the Self might not be "an epidemic of the times." As an indication of what this tendency has produced, consider the heroes of André Dhotel, Georges Leban of *Les Rues dans l'Aurore,* Sébastien of *Mémoires de Sébastien,* etc., who are totally devoid of "depth." We are told, or they tell us themselves what they *do,* and that is as much as we ever learn about what goes on "inside."

real nature of his Self. It is a point we need hardly insist upon, any reader of the *Journal* will have been struck by the persistence with which Gide returns to this subject. Here is one of the most noteworthy of these passages:

> Nothing holds, nothing is constant nor sure in my life. I resemble and differ in turn; there is no creature so foreign to me but what I could swear to feel a kinship with it. I still do not know, at thirty-six, whether I am miserly or prodigal, abstemious or a glutton . . . or rather, feeling myself carried suddenly from one extreme to the other, in this very oscillation I have the impression that my fate accomplishes itself.[79]

Gide believed that good writing was not possible apart from complete sincerity, and it is sincerely that he portrayed his most divergent characters; he is both Alissa and Michel, the pastor of *La Symphonie Pastorale* and Lafcadio, the author of both *Numquid et Tu . . . ?* and *Les Nourritures Terrestres*. Nor must it be supposed that it is a question here of a *succession* of Selves. It is simultaneously that man entertains his two desires, one leading toward God and the other toward Satan. It is simultaneously that Michel of *L'Immoraliste* loves and seeks to destroy his wife; simultaneously that the prodigal son loves his parents and longs to abandon them; and simultaneously that Thésée loves his father and provokes his father's suicide.

In the same way that man has, by logic, attempted to deny the absurdity of the exterior world, he has, by the invention of the Self, tried to ignore the chaos within, which Gide, on the contrary, insisted upon emphasizing. It will be instructive to return for a moment to our comparison of Proust and Gide. Proust was completely indifferent to religion. However, the religious sentiment, if we define it as the need to believe that the universe makes sense, and in a way that is comprehensible to men, has assumed many

[79] 24 August 1905.

forms. Chased out the door, it returns through the window. Proust has sacrificed one of the elements of the couple Ego-Absolute, but greatly inflated the other. The order of the universe is transferred from the outer to the inner world. Not only does matter possess no qualities not attributed to it by the human mind, people themselves, and conspicuously in the case of love, have no qualities independent of the opinion of others. There is perhaps no work of literature which creates more strongly in the reader than does *A la Recherche du Temps Perdu* the impression that he has entered another world; not a world which is other by the strangeness of its customs, but by its "interiority." The reader is introduced into the subjectivity of Marcel as one might enter the residence, full of rare bibelots and precious works of art, of some affable prince. No absolute, however, can be satisfactory that does not endure, there is no spiritual peace in an order that is only temporary; and yet nothing would appear more fragile than the Self divorced from the transcendental principle which it is its function to represent—a fact which disquiets Marcel:

> It is called a leaden sleep; it seems that, for a few moments after such a sleep has ended, we have ourselves become nothing but leaden men. We are *no longer anyone*. How, then, looking for our thought, our personality, as we hunt for a lost object, do we in the end recover our own Self rather than that of some quite other person?[80]

But the significance of Marcel's mystical experiences is precisely that they prove the *continuity of the Self*. The *madeleine* and the tisane evoke for him not merely a recollection of Combray, but the same *emotions* and *sensations* which had been his as a child. Marcel the adult is therefore in some essential way linked to the child he was at Combray many years before. The "interior Self," untouched by the "voluntary memory," and effaced for long periods of time before the development and wasting away of more superficial Selves, guarantees our integrity as persons.[81]

Nothing could be more foreign to Gide than this conception of the Self as the supreme reality. His efforts are directed towards achieving the greatest possible "nudity," or "penetrability" to sensation which is a property *not of man but of things*. Consider this passage from his preface to the second edition of *Voyage d'Urien:*

> This emotion, therefore, because I did not describe it in *itself*—too *abstract* as it was—or because I did not submit it to this or that fact which might have motivated it as others are accustomed to do in their novels—because, in order to manifest it, *I placed it in landscapes* —in all this you saw only idle description. And yet it still seems to me natural that an emotion we owe to a landscape should be able in turn to make use of that landscape—as of a word. . . .

This process of emptying the Self to the profit of the exterior world was to continue to a point where Gide could write ". . . to be alone in myself, is to be no longer anyone."[82] For Gide, Montaigne's greatest originality was to have recognized: ". . . the non-stability of the human personality which never *is,* but is conscious of itself only in a becoming that cannot be pinned down."[83] Montaigne's experience was Gide's own: "I am never; I become,"[84] and he defines the soul as ". . . this bundle of emotions, tendencies and susceptibilities, whose bond perhaps is only physiological."[85]

We are now in a position to be quite explicit as to the nature of Gidean sincerity. To be sincere is, quite simply,

[81] See, for example, *Le Temps Retrouvé* (II), p. 16, NRF, 1919–27.
[82] *Les Nourritures Terrestres*, NRF, 1944, p. 171.
[83] *Pages Immortelles de Montaigne*, Corrêa, 1939, p. 17.
[84] *Journal*, 8 February 1927.
[85] *Ibid.*, 16 September 1942.

to admit that we can discover within ourselves no immutable core, but only a phantom self which dissolves when we try to seize it. Hence the futility of introspection; the attempt to find out what sort of person we "really are," can result only in a paralysing uncertainty. Gide's youth was tormented by a mania for introspection which he had the lucidity to deplore many years before he succeeded in overcoming it. In 1893 he writes: ". . . This perpetual analysis of one's thoughts, this absence of action, this moralizing, are of all things in the world the most wearisome, insipid and almost incomprehensible, once one has got clear of it."[86] Time and experience reinforced his belief: "After a little while, what one understands least is oneself,"[87] and that because ". . . there is no feeling so simple as not to be immediately complicated and falsified by introspection."[88] To be sincere with oneself is to have the honesty, not to confess that one is base, but what is even more difficult, to confess that one is nothing at all. Nothing, that is, except what we wish to make of ourselves. We are no more "determined" from within than from without. "I never am; I become. I become what I believe (or what *you* believe) I am."[89] And elsewhere he remarks: "I am never other than what I believe myself to be."[90] These ideas lead us directly to the secret of Gide's importance which seems to many out of proportion with the intrinsic value of his writing. If he appeared as the devil incarnate to some and as the deliverer to others it is because he proposed that instead of looking for a Self, or submitting to an imaginary one, we accept the fact that the only Self we will ever have is one which *we ourselves create*. After centuries of unsuccessful attempts to define man, it is time to understand that we are free to create him. The soul is given not as a ready-made object but as

86 *Ibid.*, August 1893.
87 *Ibid.*, 1889–1939, La Pléiade, 1948, p. 105.
88 *Ibid.*, 20 August 1926.
89 *Ibid.*, 9 October 1927.
90 *Les Faux Monnayeurs*, NRF, 1949, p. 93.

unfinished material to be worked upon to the best of our ability. ". . . Man is responsible for God."[91]

Human freedom is limitless because it is that of self-determination. ". . . We become whatever we are persuaded we are."[92] We do not "gain" our freedom; we do not "protect" it by refusing to engage ourselves in enterprises which involve responsibility and constraint; freedom is thrust upon us, we are "condemned" to it.[93] This being the case, Gide argues that instead of accepting the "human nature" that religion and society are but too eager to propose, and wherever possible impose, it is our duty to realize as many as possible of man's unsuspected potentialities whose development is at present impeded by our readiness to accept someone else's word for what we are. This is the significance of "disponibility" (*disponibilité*) in Gide—events should find us ready to exchange one Self for another and better one. The only qualities we possess are those that the event offers us the opportunity of inventing.[94] The greatness of Gide is to have resisted throughout his life the temptation *to be*—to enter into the repose of "thinghood." "This contemptible comedy that we are all more or less engaged in; I would like to lend myself to it less than do so many others, so that my writings may find their principal value in this very abstention."[95]

The people for whom Gide has the least esteem are those most deeply engaged in playing their "contemptible comedy," the object of which is to conceal the nothingness which more sincere people have the courage to admit.

91 *Journal*, 10 April 1942.
92 *Ibid.*, 29 August 1938.
93 This is Mathieu Delarue's first important discovery. (See Sartre's *L'Age de Raison*.) He had passed his life protecting his liberty only to find that man's liberty is inalienable. His next step will be to discover how it is to be employed.
94 In "Autour de Monsieur Barrès" (Prétextes), Gide cites Laclos's *Les Liaisons Dangereuses*: "One rarely acquires the qualities one can get along without."
95 *Journal*, 12 March 1938. "I am beginning to tire of *not being* . . . sometimes my pride suffers from a veritable despair." (*Ibid.*, 24 October 1907.) "Why should I give an artificial unity to my life by artificially imitating myself?" (*Ibid.*, 24 August 1905.)

One of Gide's deepest insights and one of which Sartre will make extensive use, is to have seen that men pretend to be what they are not, not out of vanity,[96] but out of cowardice. It makes little difference to men *what* they are, the essential is *to be something*. Something that is delimited, defined, something which fulfils a definite function and which is therefore without responsibility for the rest. Something, in brief, which is justified, protected from outer absurdity and the inner void. When someone is able to convince himself that he is a senator or a business man in the same way a chair is a chair, he simultaneously creates order out of chaos, society immediately assumes an inalterable form, "contingency" in the universe is exorcized. Men become, for example, fascists not because they are attracted by fascist political philosophy but *to be* a fascist, and a fascist in preference to other things because fascism offers along with a minimum of intellectual exertion the maximum determination.[97] There is no justification, on the political level, for equating fascism and communism; if their effects are sometimes similar it is because political leaders like so many others, find absolute authority an easy way out of the inevitable uncertainty and limitless responsibility of man's estate.

It is to be noticed that Gide's Robert, the ancestor of the Sartrean "swine," is essentially not a vain man, but an authoritarian. If the Self is to exist, there must be an exterior order of some kind, a fixed point in relation to which the Self can be determined. But since all order is necessarily arbitrary, it cannot survive without respect for authority. *Robert* is full of statements like these: "Man needs to be directed, organized, dominated."[98] and "Rebelliousness is always blameworthy."[99] etc. The authoritarian is fundamentally a man who is afraid. He knows that order

---

96 Lucien Fleurier, of Sartre's *L'Enfance d'un Chef*, becomes an anti-semite not because he felt himself "better" than the Jews, but to escape the misery of man's basic indetermination.
97 In Simone de Beauvoir's *L'Invitée*, one character says of another: "She doesn't want to write, she wants to be a writer, it's not the same thing."
98 NRF, 1929, p. 29.
99 *Ibid.*, p. 33.

is fragile, and that once it is overthrown he will be obliged to face up to the fact that there is nothing either eternal or necessary in the world or in himself. "I could not manage to persuade her," Robert writes, "of the danger that may lie in abandoning oneself to oneself, in accepting oneself for what one is—which, take it all in all, does not amount to much."[100] It is this dread of being "not very much" that causes the "swine" to insert himself into a hierarchy where he will count for something, where he performs a "necessary" function, where he "does his duty." The person who does his duty is entitled to "respect himself," and the Roberts of the world are revolted by moral licence because it indicates a lack of "self-respect."[101] This is one of the obstacles that Gide himself had to throw down to effect his return to sincerity: ". . . To be able to escape from myself! I would overleap the constraint that self-respect has imposed upon me."[102] The authoritarian who is what one might call a "metaphysical coward" is also, frequently, a physical one; a fact that must at all costs be concealed if self-respect is not to suffer. So it is that Robert enters the army, but not until he has taken measures to ensure against his being sent to the front. Sartre's Jacques Delarue in a moment of panic flees Paris; then, in a conversation with his wife that might have taken place between Robert and Geneviève, he declares that it was for her sake that he thought it advisable to leave the city before the advancing Germans.[103]

Having followed Gide this far, we seem to have been led into an *impasse*. In a world where there are no fixed principles and no Self to guide us toward them even if there had been, is not human life a labour of Sisyphus toward which the only justifiable attitude is that of Camus's Meursault?

[100] *Robert*, NRF, 1929, p. 63.
[101] The fascist is "self-respectful," contrasting his virtues with the degeneracy of the democrat. The Vichy régime issued coins bearing the device: "Work, Family, Fatherland," indicating that it was founded upon the proved homely virtues.
[102] *Les Nourritures Terrestres*, NRF, 1944, p. 209.
[103] See *La Mort dans l'Ame*, NRF, 1949, p. 162.

Was Gide ever really aware of how difficult life can be for people with neither genius nor an independent income? Marcel Arland once wrote that there was a great lacuna in the work of Gide—suffering is almost entirely absent from it.[104] The observation is a just one.[105] Gide was perhaps the last great representative of a society which possessed a leisure class, a class not reduced to making life simply endurable but one for which it was possible to make life precious. It is with some impatience that we listen to a wealthy man urging us to dispossess ourselves when we possess nothing, and to set out on a voyage when we ask nothing better, but lack the means with which to do so. Gide sometimes makes us think of the *philosophes* who destroyed and rebuilt worlds in Parisian *salons*. But if Gide is perhaps often unaware of how difficult it is to be a man, if part of his message is lost as a result of having been addressed to a disappearing leisure class, the rest of it can be and has been of great use. It is time to consider what is constructive in Gide's thought.

Introspection can be a disease for which the only remedy is to act. Disillusioned by the completely negative results of his soul-searchings, Gide writes: "In reaction, I have got to the stage of no longer wanting to be concerned with myself at all. I do not worry, when I want to do something, whether I do well or ill. My sole concern is to do it, and that's that."[106] If man possesses no internal principle, then his only Being can be that which, through action, he gives himself. Contemporary thought has passed, along with Gide, from Being to Existence, from contemplation to action. But the question remains, how are we to choose an action in an absurd world, in a world where, presumably, the nature of the act is perfectly indifferent? The answer is that an action, to be legitimate, must be a re-

104 *Essais et Nouveaux Essais Critiques*, NRF, 1950, p. 64.
105 Despite the revelations of the *Journal Intime*. Conjugal unhappiness is the common lot, and it is an unhappiness of which, given the present state of the world, one is less and less inclined to complain.
106 *Journal*, August 1893.

sponse to a concrete thing or situation, it must not be determined by a "non-existent" concept or generality. Gide must here be quoted at length. He has just explained that, as a result of a puritan upbringing, the abandonment of his moral scruples was, in his early years, not a *laissez-aller,* but a conquest. However:

It soon became clear to me that I had hardly made any advance. I was still acting only in accordance with the better motive, inasmuch as I was submitting my acts to that approval which implied, prior to action, a kind of imaginative deliberation and balancing, as a result of which action was proportionately slowed down and impeded. Thenceforward the promptest, the suddenest, action seemed to me to be preferable. My action appeared to me the more sincere in so far as I swept before it all the preliminary arguments with which I tried to justify it to myself beforehand. Now and henceforth, acting as I do anyhow and without allowing myself time to think, my smallest acts seem to me more significant, now that they are no longer reasoned out.[107]

We have argued that the natural concomitant of a religious or philosophical absolute is the idea of a Self. But since we have substituted things-in-themselves for the Absolute, we would expect the Self also to change. And, in fact, in the passage just quoted, it has disintegrated into a succession of acts; but the essential point is that these acts, being responses to individual things must themselves be considered *individually.*[108] The gratuity of the particular is echoed by the *gratuity of the act* which it provokes. Just as there is no logical relationship between things, so there is none, if we are sincere, between our acts.[109] Our actions, like things, are in themselves meaningful, and to make use of them

[107] *Ibid.,* 1889–1939, La Pléiade, 1948, p. 776.
[108] "Let no thing, be what it may, be done in the least for some other thing, be what it may. Every act must find its justification and its end in itself. . . ." (*Ibid.,* La Pléiade, 1948, p. 46.)
[109] "It is by his contradictions that a being interests us and gives evidence of his sincerity." (*Ibid.,* 29 October 1922.)

to accomplish this or that purpose is to impoverish them
just as we impoverish objects by looking not at them but
through them to discover a putative essence or law. Consequently Gide endeavours to act without giving himself the
time to reflect; that is, without giving himself the time to
tarnish the purity of his act with self-interest. All this is
worth a closer investigation.

Gide has several times been quite explicit as to what
he meant by a gratuitous act,[110] it is simply an act not
dictated by self-interest. It is *not* an unmotivated act, but
one whose motive is often obscure because it is totally unconnected with our personal well-being. As always with
Gide, the idea is not a story-teller's device,[111] but the exploitation through art of a psychological problem, which
his personal experience had suggested. *A propos* of a conversation with Jaloux and Miomandre, Gide writes: ". . .
I don't know how or why—by the same absurd fatality that
makes Muiçhkine draw near the fragile vase he is so afraid
of smashing—I bring up the question of Suarès (a delicate
subject, about which I know we shall not be able to
agree)." Gide had in his pocket a letter he had just written about Suarès and which he should have kept to himself; however: "Fully conscious of my mistake and my
offence, I hold in my shaky hand the sheet I am reading,
and, stumbling at every phrase, I read. I read with difficulty. Sweat starts on my brow. I *drive* myself . . ."[112] On
another occasion, at an auction, he outbids everyone else
for a painting he does not want.[113] The *Journal* tells of several other such occurrences.[114] Gratuitous acts are more
common than most of us think because the motives we
attribute to our acts we frequently discover only *after* the
act has occurred. When we identify the "cause" or motive
of a given act, we forget that at the moment it took place
we were not in the least aware of being "compelled" to act

110 See *Journal*, 1 May 1927; *Dostoievsky*, Plon, 1947, p. 212; *Journal*, November 1947; *Les Caves du Vatican*, NRF, 1924, pp. 206–14.
111 As *Les Caves du Vatican* too often leads people to suppose.
112 *Journal*, 17 May 1907.
113 *Ibid.*, 16 May 1908.
114 See, for example, 30 October (Dimanche) 1915.

as we did. We are, in regard to our past, in the same position as is the historian who, confronted by the historical past, works out elaborate causal patterns which satisfy him, but which would appear highly fanciful to the persons supposed to have been "determined" by them. "The hidden motive of our actions," writes Gide, "—our most decisive actions, I mean—escapes us. And this not only in our recollections of them, but at the very moment of action."[115] So convinced are we that every act is preceded by a decision that we fail to remark that our deliberations, when they do not altogether replace the act, are a mere formality whose purpose is to legitimatize a decision already taken. The novelist who causes his hero to torment himself with questions is not a careful observer, or else ". . . his hero is a poor thing. We instinctively begin by resolving all these questions. We ask them only afterwards, and then only if we are quibblers. They precede action less often than they replace it."[116] The classical picture of mind or Self as being that which "directs" or "motivates" is a simplification. Life admits no clear and distinct divisions; it is its nature to be ambiguous; so that instead of a clear and logical Self determining an action, it is the action, uncertain and partly blind as it necessarily is, that determines the Self. "Being," writes Sartre, "comes down to doing."[117] An event of Gide's own life will serve to illustrate this idea. In *Si le grain ne meurt,* Gide recounts the meeting with Oscar Wilde which took place during Gide's second sojourn in North Africa. Returning to their hotel one evening after visiting several Arab cafés, Wilde asked Gide whether he would like to become more familiar with one of the Arab boys they had seen in the course of the evening's entertainment and whom Wilde knew. In answer-

115 *Si le grain ne meurt,* NRF, 1949, p. 301. Also: "I do not think there is much profit to be drawn from these examinations of conscience, in the course of which, whatever the conduct involved, we always succeed in discovering a shabby motive. We might even invent one, for the satisfaction of appearing more perspicacious to ourselves. . . ." (*Journal,* 29 August 1938.)

116 *Journal,* 9 October 1927. See *Le Sursis,* p. 303, where Sartre says of Boris: ". . . an icy shiver ran down his sweating back: he had just realized that he had decided to enlist the next day," and *L'Etre et le Néant,* p. 527.

117 *L'Etre et le Néant,* NRF, 1943, p. 555.

ing "Yes," Gide suddenly realized for the first time that he was a pederast.[118] One of the reasons for Gide's critical attitude toward the family is that only by being thrown upon our own resources, only by being forced to act can we cease being nothing at all. The young men of *Voyage d'Urien* undertake their adventures in order to be forced to: "revealing acts."[119] Oedipus tells that he set out from home: "not yet knowing who I was."[120]

There are, in the work of Gide, two exemplary gratuitous acts—that of Oedipus and that of Philoctetes. Oedipus, appalled to learn that his acts had been "stolen" from him by the gods, that his destiny, of which he took pride in being the sole architect, had been fashioned by others, puts out his eyes in a great gesture of defiance which recalls the suicide of Kiriloff. Philoctetes, although he is not in the slightest interested in the fate of the Greek army, and indeed has cause to wish it ill, surrenders to the Greeks the bow upon which his life depends and which they need to win the war against the Trojans. Oedipus and Philoctetes reveal to us the highest reaches of the gratuitous act because their acts were inspired by the lowest possible amount of self-interest. They saw that human value depends upon the extent to which men are capable of doing what they are *least compelled to do*. There is no virtue in obedience, no virtue in doing what we will be recompensed for doing, no virtue in a sacrifice however great which is not *gratuitous*.

This is the positive element of modern atheism. It is founded upon Nietzsche's remark: "The world is divine because it is gratuitous." The existence of God is incompatible with human virtue, for if God exists our acts are either determined by predestination or motivated, if not by the hope of reward, at least by the reluctance to offend, the desire to obey. The glory of man and the source of his

---

[118] ". . . To tell the truth, I didn't know it myself; it was, I think only in answering 'yes' to him that I suddenly became aware of it." (*Si le grain ne meurt*, 1949, p. 343.)
[119] NRF, 1929, p. 99.
[120] *Oedipe*, NRF, 1932, p. 90.

uniqueness in the scheme of things is not his reason, considered as a means of attaining an Absolute, that is, of suppressing the gratuitous, but his freedom to be totally disinterested. Here is the answer (if one is needed) to the old fear that when men cease to believe in God "everything will be permitted." On the contrary, the events of the past few years revealed no lack of men ready to sacrifice themselves for the very reason that their act was neither obligatory nor ever likely to be rewarded. The quality of man was at stake; something had to be opposed to the fascist subman, and the fact that the struggle had to be engaged in the name of nothing at all made it that much more worth the attempt. Those who were not communists, and who, with "iron in the soul,"[121] chose to resist fascism at the height of its power were acting gratuitously.[122] It is upon such tiny groups of men who have no permanent "solution" and yet who refuse to submit to evil, who, in other words, have passed to the "other side of despair" without having their spirit broken, that the future of our society may well depend.

The function of "gratuity" in modern thought is now clear. It is the answer to the Absurd. The fact that there are no ultimate goals to be attained, no "eternal truths" to be discovered, instead of condemning us to a sterile indifference, constitutes the only possible incentive to action which leaves intact the dignity and autonomy of man.[123]

[121] See Sartre's *La Mort dans l'Ame,* NRF, p. 264, where Schneider says to the communist Brunet that it is easy to fight back when one has the Party and all it stands for to lean upon.
[122] Doctor Rieux of Camus's *La Peste* is one of these men, the hero of Koestler's *Arrival and Departure* is another, and Ibbieta of Sartre's *Le Mur* a third.
[123] "Metaphysical and moral consciousness dies upon contact with the absolute." (Merleau-Ponty, *Sens et Non-Sens,* Nagel, 1945, p. 191.) In any case, the existence of an absolute is logically inadmissible: ". . . any quite ordinary thought may be a 'supreme thought.' If it were otherwise, if there were one *supreme in itself* and *by itself,* we might find it by reflection or by chance; and, having found it, we should have to die. This would mean being able to die of a certain thought, simply because it could be followed by no other." (*Monsieur Teste,* NRF, 1948, p. 59.) And Gide ". . . we should protect all the natural antinomies in ourselves and understand that it is thanks to their irreducible opposition that we live." (*Journal,* 1 January 1925.) Malraux writes, "Total consciousness of the world is—death. . . ." (*Tentation de l'Occident,* Grasset, 1951, p. 175.)

". . . To do each thing for itself," writes Gide, "is the only way to establish its value."[124] As the Absolute is complemented by a Self which is necessarily "selfishly" motivated, the Absurd is complemented by the *Act itself,* an "unjustifiable" response to a thing or situation itself unjustifiable. The return to things-in-themselves has resulted in a return to acts-in-themselves.

In the philosophy of Gide a gratuitous act is, as we have explained, essentially an act uninfluenced by self-interest. But such an act is not necessarily one of which society can approve; a selfless act is not necessarily a charitable one.[125] Indeed, since the gratuitous act is frequently a spontaneous yielding to impulse, one readily imagines it producing disastrous results.

For many people, Gide is "l'Immoraliste," someone who invented an ethic with which to justify his sexual self-indulgence. His "influence on youth" is universally deplored, and almost everyone subscribes to Gabriel Marcel's objection: ". . . What disturbs me here is the equality of rights that seems to be accorded to the best and to the worst. . . ."[126] How is "gratuity," considered from this point of view, to be justified?

It is justified, first of all, by the satisfaction it gives. Gide tells of ". . . that state of joy that made me know my act to be good, simply by the pleasure I found in doing it."[127] The joy of gratuitous acts is that of a liberation; liberation from the barren unrest of introspection, liberation of desires and instincts suppressed—in the name of what?—since we have refused existence to everything but the particular.[128]

[124] *Journal,* 1948, p. 46.
[125] Referring to the *acte gratuit,* Gide writes: "I simply meant that the disinterested act might well not always be charitable . . . and what you call the forces of evil are not all egocentric." (*Journal,* 1 May, 1927.)
[126] *André Gide et Notre Temps,* NRF, 1935, p. 34.
[127] *Journal,* 1889–1939, La Pléiade, 1948, p. 777.
[128] See *L'Age de Raison,* p. 55. Mathieu recalls having smashed a valuable Chinese vase for no particular reason, but immediately afterward ". . . he had felt thoroughly proud, liberated from the world and unattached, without family, without an origin." However, as we shall see, *L'Age de Raison* is in some respects a criticism of the gratuitous act as envisaged by Gide, and there is probably a touch of satire in the passage from which we have just quoted.

This, of course, is no answer to the problem. Joy is legitimate only when it is not totally destructive of that of others, and what guarantee have we that gratuitous acts will not usually be of that nature? Gide answers indirectly by a criticism, which occupies an important place in his thought, of the hoary opinion that man has the good fortune to be a "reasoning" animal and that the main function of his reason is to exercise a discipline over his passions and instincts which, even when they are not "immoral," are "anti-social." The Devil is the "tempter"; he tempts us to give free reign to our instincts, particularly the "baser" ones. The Devil appeared to Gide, however, not as the Tempter, but as the Reasoner—". . . for the Evil One is the Reasoner . . .,"[129] and: ". . . he [the Devil] conceals himself nowhere so well as behind these rational explanations."[130]

We have already seen that reasoning does not precede our acts, it follows them, and its function is to find a motive for what was done.[131] This being the case, it is clear that unless we are watchful, our reason will be used to discover the motive which flatters us most. Since there is no Self, there can be no clearly discernible motive; it is therefore always easy to invent one; it is, in other words, always easy to justify by use of the reason *whatever it pleases us to do*. We could wish no more striking example of this than that offered, as could have been expected, by an event of Gide's own life. It was *after* discovering that his sexual instincts were such as to make a marriage unadvisable that he married his cousin Madeleine. If Gide had been sincere with himself he would have admitted that there was an absolute incompatibility between the happiness of his wife and the life he wished to lead. He refused to surrender either his love for Madeleine or the determination not to allow what he considered an absurd prejudice against

129 *Journal*, 1889–1939, La Pléiade, 1948, p. 607.
130 *Journal des Faux Monnayeurs*, NRF, 1934, p. 142.
131 For a philosophical demonstration of this idea, the reader should refer himself to Sartre's article "La Transcendance de l'Ego." (*Recherches Philosophiques*, Vol. VI, 1936–7.)

homosexuality to poison his existence. He was able to do so by convincing himself that the less there is of sensuality in our conduct with "honest" women, the more they are honoured and the better they are pleased. A childhood narrowed by the watchfulness of two puritan women and no doubt also the probably excessive reserve of Madeleine herself, does not suffice to explain such a naïveté in a person of Gide's perceptiveness. The more intelligent the person the more monstrous the error, because the more clever the arguments proposed to justify it. No one more blind than he who does not wish to see. Gide, of course, was not long in understanding what had happened and in drawing the moral. He writes in *Si le grain ne meurt*: ". . . If the Devil fooled me by making me consider as an insult the possibility of mingling with it [his marriage] any element of the sensual, that was something I could not yet realize."[132] The book most obviously inspired by this experience and his reflection upon it, was *La Symphonie Pastorale*. It is simply the story of a man with a gift for finding good motives for bad actions—for converting bad actions into good or necessary ones. The pastor first refuses to admit to himself that he is in love with Gertrude and accounts for his excessive interest in her by the fact that for the good shepherd the strayed lamb is more precious than the rest of the flock in its entirety. Eventually compelled to recognize the real nature of his sentiments, he comforts himself with the thought that the Christian religion, properly interpreted, is one that bids us to love and be joyful.

Nothing could be less typical of Gide himself than

132 NRF, 1949, p. 289. Gide is more explicit about this in *Nunc Manet in Te* (Ides et Calendes, 1951), p. 22, but it also seems that he continued to try to reason his way out of an impossible situation, for on p. 26 we read: "To be sure, I tell myself, and how remorsefully! that she would have wished to be a mother, I also tell myself that we should not have been able to agree about the education of the children and that other sorrows, other bitter disappointments, would have been the price of motherhood for her." Reason serves far less often to guide than to justify conduct adopted for extra-rational reasons. Thus Faulkner has persuaded himself that the Negro's best friend is, in reality, the southerner; and the believer persuades himself that the Church is the best friend of the poor.

self-abandonment, and of nothing is he less tolerant in his writings. He is a sinister teacher only for those who continue, anachronistically, to confuse sexual comportment with morality. No one is more aware than is Gide of the danger of a liberty without employment. ". . . The happiness of man lies not in freedom, but in the acceptance of a duty."[133] And to choose one remark out of many similar ones in his *Journal*: "I have always had a horror (or fear) of freedom and . . . I have always sought to limit, to compromise and to restrict it."[134] Gide nowhere gave a more succinct expression to his ethic than in *Les Faux Monnayeurs*: "You must follow your bent, provided it leads upwards." The pastor of *La Symphonie Pastorale*, the Saul of Gide's drama, and Daniel of *Les Thibault* (who misinterpreted *Les Nourritures Terrestres*) all followed their bent, but downwards rather than upwards. In contrast, those characters of Gide's books of whom he approves, exact the best of themselves by a self-imposed discipline. And need we recall here Gide's often repeated belief that self-abnegation is the noblest form of self-realization?[135]

Just as reason serves to conceal from us the "contingency" of the material world, so it serves on the moral plane, with its ancillary duty (unless it be a *self-created* duty), to protect us from our immediate reactions to things, upon which alone our conduct should be based. Several times in the course of his story, the pastor unconsciously puts his finger upon precisely the fault he is committing. "My wife nevertheless was a help to me. Her most natural impulse is always the best. But her reason constantly struggles against her heart, and often wins."[136] And Gide writes of himself: "All the really absurd things I have done in the course of my life have always been done in the name of 'reason.'"[137] It is in the name of reason that

133 Gide's preface to *Vol de Nuit*, in *Préfaces*, Ides et Calendes, 1948, p. 57.
134 5 August 1922.
135 See, for example, the *Journal*, 16 February 1916, and *Incidences*, NRF, 1948, p. 38.
136 *La Symphonie Pastorale*, NRF, 1920, p. 21.
137 *Journal*, 7 May 1937. "What is inconsistent for the reason is often consistent for the heart." (*Ibid.*, 14 March 1943.)

we accept artificial Selves to which it is our "duty" to conform. Reasonable people are those who accept their "limitations," those who accept to model their lives upon a form presented by their society. "Sensation is always sincere. . . .";[138] but, as we have seen, it is precisely that sincerity we wish to avoid, for it reveals to us that we do not exist as things, but only as action; sensations cannot be organized into Selves any more than the things that excite them can be organized into Absolutes. To accept the legitimacy of sensation is to accept our own non-existence.

If the gratuitous act is not the social menace it might appear to be, it is because it precludes Evil as a career, just as it precludes the Good established by usage. Man is by nature (since he possesses no Self) neither good nor bad. The confirmed criminal is a man whom society has forced to adopt an artificial Self; his conduct is as far removed from "sincerity" as is that of Robert.[139] The only really bad sentiments are those that are counterfeited. The gratuitous act, therefore, is not, as is so commonly supposed, a means of reaching the "real Self" which, inhibited by convention, is unable to give expression to its "natural goodness." There is nothing of Rousseau in Gide. In general, an act which is a spontaneous reaction to a given situation will be a "good" one. Our first impulse upon see-

---

[138] *Ibid.*, 8 August 1905.

[139] ". . . there is no *essential* difference between the honest man and the scoundrel." (*Journal*, 3 December 1909.) Jean Genêt *forced* himself to adopt the Self that society had imposed upon him. (See Sartre's book on Genêt.)

When Sartre's work on ethics appears, the manner in which he fills out and completes Gide's reflection on these matters will become more evident. We may be sure that an important place in that book will be reserved for the idea that Good bears to Evil the same relationship that being bears to nothingness; one cannot exist without the other. "Every spoken word suggests its opposite" writes Goethe; and he who is most unremittingly given to the expression of what Gide calls "the good sentiments" is precisely he who is most constantly preoccupied with evil. Conversely, to devote oneself to evil is, as in the case of Genêt, to be obsessed by the Good. It is the stern moralist and not the criminal who makes possible the prosperity of evil which was never greater than in Thebaid and in Calvin's Geneva. "Is it not surprising," writes Gide, "that the Christian peoples alone should have been capable of creating the civilization most removed from the precepts of the Gospel, the most contrary to all forms of Christian life?" (*Un Esprit non Prévenu*, Kra, 1929, p. 93.) An amusing but none the less significant illustration of the Christian's preoccupation with "evil" are the fig-leaves with which all the antique statuary in the Vatican has been defaced.

ing a person fall in the street is to help him up, and when we fail to do so it is because we have stopped to think— of our dignity, of soiling our clothes, etc.[140] Also, as we have already seen (and we are aware of passing from Gide to Sartre, but is not one of our aims to show that this is unavoidable), acts of passion are not uncontrollable, gratuitous outbreaks, but a means adapted to deal with a situation that has gone beyond us. "The man," Sartre writes, "had found what he was looking for—anger."[141]

It will be objected that Gide himself never talks about the "suppression of the Self" in so many words; on the contrary, the goal which each of us is to set for himself is that of the greatest possible self-development. It is to be remarked, however, that Gide seldom uses the word "Self" in this connection. What we should strive to bring to its fullest fruition is that which is unique in us.[142] Consequently: "One must 'bear witness,' " but there would be no point to "bearing witness" to a Self (which in philosophical and religious thought we share with everyone else). Gide repeats that: "We must surpass ourselves," but if he held the opinion that the Self is of the nature of an "essence," his exhortation would be a nonsense.

That said, it is nevertheless true that Gide was not aware of the precise nature of the revolution he had been instrumental in bringing about, and the result was a serious flaw in his moral thought—a flaw which the war, and events leading up to it, throw into clear relief; and which is the source of most of the perplexity we find in the *Journal* from 1939 onwards.

We have seen that the philosophy of Gide tends toward the replacing of the immemorial ideal of a "contemplative life" by the idea of a life held in constant readiness to dis-

[140] See Sartre "La Transcendance de l'Ego," *Recherches Philosophiques*, Vol. VI, 1936–7, p. 98. In his *Mémoires d'un Touriste*, Stendhal remarks: "Mistrust your first impulse; it is always generous." (Calmann Lévy, Paris, 1879, Vol. II, p. 295.)

[141] *La Mort dans l'Ame*, NRF, 1949, p. 19.

[142] ". . . I cannot say something other than what I have to say, what can be said by no one else." (*Journal*, 19 January 1912.) "Only attach yourself to that in you which you feel is to be found nowhere else but in yourself. . . ." (*Les Nourritures Terrestres*, NRF, 1944, p. 185.)

cover itself through action.[143] Unfortunately Gide did not always bear in mind that there is nothing in man to be "realized," no fixed thing about which he can organize his action. It is very well to say that we must develop that in us which is unique, but how are we to know what it is or even if there is within us something which is unique to begin with.[144] We have come upon a fundamental contradiction in Gide's thought: *he simultaneously helped to destroy man's "interiority" and tried to maintain it as the goal of action.* He failed to see that if there is no essence Man, then action must be turned outward and not inward, it must be directed toward the achievement of social, not individual aims. Here is the source of Sartre's criticisms of Gide. The metaphysical orientation of the two men is identical; they differ on points of procedure alone and that less than commonly supposed. Sartre simply pointed out that our particular "historical context" (to borrow Sartre's phrase) cannot permit itself the luxury of totally gratuitous acts; that such acts, while remaining gratuitous, in so far as permanent solutions are not possible, must be made to serve some immediate social need. The philosophy of Gide, therefore, finds its natural complement in that of Sartre. Gide sought to liberate man, but he liberated him "for nothing." The theme of *L'Age de Raison* is that Gidean liberty is not enough. Mathieu was free, but his liberty had a sour taste because it existed "for nothing"— like a sharp sabre which one is too feeble to wield. He was free to act gratuitously, to break precious vases, to thrust knives into his hand, to steal, but it was a freedom of no value until Mathieu had found a use for it, until he had "engaged" it by firing upon the Germans from the top of a church steeple. No act more gratuitous than that of standing alone against the advance of a German battalion, and yet Mathieu had an immediate purpose—that of kill-

---

[143] "Seek away. Nevertheless you will not act at all." (*Les Nourritures Terrestres*, 1944, NRF, p. 235.) "Know thyself. A maxim as pernicious as it is ugly. Whoever observes himself halts his own development." (*Ibid.*, p. 266.)
[144] According to existentialism every man is unique, but by his "position" and not by any inherent quality.

ing as many Germans as possible so that his death would have counted at least for that. The members of the resistance in *Morts sans Sépulture* wish above all that their death may serve a purpose, not that of "making the world safe for democracy," or that of hastening the reign of the proletariat but simply that of protecting a certain number of their comrades in arms. Such is one aspect of the existentialist "project." Sartrean liberty is the Gidean gratuitous act rendered socially effective by the existence of a project, the nature of which will depend upon the historical context.

We referred to a perplexity which seems to us to mark the closing years of Gide's *Journal*. It is that of a man lucid enough to see that his philosophy had, in the light of events, developed some grave defects, and yet who has not enough time remaining to him to be able to work out the necessary modifications.

Gide was all his life easily troubled by political events[145] and it was often with an uneasy conscience that he applied himself exclusively to his art. His interest in communism was not an anomalous irruption in his life, but the result of coming to understand that if the individual is to develop what is unique in him, he must first be free to do so, and that the social order must be altered accordingly. Gide abandoned communism when he discovered that it was interested in theories, and not in men, in *generalities* and not in *individuals*,[146] but he was never again as detached from such matters as he had been before. Thésée's declining years are devoted to Athenian politics.

There is only one political problem for the nations of the West, which they must solve or disappear—the organization of a genuinely revolutionary movement not dominated by faith in an Absolute, driven less by hope than by indignation. Gide belonged to a past for which action was

---

[145] As early as 1905, we can read in the *Journal*: "The most disturbing news from Russia. It is like a *basso continuo* running through my thoughts, cutting across all the occupations of the day." (2 December 1905.)
[146] See Gide's *Journal*, 7 February 1940. This is precisely the lesson that Brunet learns from Schneider in *La Mort dans l'Ame*.

inconceivable apart from hope, for which only a utopia was worth fighting for; to a generation which, having lost its hope in communism, lost its hope in action itself. There is, however, in Gide the constant feeling that action is somehow good and necessary in itself. He had a deep and envious admiration for men like Jef Last, Malraux and Saint-Exupéry.[147] The one "disharmony" of Gide's life appears to us to be a longing to act, constantly frustrated by an ingrained incapacity to act: ". . . But the feeling of being out of the running for the grand battle about to be engaged . . . a first-class spectator still, but taking no part in the struggle, and acquiescing too readily in whatever the outcome may be." And then the inevitable excuse: "A 'nature' like mine is totally unsuited to politics . . . it's pitiful."[148] And yet, in his own way, he was able to serve the "cause" in the three or four years before his visit to Russia. What has happened is that there are no longer any "causes" and the ethic of "surpassing oneself" is sadly dated.

It was left to the next generation to reflect: "Strange nevertheless that there should be no way out,"[149] and to continue the struggle just the same.

[147] See Claude Mauriac's *Conversations avec Gide*, Albin Michel, 1952, p. 194.
[148] *Journal*, 13 April 1943.
[149] Sartre, *Le Diable et le Bon Dieu*, NRF, 1951, p. 266.

Chapter 2

Malraux

Je travaille dans l'absurde.
VALÉRY

PHILOSOPHY AND literature have often acted upon one
another in the past, but they have never lost their identity
in one another. Writers who were not philosophers wrote
about philosophy; what they wrote was not in itself philosophy in the strict sense of the word—Descartes's system
would have been substantially the same had Montaigne
never existed. It is with Nietzsche, in whom the author is
often difficult to distinguish from the philosopher and who
spoke admiringly of Stendhal and Dostoievsky, that this
situation begins to change. If we have found much criticism of Gide inadequate or misleading, it is because the
evolution of modern philosophy, which declares existence
to be not a derived phenomena but the truth, has made of
Gide a philosopher as well as a writer. Gide refused to submit his life to any principle which he had not himself
established as a result of some personal experience—an
attitude perhaps not unique in literary history, but one
which has acquired a new importance because a number
of genial philosophers have come to believe that only such
principles—those derived from existence—may be considered valid.

If the philosopher Gide has been obscured by the "artist" and to some extent by the personality, the philosopher
Malraux is too often sacrificed to Malraux the "adventurer" and the anti-fascist. An adventurer is one who seeks
action for its own sake. Action, for Malraux, is an instrument of metaphysical investigation; he acts as the classical
philosopher meditates. Even in *La Voie Royale,* it is clear
that the story is being told less for itself than for the re-

175

flexions to which it prompts the two leading characters. "What," writes Malraux, "has obsessed me as a writer these ten years past, if not man?"[1] This "obsession" is present in all of Malraux's books, and it is one not at all typical of the "adventurer." Malraux was all but alone among French writers of the years between the wars to understand the gravity of the fascist threat and to oppose it not with words, that was common enough, but with arms. For it is surprising how little this great anti-fascist speaks of the fascists in his books. It is as though his heroes were fighting not against other men, but against some inhuman and absurdly hostile force; the same which, Malraux will come to believe, the painter and the sculptor have, from cave art to the present, sought to encompass; the efforts of the artist being supplemented from time to time by the weapons of the revolutionary. The fascist appears in Malraux's novels (with the exception of Ferral of *La Condition Humaine*) only as the executioner, between whom and his victims there is no dialogue. The struggle, in the books of Malraux, is not one between men of opposite political convictions, between two arguments or two ideologies—Malraux knows what talk of this kind is worth—but between man and the absurd. It is no small distinction for Malraux that we find in his work and in his alone the true atmosphere of the inter-war years, the bloodshed of China and Spain and not the somnolence of the Western democracies. Malraux is, nevertheless, not Koestler; we feel that in some way his genius transcends the events to which it was a response. The "historical context" has changed radically since *La Condition Humaine* and *L'Espoir,* but these books have lost none of their fascination.

Culture in the Occident, and to an even greater extent in the East, defines itself by opposition to existence. "Our cultural heritage" has been transmitted and safeguarded (but not created) in the main by men repelled by the transient brutality of life, attached to saving whatever pos-

[1] *Les Noyers de l'Altenburg*, NRF, 1948, p. 29.

sible from the succession of shipwrecks brought about by
human folly to which it is their "mission" never to con-
tribute. The culture of the Middle Ages is said to have
been shared by all.[2] However that may be, it is certain
that with the Renaissance it became the appanage of a
small group of specialists in the classical languages; and
to this day the "cultivated" man is frequently a specialist
in the study of whatever serves no practical purpose. Indeed, he is probably further removed from the factory
than was the humanist from the artisan.

Gide was aware of how fragile and artificial is a culture
too far removed from any practical activity. Ménalque
remarks in *L'Immoraliste*: "Do you know what makes
poetry a dead letter today—philosophy even more so?
They have cut themselves off from life."[3] A philosopher's
life was once ". . . a practical application of his philosophy."[4] Nevertheless, there is, as we have seen, a fallacy
in Gide's ideas about action. He conceived it as had the
cultivated man of previous ages as leading towards an
"exemplary life," although one of a new kind. If we cannot take Ménalque seriously (as we can a Garine or a
Perken in the novels of Malraux), it is because his action
aimed at the development of a Self that did not exist. It
was futile without being gratuitous. In the absence of any
preconceived notion of man, action can no longer be an
attempt to lead a "model" existence for the edification of
one's fellows and future generations—its purpose must be
to "leave a scar on the face of the earth."[5] But the *sine
qua non* of an action of this kind is that it be conducted
with other men.[6] Before the appearance of Malraux's

2 But if this is true, it is surely only because mediaeval culture was so limited
in scope; and if we mean by this culture, scholasticism, then there was no
"mediaeval synthesis."
3 *Mercure de France*, 1948, p. 170.
4 *Ibid.*
5 *Les Noyers de l'Altenburg*, NRF, 1948, p. 64. Perken, of *La Voie Royale*,
makes the same remark.
6 For the intellectuals assembled at the Altenburg ". . . man was the individual,
if not the self. . . ." But Vincent Berger ". . . had had too much experience
of command and of carrying conviction to be able to see man primarily as
anything but other people." (*Les Noyers de l'Altenburg*, p. 114.)

novels "masculine brotherhood" (*la fraternité virile*), as he calls it, had been absent from French literature for fifty years.[7] Writers were given over to "the fanaticism of difference," to an "individualism of artists, preoccupied above all with safeguarding the 'interior world.'"[8] No action involving practical efficiency could interest those generations devoted to "the cult of the Self," because such an action cannot be undertaken alone. The existentialists are finding the difficulty of communicating with the masses almost insuperable, and Malraux once complained of the same impotence.[9] This tragic division between culture and the people, which in recent years has had such catastrophic consequences, can, however, be bridged by action. There is nothing concealed in man which makes him what he really is.

"It is our old struggle against the demon . . . which causes us to confound knowledge of man with knowledge of his secrets. To the question, what is man? we are confusedly ready to answer—what he hides. . . ." But "A man's secrets disclose him to us . . . very much as science has disclosed to us the meaning of the universe!"[10]

Man is what he does. He is not his thought, or his intention, or his "subconsciousness," and therefore a common action is a common bond; the intellectual and the labourer freely engaged in the same combat do not need to "communicate" with one another, for they are no longer separated.

Action which has as its object not the moulding of the Self, but that of the world, has always been regarded by intellectuals with the utmost suspicion; and that for the

7 See his preface to *Le Temps du Mépris,* NRF, 1944.
8 *Ibid.*
9 In a review of Guéhenno's book *Journal d'un Homme de 40 Ans,* Malraux remarks that Guéhenno is ". . . a quest for fraternity; but few of those he teaches can read him. (Several of us share his predicament.)" (NRF, January 1935.)
10 *Les Noyers de l'Altenburg,* NRF, 1948, p. 126.

simple reason that upon contact with reality their systems immediately declare the grossest inadequacies.[11] In the last analysis, systems exist for the purpose of explaining Evil, in other words for the purpose of denying that there is any; for if Evil can be shown to fulfil a function, it ceases to be `Evil. The first lesson of action is that Evil exists on an equal footing with Good, and that only in the airy realm of thought can it be eliminated. "The great intellectual is a man of fine shades of difference, of degree, of quality, of truth as such, of complexity. He is by definition, by essence, antimanichean. But the means of action are manichean, because all action is manichean."[12] The elliptical sentence or thought so frequent in Malraux which often results in obscurity is a reflection of the ambiguity of existence. Malraux's intelligence functions not as a creator of systems, a finder of "solutions," but as *lucidity;* it tells more easily what is not than what is, because action is not something "added" to life, it is life itself.

According to Pascal, human existence is such a sorry affair, that even he who has little belief in an eternity of bliss after death, would do well to conduct himself as a Christian. Risking next to nothing, he may gain everything. During the two following centuries rationalism reversed the argument. As man's confidence in his ability to fashion the world as he pleased grew stronger, eternity became a poorer risk. Kant said that there would never be a greater man than Newton, since the discovery of one of the "basic laws of the universe" could not occur twice. After Newton's achievement, anything seemed possible, and the "pursuit of happiness" became the chief occupation of people in the West. Life came to be its own goal, a good in itself. Malraux is one of the first non-Christian writers to seriously challenge this view. If his books make painful reading for so many of us, it is not because they are full of scenes of atrocious suffering, but because he manages

11 And as a result: "Ordinarily we find among the intelligent only people incapable of action, and among men of action only fools." (Gide, *Journal,* 3 June 1924.)
12 *L'Espoir*, NRF, 1948, p. 279.

to convey to us his conviction that life is not "sacred," not a possession, but a simple instrument, of value only to the extent to which it is utilized. Thinking in terms of progress, we have acquired the habit of looking to the future (instead of eternity) for the explanation of the inexplicable, for the establishment of our "happiness." In Malraux, we discover that the present, with all its agony and uncertainty, *is the future;* it is life itself. In *Les Conquérants* Malraux says that: "everything that is not the Revolution is worse than the Revolution";[13] everything that is not suffering is worse than suffering, for it is a refusal to participate in the present, in life; it is a form of non-existence. Malraux thinks a great deal about death in his early work, and we realize with surprise that the theme of death, except as a stereotyped Christian meditation, was almost altogether absent from French literature before Malraux and the existentialists.[14] There is no place in rationalist thought for the idea of death, for it is one that reduces the boundless pretensions of rationalism to absurdity.[15] Death is the form under which Malraux envisages the absurd—against which our only recourse can be, through action, to leave a human footprint in the formless sand.

With Malraux, therefore, we will be able to take up the story where Gide left it. The significance of Malraux's work is that it contains a philosophy of action.[16]

Malraux's encounter with the Chinese was the starting point of his reflection, and *La Tentation de l'Occident* may be considered a kind of philosophical introduction to the novels—indeed, to contemporary thought in general. It is an astonishingly prophetic book which bears comparison

[13] Grasset, 1949, p. 171.
[14] It plays a very important rôle in the philosophy of Heidegger; a negligible one, however, in that of Sartre.
[15] It is in America that the rationalist "happiness myth" is still most alive. See Lionel Trilling's *The Middle of the Journey* in which the Crooms, representative American liberals, consider it in extremely bad taste to talk, or even think, about death. But unfortunately ". . . life is possible only on condition of accepting the prospect of death." (Michel Leiris, *L'Age d'Homme*, NRF, 1946, p. 231.)
[16] See *Les Noyers de l'Altenburg*, NRF, 1948, p. 47.

with Valéry's *Introduction à la Méthode de Léonard de Vinci.*

Nothing could be more revealing of the new intellectual temper of Europe than this: that a man capable of writing *La Tentation de l'Occident,* certain parts of *Les Noyers de l'Altenburg,* and *La Psychologie de l'Art* should have chosen the novel as his favourite mode of expression. What is most alive in French thought between the two wars is to be found with very few exceptions not in the labours of the philosophers, but in literature. The work of men like Valéry and Gide extends far beyond the confines of what we usually mean when we say "literature," although the predilection of both men for aesthetic theorizing still tends to obscure the fact for many critics. With Malraux, however, considerations of art were no longer permitted to insert themselves between the author and things; all trace of "contemplation" and of system disappears so that the philosopher in Malraux might think, not like the classical philosopher in terms of ideas, but of existence—in terms of our commerce with particular things. An author, Malraux believes, is not a style but a life. A writer's genius resides less in what is said or how it is said than in the strength of the personality which lies beneath. Tolstoy could have converted the humblest subject into a literary masterpiece: "Because he had the talent of a Tolstoy, but primarily because he was Leo Nicolaievitch. The force of Christ's answer, when faced with the woman taken in adultery, is not due to the talent of the evangelists."[17] For Malraux, the quality of thought depends upon the quality of existence.

La Tentation de l'Occident is a brief exchange of letters that Malraux imagines taking place between a Frenchman in China and a Chinaman visiting Europe. Through the Chinaman, Malraux is able to comment upon the final stages of the decomposition of all of Europe's traditional values, while his observations of the Chinese suggest to the

17 Quoted from an excerpt from Malraux's unpublished *Le Démon de l'Absolu* appearing in Gaetan Picon's *Panorama de la Littérature Française,* 1949, p. 278.

Frenchman two possible means by which Europe might re-
invigorate her culture. The first is one to which Malraux
will give no further attention until many years later in his
La Psychologie de l'Art, which is essentially the exploitation of an idea touched upon in *La Tentation de l'Occident*:

> . . . It is no longer Europe nor the past that is invad-
> ing France in these opening years of the century, it is the
> world that is invading Europe—the world with all its
> present and all its past, its heaped-up offerings of living
> or dead forms of meditations. . . . This great confused
> pageant now beginning . . . is one of the temptations of
> the West.[18]

The second concerns us more immediately, for it constitutes the philosophical basis of the novels.

Malraux was one of the first to see that the "death of
God" involves that of Man.[19] God understood not only as
the Deity, but as any principle purporting to render the
universe intelligible: "Europe is dominated by the idea,
more or less clearly defined, of the impossibility of grasp-
ing any reality whatever."[20] Despite the loss of all the
"coherent myths"[21] with which Europe has attempted to do-
mesticate the universe, she clings desperately to a conception which is a nonsense without them—that of the "inner
world," of the individual *per se.* "Undoubtedly the final impression I shall take away with me from the West is of so
many men intent on maintaining a conception of man that
permits them to master thought and to live, while the world
over which man rules becomes daily more foreign to
him."[22] Malraux's most important discovery in China was
that of a kind of mentality so different from the occidental,
as to make him wonder whether it is possible to speak of

[18] Grasset, 1951, p. 143.
[19] "For you absolute reality has been God, then man. But *man is dead,* after
God. . . ." (*Ibid.,* p. 174.)
[20] *Ibid.,* p. 209.
[21] *Ibid.,* p. 155.
[22] *Ibid.,* pp. 175–6.

the "human mind" in the abstract. The Chinaman, for example, does not conceive himself as an individual, the notion of "personality" is foreign to him; to such an extent that until the revolution, parents were punished with their children when the latter misbehaved, even when the parents were in no way responsible.[23] The Chinese feel themselves far less distinct from others and from things than does the westerner; and Malraux, in a passage remarkably reminiscent of Gide and Valéry, admits that the Chinese attitude appears to him the more convincing.

For this mode of consciousness [the Western, that is] fed on all the honeydew of delirium—along with the hopes, or promises, of a human existence—being (being someone, that is) cannot descend to more becoming. This mode evades all discussion. If it has never been examined, it is because the thinking, in the West, with the Self as object, has fastened mainly on its permanence. All such thinking assumes implicitly that the Self is momently distinct from the rest of the world. The Chinese I meet do not accept this antithesis at all. And I must own it does not affect me. However strongly I may wish to become conscious of myself, I feel myself subjected to an unregulated series of sensations on which I have no hold whatever, and which depend only on my imagination and the reactions it calls forth.[24]

Malraux saw more clearly than had Valéry or Gide that if there is no Self,[25] a man exists only to the extent in which he acts. Since nothing from either within or without is able to impose a direction upon human life, then its only mean-

23 See *ibid.*, p. 151.
24 *Ibid.*, pp. 101–2. How the following sentence recalls the theme of *Le Cimetière Marin*: "This defence against the continuous solicitation of the world is the very mark of European genius. . . ." (*Ibid.*, p. 103.)
25 Malraux writes of ". . . the consciousness we have of ourselves, so obscure, so contrary to all reason, that the very effort of the mind to seize it causes it to disappear. Nothing defined, nor anything which permits us to define ourselves. . . ." (*Ibid.*, p. 100.)

ing must be in its intensity. "I can no longer conceive man apart from his intensity."[26] Many years later, in *L'Espoir*, Malraux will repeat this idea when he defines the best life as one which had "transformed into consciousness the widest possible experience."[27]

Before the débris of its civilization, Europe has fallen back upon either faith or reason, the Church or leftist political absolutism, and so divided itself hopelessly into warring camps because faith, on the political level, is conservative. Malraux, like Gide, like the existentialists, refuses the choice;[28] and, like them, refuses it in the name of the unprecedented freedom and prestige which the collapse of the religious and rationalist Absolutes confers upon man. Like them, he is persuaded that we have reached the point where reason exacts the abandonment of Reason; not for unreason, but so that we may reconcile ourselves to life's ineluctable ambiguity. If this is to be accomplished, we must learn an uncompromising lucidity, and surmount the temptation of despair to which it leads.[29]

For the very reason that no system (except those of fanatics) survives the test of action, the test is as often as possible avoided. Consequently, the belief in the absurd is a condition of action. ". . . No strength, not even a *real life* without the certitude, without the obsession of the vanity of the world," and Malraux goes on to say of Garine, of *Les Conquérants,* ". . . if the world is not absurd, his whole life is dissipated in vain gestures. . . ."[30] If the universe is, after all, a rational one, then Garine's work for the revolution was a needless agitation. It is pointless to act unless we

---

[26] *Ibid.,* p. 168. "To know the world is not to make a system of it, any more than to know love is to analyse it. It is to be intensely conscious of it." (*Ibid.,* p. 159.)

[27] NRF, 1948, p. 282.

[28] "To be sure, there is a higher faith—that proposed by all the village crosses, and those same crosses placed over our dead. It is love, and peace is therein. I will never accept it; I will not lower myself to ask of it the peace to which my weakness calls me." (*La Tentation de l'Occident,* Grasset, 1951, p. 217.)

[29] See the closing lines of *La Tentation de l'Occident*: "Europe . . . you leave around me nothing but a bare horizon and the mirror brought by despair . . ." (p. 217). "Avid lucidity, I still burn in your presence. . . ." (*Ibid.,* p. 218.)

[30] Grasset, 1949, p. 229. "The absence of finality in life had become a condition of action." (*La Voie Royale,* Grasset, 1945, p. 54.)

can be sure that what we do is in harmony with the requirements of the divine Plan. We use our ignorance of the nature of this Plan to excuse a "philosophical" refusal to engage in any vital and dangerous action, while our hope or our certitude that such a Plan exists, enables us to lead a life which we may suppose not altogether bereft of significance. The common belief, therefore, that only in a world that is *not* absurd can human activity have a meaning, is simply a means of refusing to act by refusing to admit that the occupations of our daily lives are entirely without importance and that the only "Plan" the world will ever possess is one which we force temporarily upon it. ". . . The ordering of the world is not destroyed to the advantage of chance, but to that of the will to profit by it."[31] If there is no great Plan, and most of contemporary thought which is not theological has long since ceased to believe in one, then a life is to be judged not upon the "place it occupies," but upon the "intensity" with which it consumes itself. *La Voie Royale,* like *Les Nourritures Terrestres,* is the criticism of a way of life, but while Malraux's disapproval of his society extended to a refusal to take any part in it, Gide preferred to conduct his opposition from within its framework. Gide was able to make his life with the absurd, Malraux could not. If the absurd exists, then whoever is not in revolt against it, has accepted defeat. "The submission to order of the man without children and without God is the most profound submission to death."[32] But it is a defeat that, thanks to the illusion of the primacy of culture, we need not acknowledge: "He had thought in the past, . . . about the conditions of a civilization which assigns to the mind so great a place that those who feed upon it overfeed probably, and are gently led to be content with poorer fare."[33] Malraux is in revolt not against a given social order, but against the idea that there is an order. His revolt is metaphysical before being political. Perken and Garine are

31 *Ibid.,* p. 55.
32 *Ibid.,* p. 54.
33 *Ibid.,* p. 54.

"nothing"; the first is not an adventurer, the second not a revolutionary. Malraux is careful to indicate at the beginning of *La Voie Royale* that Perken is to fill no known place in the social order. "Every adventurer is born of a mythomaniac . . . but the precise action of Perken, his sense of organization, his refusal to talk about his life . . . were surprising."[34] *Les Conquérants* was suppressed in Russia because its central figure, Garine, was a revolutionary of no recognized species. "If I threw in my lot with the Revolution so readily," says Garine, "it is because its results are distant and always changing."[35] His action is not sustained by illusions as to the happy result it may produce: "Yes, they [the poor] have, as a whole, more heart, more humanity than others. . . . But . . . I know so well that they would become contemptible as soon as we had triumphed together."[36] He is convinced that no future system of government will offer any marked improvement over its predecessors, for he considers society absurd, and not simply bad.

Perken and Garine in particular, but also all the other heroes of Malraux refuse *to be* so that they may *exist*. They are pure act. If they reject the "place" which society assigns to them,[37] it is not to accept another in a different society, but to assert that no acceptance is tolerable because it is necessarily acceptance of the absurd. To be as a thing is, is to be absurd, and the only alternative is to act. More than death, Perken fears age because it will limit his activity, oblige him to accept. "To grow old is . . . so serious a matter! To accept one's destiny, one's function, the dog-kennel built for the only life one has. . . ."[38] Death, on

---

[34] *Ibid.*, p. 24. Malraux makes the same point in *Les Noyers de l'Altenburg à propos de* Vincent Berger. "He had heard my father spoken of as a man with a sharp and untrammelled mind, and also as an adventurer. A romantic? Certainly; but romantics show neither this precision of mind, nor this mastery of their means. . . ." (NRF, 1948, p. 63.)

[35] Grasset, 1949, p. 216.

[36] *Les Conquérants*, Grasset, 1949, p. 216.

[37] Malraux remarks that Perken is above all "refusal." (*La Voie Royale*, Grasset, 1945, p. 25.)

[38] *Ibid.*, p. 53. See also, pp. 84–5.

the other hand, can be to a certain extent circumvented if, rather than submitting to it, we make of it a means. The only way to dominate the absurd is to understand that "life is a material. It is a question of knowing what we are doing with it."[39] The personages of Malraux are so closely bound up with their action that they dread idleness as a rich man dreads bankruptcy—for no longer wealthy, he is no longer anything at all. ". . . This vanishing of the tragedy of the night fell upon Claude like the awareness of his own nothingness."[40] Claude is nothing more than his will to act: ". . . It seemed to him that his reasons were fading away . . . that, of himself, he would never know anything but his will."[41] Forced by illness to rest, Garine is assailed by the absurdity of everything that is not his protest against it: "It's idiotic, sickness. . . . And yet, it seems to me that I am fighting against human absurdity, in doing what I am doing here . . . the absurd is recovering its rights. . . ."[42] There is little joy in Malraux's books, and what there is derives from the completeness with which a man is absorbed by his action, for that is the extent to which he exists. Hernandez, fighting his way out of Toledo which had fallen to the fascists ". . . thought about nothing, pressed his machine-gun against his shoulder, and was fully happy."[43] Such moments are certainly not always productive of a feeling of well-being, however, and the essential point is that since man is what he does and not what he thinks the greater his absorption in action the greater his realization of Man's Estate, which is to be and to know nothing beyond his action, nothing beyond the immediate. Malraux writes of Gonzalez, watching with his friends the approach of fascist tanks which they propose to stop with

[39] *Ibid.*, p. 159.
[40] *La Voie Royale*, Grasset, 1945, p. 214.
[41] *Ibid.*, p. 229.
[42] *Les Conquérants*, Grasset, 1949, p. 169. "We defend ourselves only by creating." (*Ibid.*, p. 231.)
[43] *L'Espoir*, NRF, 1948, p. 180. In Sartre's *Le Sursis* (NRF, 1947, p. 230) Gomez, returning to fight in Spain, thinks: ". . . I may well be killed tomorrow. . . . I have given up everything, painting, renown, and I am perfectly happy."

188 / Literature Considered as Philosophy

sticks of dynamite: "He was never to know more fully what it means to be a man."[44] Gonzalez is at the farthest possible remove from the domain of ideas and generalities in which alone it has always been supposed man arrives at his truest expression, it being in his mind and not in his body that man is most man. But we no longer have the same confidence in mind (or, more exactly, we no longer consider it profitable to think of mind as a separate entity). ". . . Nothing but what we experience for ourselves instructs us,"[45] writes Gide. There is no understanding apart from experience, because what is not accessible to sensation does not exist. History for example is not what men write about events, but the events themselves. The men of the International Brigade awaiting a Moorish attack: ". . . are history,"[46] and Hernandez, watching the execution of his comrades, thinks that history—that of the historians—is: ". . . not much compared to flesh and blood. . . ."[47]

As we have already seen, there is no communication in the novels of Malraux between the fascists and the "new man" who opposes him—nor is there any between this "man of act" and the communists. Garine and Borodine disagree violently; and another communist, Nicolaieff, concludes that there is no place in the Party for men like Garine.[48] In L'Espoir, Manuel is the only communist with whom we become at all well acquainted and when, towards the end of the book, he remarks: "Drawing closer to the Party is worth nothing if it means being cut off from those the Party is working for,"[49] we understand that Manuel is no longer an orthodox communist. Both communism and fascism are part of the Absurd upon which Malraux's characters struggle to leave a human imprint. But the Absurd, as is fitting, is mute; and the dialogue is engaged between the two different types into which Malraux has divided these characters: Garine and Hong; Kyo and Tchen; Garcia and

44 L'Espoir, p. 171.
45 Preface to Saint-Exupéry's Terre des Hommes.
46 L'Espoir, NRF, 1948, p. 238.
47 Ibid., p. 185.
48 See Les Conquérants, Grasset, 1945, pp. 224–8.
49 NRF, 1948, p. 290.

Hernandez; the first arguing that action must to a certain extent be organized, the second insisting that the act itself is the only realization possible for men, and that to organize is to reintroduce the Absurd. The point we wish to make, however, is that the work of Malraux is the first of any importance which is at the same time concerned with social problems and in which the intellectual with his "solutions" plays no rôle whatever. Listen to Malraux conducting a post mortem upon the European intellectual: "For a long while, the sage—let us call him that—was considered, more or less explicitly, as the best Europe had to offer. Intellectuals were the clergy of a world whose nobility, clean or soiled was constituted by politics. The unopposed clergy."[50] This "clergy" is best characterized as a class by its fondness for the idea of "totality," but unfortunately, ". . . the only man who *seeks* a real totality is precisely the intellectual.

"—And perhaps only he needs one. . . . All the last part of the nineteenth century was passive. The new Europe really seems to be constructing itself upon action. Which implies a number of differences."[51]

From this premise, that Man is act and not thing, existence and not essence, can be deduced all the major tenets (the "number of differences" of Malraux's ironical understatement) of that thought which is furthest to the philosophical left in present-day Europe and whose influence is steadily expanding. Two of the most important ideas to

50 *L'Espoir*, NRF, 1948, p. 281.
51 *Ibid.*, p. 281. One of these differences must be a reconsideration of some of our ideas about art. Art should no longer be considered as having precedence over life. Scali (a former art historian) says to Alvear: "Art confronted by pain, amounts to little, and unfortunately no painting stands up to blood stains." (*Ibid.*, p. 231. See *La Mort dans l'Ame*, p. 29: "If painting isn't *everything*, it's just a laugh.") In this conversation between Scali and Alvear, critics have been over-hasty in conceding the advantage to Alvear. Malraux makes it clear that Alvear's attitude is in part due to the fact that his son has lost his sight in the war. "Scali wondered whether he had to deal with Alvear's thought or his pain." What Malraux intended us to think of this conversation becomes evident later on when we read, "Scali thought of Alvear's argument, and took it up again. 'And if, in order to liberate them [the poor] economically, you had to make a State which would enslave them politically?' and Garcia replies, 'In that case, since no one can be sure of his future purity, we have only to let the fascists do as they please.' " (p. 282.)

follow from our premise are those of human freedom and of "gratuity"; ideas no less present in the work of Malraux than in that of Gide.

The freedom of the Gidean hero is, and in our opinion illogically, turned inward. In Malraux, on the contrary, it exists so that man may shake off the tyranny of the absurd, so that the human may defend itself against the inhuman. Malraux does not think highly of the *Clerc*, whose defence of the Good limits itself to words, and to the non-participation in Evil; who allows himself to be paralysed by the knowledge that action is "manichean," that the only effective defence against Evil is Evil; who refuses to incur the risk of having "dirty hands." That Good is easily distinguishable from Evil is one of the happy illusions of the moralist, perhaps not altogether unconnected with that of the philosopher who invents separate compartments for mind and matter. Tcheng-Dai, of *Les Conquérants,* attempts to combat wrong by making of his life, in conformance with an ancient oriental tradition, a model of purity and disinterestedness; of him Malraux writes: "He is believed to be capable of action: but he is capable only of a particular sort of action, that which requires the victory of man over himself."[52] There are actions of greater urgency. Unamuno was an occidental Tcheng-Dai. His opposition to Evil was an "ethical," and therefore ineffectual one. Scali, in *L'Espoir,* remarks that Unamuno's place was in Madrid, but Garcia replies: "Here he would have found another kind of drama, . . . and I am not sure that he would have understood."[53] Madrid had taken up arms, and the only drama that Unamuno understood was that of the "inner life." The freedom of the intellectual to "rise above circumstances" by ignoring them is not one that interests Malraux for whom the only freedom that matters is that which enables us to alter the circumstances themselves. On several occasions, though briefly, because only existentialist theory could provide a sound foundation for the idea, Malraux

52 Grasset, 1949, p. 99.
53 NRF, 1948, p. 279.

wonders whether man's power to change things might not
be limitless; whether, in the stress of action and after, it is
not he who changes, but the world.

> The murderer of a life [we read in *La Tentation de
> l'Occident*], or of other more secret things unknown to
> the coarse hand of the law, may find himself transfixed
> by his crime, *or* by the new universe it forces upon him.
> Strange faces unveil themselves in the mirror of wars.
> Is it we who change, or the world, when passion, like the
> sea, ebbs from the passionate act which set us against
> it?[54]

The suggestion that it is the world that changes, we may
think, can be only an idle fancy; and yet Malraux seems to
return to it in *La Condition Humaine*. The book opens on
the scene of Tchen's assassination of a man asleep in a hotel bedroom. His act seems to place between him and the
world he once knew a gulf that will never be bridged. Tchen
himself, however, has not changed. "The murder left no
trace upon his face . . .,"[55] and, showing his passport to an
official, Tchen thinks to himself: "What I have just done is
decidedly not visible."[56] Language is perhaps closer to the
truth than the old epistemology, for we speak of an extraordinary experience causing us to "see the world in a different light," as though some aspects of it had, until then,
been hidden from us. This is the case with Tchen. "There
existed a world of murder, and he remained in it, as in the
heat."[57] Returned to his comrades, Tchen discovers that
they also are no longer the same: ". . . He seemed to be
discovering them—as he had discovered his sister the first
time he had come home from a brothel."[58] Vincent Berger,
after an absence of six years passed in the Near East returns
to France; and, disembarking at Marseilles, finds, instead

54 Grasset, 1951, p. 214.
55 NRF, 1933, p. 17.
56 *Ibid.*
57 *La Condition Humaine*, NRF, 1933, p. 18.
58 *Ibid.*, p. 20.

of the city once familiar to him, one that is strangely altered. It is not that the fashions in clothing have changed, or that the advertisements in the streets are different. The newspapers were full of the trials of the anarchists, and a remark that one of them makes to a doctor who had been questioning him comes to Berger as a revelation: "The individual who has been killed is not in the least important! But afterwards, something unexpected happens: everything is changed, the simplest things, the streets, for example, the dogs. . . ."[59] Berger's life in the Near East had been one of intrigue and warfare, and whatever the other effects of his action, one of them was to reveal to him now that matter is less implacable than it appears, that what face the world presents to us depends upon us alone. As a result, Berger ". . . felt himself free—with a piercing freedom not to be distinguished from abandonment."[60] The absurd (or, in the present context, the "inexhaustible") cannot constrain, we are therefore free; nor, on the other hand, can it indicate direction, we are therefore abandoned to a perpetual and anguished uncertainty as to how our freedom is to be employed. "The story of man, the earth. And all that, like the completed destiny of my father, might have been different. . . . He felt himself little by little overwhelmed by an unknown feeling. . . . It was, . . . the anguished liberty of that evening in Marseilles."[61]

This freedom, so total that it is abandonment, so heavy to bear that the entire history of human thought is an attempt to evade it, is nevertheless what gives life its price. We remarked that if Malraux makes disconcerting, at times terrifying reading, it is because he refuses any *intrinsic* value to life. We need not insist upon the contempt in which the heroes of Malraux hold their own and others' lives; but this is not to say that life is valueless. A life is worth what it *does* and not what it pretends to *be;* how-

[59] *Les Noyers de l'Altenburg,* NRF, 1948, p. 78.
[60] *Ibid.,* p. 79.
[61] *Les Noyers de l'Altenburg,* NRF, 1948, p. 91. *Les Noyers de l'Altenburg* is not a book that is easily interpreted—we shall have occasion to discuss it further on.

ever, it can do nothing of any consequence without risking itself. Here is the explanation of most of what appears paradoxical in the careers of Perken and Garine, of the way in which they unite in themselves a gift for carefully organized, effective action and a supposedly incompatible despair.[62] "It is not for the sake of dying that I think of my death," says Perken, "it is in order to live."[63] And Garine: ". . . A life is worth nothing, but . . . nothing is worth a life."[64] However little a life is worth, there is nothing else to contest the universal triumph of absurdity, and that resistance is what counts for Garine: ". . . There is one thing that counts in life just the same: it is not being beaten."[65] In one sense, no life is ever a defeated one, because whatever our life is, we *chose* it to be so; and the only way to lose one's life altogether is to deny this fact. A few days before committing suicide, Vincent Berger's father had said to him: ". . . If I had to choose another life, I would choose mine,"[66] and in that sentiment, writes Malraux: ". . . the whole starry sky was imprisoned. . . ."[67]

The foregoing considerations will have little meaning for those who cannot sympathize with the ideal of "gratuity" as exposed in our last chapter. Of what possible value is freedom in a world where nothing durable can ever be achieved? Action, under these conditions, is mere restlessness. With Christian opinion in particular "acts in themselves" find little favour.

It is because he engaged himself without becoming a partisan [writes Gabriel Marcel of Malraux], because to the fullest extent he paid in his own person, first in the

[62] Malraux's opinion has not changed. See his *Postface to Les Conquérants* (Grasset, 1949, p. 259) written in 1949: "The end of nineteenth-century optimism is not that of human thought. Since when was will founded upon optimism in the immediate? If such were the case, there would never have been a resistance movement before 1944. According to an old and illustrious phrase: 'It is not necessary to hope in order to undertake. . . .' "
[63] *La Voie Royale*, Grasset, 1945, p. 161.
[64] *Les Conquérants*, Grasset, 1949, p. 216.
[65] *Ibid.*, p. 211.
[66] *Les Noyers de l'Altenburg*, NRF, 1948, p. 100.
[67] *Ibid.*, p. 99.

resistance, then in the army of Alsace . . . that he enjoys
a privileged place in public opinion today. To be sure,
everyone has not forgiven him his strange beginnings.
It cannot seriously be argued that he did not at first conduct himself like an adventurer. . . .[68]

The incredible judgment of *La Condition Humaine* and
L'Espoir as books of an "adventurer" is possible only on
the part of someone who absolutely rejects the idea that an
act is admirable for the very reason that it has cast off the
support of hope, that it refuses to be recompensed, that its
raison d'être is not human *profit*, but human *value*.

Perken is fascinated for a moment by the possibility of
pushing the gratuitous act to its last possible extremity, to
submit unnecessarily to the torture of the savages into
whose hands he had fallen. "He experienced so furiously
the exaltation of risking more than his death, it became to
such a point his revenge against the universe, his liberation
from man's estate, that he felt himself struggling against
the fascination of a kind of madness. . . ."[69] There is very
little difference here between Perken and Gide's Oedipus
—the same defiance, the same hatred of whatever it is that
condemns man not to tragedy, which is a human invention,
but to a perpetual, inglorious defeat; the same determination that man shall dispose of himself in his own way. No
character more Gidean than Tchen of *La Condition Humaine* who, in his every act, attempts to "surpass" himself.
He has a horror of bloodshed,[70] and therefore becomes an
assassin—with a knife. What is difficult about killing, he
remarks, is rising above what goes on in oneself at the
moment of the act.[71] What Tchen seeks in terrorism is ". . .
the complete possession of oneself,"[72] and how can we
avoid thinking of Lafcadio when Tchen picks up a sliver

[68] "Prestige de Malraux," *Gazette de Lausanne*, 19 May 1946.
[69] *La Voie Royale*, Grasset, 1945, p. 193.
[70] See *La Condition Humaine*, NRF, 1933, p. 74.
[71] *Ibid.*, p. 175.
[72] *Ibid.*, p. 219.

of glass and thrusts it into his thigh?[73] But Malraux, less encumbered than Gide by nineteenth-century moral and aesthetic judgments[74] was able to react more vigorously to European events of the thirties. He saw more clearly than Gide that this time "protestations" and "examples" were not going to be sufficient. If men of good will were going to survive, their "defiance" would have to become more precise, more effective, less totally gratuitous. The result was *Le Temps du Mépris,* whose hero, Kassner, is a leading communist working in Germany, where his activities, owing to the Nazi accession to power, had become extremely hazardous. But for the very reason that Kassner is a militant, a "believer," an anti-fascist pure and simple, he is unique among Malraux's heroes, and *Le Temps du Mépris* is the least characteristic of his books. In *L'Espoir,* the personages of Malraux have regained the lucidity of the first novels with, however, a sharper sense of the urgency of the task in hand. There is, in other words, more "hope," but it is accompanied by singularly little enthusiasm, for none of the combatants of *L'Espoir* expects the revolution to bring about a "solution." This is the function of the conversation we have already referred to between Alvear and Scali. Scali is somewhat shaken to learn from Alvear that the revolutionary government might very well prove itself eventually to be no better than the one it was trying to replace. What would have been gained if political oppression took the place of economic oppression? To Scali's doubts, Garcia (through whom, more than any other character of *L'Espoir,* Malraux expresses himself) answers in effect that acts have a validity of their own entirely apart from what they may or may not accomplish, that their "gratuity" in no way detracts from their necessity.

73 *Ibid.,* p. 220.
74 By which we mean: In morality, the rationalist belief that Good is somehow in the nature of things, and that Evil is a sporadic aberration that could never permanently prevail; in aesthetics, the belief in "immortality through art."

As long as we are in agreement about the decisive point, resistance *de facto,* that resistance is an act: you are committed to it, as to every act, to every choice. It bears within itself all its fatalities. . . . For a thinking man, revolution is tragic. But for such a man, life also is tragic. And if he is counting on revolution to rid him of his tragedy, his thinking is faulty, that's all.[75]

Apart from *Les Noyers de l'Altenburg, L'Espoir* is the least tormented of Malraux's novels. At times, even, it achieves a strange serenity—not that of hope, but of man's reconciliation with his despair.

The ideas with which we have been concerned—absurdity, "man as act," human freedom, and gratuity—are all negative ones. However, a positive moral principle is implicit in them. We encountered its origins in Gide, it is stronger still in Malraux; it is that which, for want of a better term, we may call "immediacy." A good act is one which responds to an immediate human need. Fascism is an attempt to re-establish a basis for the exercise of absolute power; it must therefore look back beyond capitalism, beyond constitutional monarchy, to divine right; to a system, that is to say, in which the needs of the people are a relevant consideration only in so far as they coincide with those of the central authority.[76] Communism, on the other hand, its eyes fixed on the Promised Land of a total solution, too often overlooks the fact that man needs more than bread to lead a human existence. It is time for us to admit that intelligence, that of the classical rationalist, intelligence as a constructor of systems has fallen far short of its promise; and this has happened because the welfare of men tends to be confused with statistics and plans.[77] Of all of

[75] *L'Espoir,* NRF, 1948, pp. 282–3.
[76] "All fascists command by divine right." (*L'Espoir,* NRF, 1948, p. 125.)
[77] The recent history of China offers a remarkable instance of the way in which the marxist's affection for theory works against his own interest. Marx thought that the revolution would have to be carried out exclusively by the industrial proletariat, since the peasantry, where not actually counter-revolutionary, had always been conservative. Whatever the case in Europe, the only group in China which could have carried the revolution to success was the

Garcia's friends, there was only one ". . . in whom intelligence had taken the form of charity."[78] If charity and intelligence are too often mutually exclusive it is because we insist that human affairs be regulated once and for all. We want *to be* either a Christian or a marxist, as though the land in between the Yogi and the Commissar were uninhabitable except by the moribund political arrangements we find there now, from which all conviction or at least all the enthusiasm that saves, is departed.[79]

Malraux has written that the main interest of *Les Conquérants* is that it portrays ". . . a type of hero in whom culture, lucidity and an aptitude for action are united."[80] There is another, however, that of the conflict of ideas between Garine and the communists. Garine is described as being ". . . indifferent to systems" and the spectacle offered by political meetings caused him to consider with ". . . a contemptuous irony men . . . who claimed to work for the happiness of mankind."[81] What divided Garine and the communists was that the latter worked in accordance with theory while Garine's success as director of propaganda was due to his readiness to adapt his tactics to the requirements of the immediate situation. Borodine's ready-made propaganda designed for use in the West by which he attempted to persuade the Chinese masses that by virtue of their numbers they should and could be masters of the state had little effect upon people whose political history was

---

peasantry. Mao-Tse-Tung was, in the early years of the century, one of the few communist leaders to understand this, and consequently he brought upon himself for a while the hostility of the Party. This question comes up in *La Condition Humaine* (p. 164), where Kyo argues for the necessity of a peasant uprising.

[78] *L'Espoir*, NRF, 1948, p. 220.

[79] Pierre de Boisdeffre sees cause to hope that Malraux has at last left the interspace where men carry no labels: ". . . his most recent work [that of Malraux] in its very ambiguity calls for conclusions which should form part of a Christian perspective." (*Malraux*, Editions Universitaires, 1952, p. 19.) One hopes that Malraux will not take the banal and easy path to a conversion; but his inexplicable adherence to Gaullism, and what has become his quasi-religious attitude toward art are a little disquieting. He appears to have forgotten his own excellent advice that one should never "let go of the earth."

[80] *Les Conquérants*, Grasset, 1949, p. 248.

[81] *Ibid.*, p. 62. ". . . in the Bolsheviks, . . . the doctrinal vocabulary, and especially the dogmatism they laboured under, exasperated him." (*Ibid.*, p. 70.)

very different from that which had produced marxism. Malraux saw that the driving force of revolutions (the Spanish as well as the Chinese) is not hunger. The poor are less interested in economic theories about the abolition of want than they are in means of acceding to the dignity of human beings. Their greatest misery is their humiliation, and not their physical need. Oriented in this way, Garine's propaganda acted upon the Chinese ". . . in a way obscure, profound—and unforeseen—with an extraordinary violence, by offering them the possibility of believing in their own dignity, in their importance, if you prefer."[82]

The terrorist is one who feels so sharply his degradation that for him the sole object of the revolution becomes the destruction of that class without which contempt, if not poverty, will at least for a time cease to exist. Such is Hong of *Les Conquérants*: ". . . Above all he hates the man who respects himself, who is sure of himself. . . . It was his disgust with respectability, the Chinese virtue *par excellence*, that led him into the ranks of the revolutionaries."[83] "Poverty" does not exist, there are only poor people; and what the poor man feels in the presence of the rich is not his "poverty," but his humiliation. Being poor is not a question of the number of calories in one's diet or the quality of one's clothing—there are wealthy eccentrics who eat and clothe themselves poorly—it is a feeling in certain individuals brought about by the attitude taken toward them by certain others. It is this attachment to the basic reality of individual relations that earned for Garine the communist opinion that he was "human, too human."[84] Dialectical materialism is as far removed from things as was the idealism with which it coexisted through most of the nineteenth century. Malraux was aware of this when he has Garine say, referring to the communists, "People who want to 'let go of the earth,' see at once that it sticks to their fingers."[85] Both the idealist and the marxist

82 *Ibid.*, p. 21.
83 *Ibid.*, p. 155.
84 *Ibid.*, p. 225.
85 *Ibid.*, p. 231.

refuse to be reconciled to the earth—the first sacrifices it to the non-existent, the second believes that, at bottom, it is neatly organized into harmlessness. Until this century, human thought had produced no realism in the true sense of the word.

The idea that the purpose of the revolution is not to convert workers into bourgeois, but to create a dignity of the worker, to abolish the middle class monopoly of "respectability," becomes prominent in *La Condition Humaine* and in *L'Espoir*. It was Péguy who first condemned in terms appropriate to the gravity of the situation the socialist conception of the revolution as an "elevation" of the proletariat to the culture and standard of living of the middle class.[86] The great preoccupation of the bourgeoisie, and the cause of the scorn traditionally heaped upon it by artists and writers, is "happiness" considered as a function of material well-being. Communism, like socialism, has always been, to a considerable extent, infected by this pitiable ideal (pitiable, that is, in countries where there is no hunger), and if *La Condition Humaine* and *L'Espoir* while being novels of the revolution render a distinctly unmarxist tone, it is in large part because, paradoxically, all trace of bourgeois values had disappeared from them.

Kyo, of *La Condition Humaine* is, of all Malraux's heroes, the least uncertain of what the revolution is to accomplish. "His life had a meaning, and he knew what it was—to give to each of these men whom famine . . . was killing like a slow plague, the enjoyment of his own dignity."[87] And that dignity is, unlike the "dictatorship of the proletariat," something that can be realized immediately, by the simple act of resistance. Malraux is never farther from the communists than when he describes

86 "Contrary to someone seeking to 'cross the colour line' or someone belonging to a persecuted minority, both of whom want to raise themselves to the level of the privileged and to become assimilated, the revolutionary wants to bring them down to himself by denying the validity of their privileges." (Sartre, *Situations III*, 1949, p. 189.)
87 *La Condition Humaine*, NRF, 1933, p. 79.

marxism as being not a doctrine but an act of will.[88] For the orthodox marxist the doctrine is the supreme reality apart from which there can be no action. What the marxist refuses to see, however, is that if he attaches the higher importance to the doctrine, it is not so that the action may be more effective, but so it may be more automatic. His purpose is to conjure away the agony of indecision and responsibility which necessarily accompanies the acts of men who have ceased to believe in any order of which they themselves are not the creators. Kyo remarks that, in marxism, "each time that fatality precedes will, I am suspicious,"[89] but lucidity, as always, is bought dearly; Kyo suffers ". . . the anguish of being only a man."[90] How much easier life would be for him if he simply accepted like a new infallibility and as a good communist should the instructions of the Internationale. Unfortunately, the Internationale in this particular instance was wrong and Kyo knew it.

It frequently happens in *L'Espoir* that one character asks another what he is fighting for. The answer is always unpretentious; so much so that Barca, for example, seems almost ashamed to admit that he is prepared to die, not because he had been dispossessed of his land, but because he refuses to have to respect people who are not respectable, and who nevertheless consider themselves in a position to despise him.[91] Magnin was a revolutionary because he wanted men to know what they were working for, because it is intolerable that they should pass an entire life losing eight hours of each day.[92] Garcia had chosen to fight so that the conditions of peasant life in Spain might be changed.[93] If these seem modest demands in exchange for one's life, it is because only the intellec-

88 *Ibid.*, p. 80.
89 *Ibid.*, p. 164.
90 *Ibid.*, p. 174.
91 *L'Espoir*, NRF, 1948, p. 74.
92 *Ibid.*, p. 64.
93 *Ibid.*, p. 282.

tual believes that any more is obtainable. Only those more conversant with ideas than with existence, believe that the millennium alone is worth dying for.

The conflicts that have torn the world since the end of the First World War are said to have been ideological ones as opposed to the religious, dynastic or imperialist wars of the past. Nothing, however, could be less true of the Loyalists as Malraux presents them to us. No character of *L'Espoir* dies for an idea, nor even for hatred of that of the enemy, since fascism, as we have seen, does not appear in the books of Malraux. One of the main reasons for the failure of the revolution in Spain was the reluctance of the Loyalists to organize and disci- pline themselves, not so much because they were incapable of doing so, but because they had a tendency to see in the revolution itself all they could hope to achieve—organi- zation and discipline, fascist virtues, would have been the first steps toward a betrayal.[94] Hernandez and le Négus are the best examples of this mentality. During a brief truce at Toledo, the Loyalists distributed cigarettes to the fascists defending the Alcazar, and Hernandez saw that a letter was forwarded to the wife of the officer in command of the fortress. The purpose of these "gratuitous acts" was the realization here and now of the revolution, whose object was not the creation of new institutions, but of new men. No one is more aware than Malraux that institutions betray the *mystique* (in Péguy's sense of the word) out of which they grow. "We want to form," says le Négus, "neither a state, nor a church, nor an army. But men."[95] In the admirable generosity of Hernandez's action (the fascists had taken women and children with them into the Alcazar as hostages), the revolution had accomplished itself. "If we win, those on the other side will appear at the bar of History with their hostages, and we with the freedom of Madame Moscardo. Whatever

[94] All this, of course, according to Malraux.
[95] *L'Espoir*, NRF, 1948, p. 149.

happens, Hernandez, you are setting a great and noble example."[96] Hernandez and le Négus ask no more of the revolution than the opportunity to conduct themselves as men should. "If we are crushed here and at Madrid, men will have lived for a while with their hearts. . . . In spite of hatred. They are free. They had never been free before. I'm not talking about political liberty, I'm talking of something else!"[97] The revolution is an end in itself. While Malraux did not altogether approve of this view, it poses a dilemma for which, as always on the level of action, there is no solution. If the revolution cannot be brought about without organization, it cannot succeed, on the other hand, without men like Hernandez who are opposed to organization and all the compromises with "immediacy" it necessarily involves. This is the real drama of *L'Espoir*; whether or not action should sacrifice its purity in an attempt to achieve something beyond the immediate.[98]

There follows from the rejection of absolutes, whatever their nature, a consequence we have not yet sufficiently discussed. The purpose of an absolute is to give the universe a meaning, so that man may know his place in it, so that his privileges and responsibilities may be clearly defined. But to go that far is, as we have seen, to define Man himself. There is, or was, a Christian Man, there is a communist Man, and there was until recently an "Aryan" Man. The degree of definition varies greatly, from the Aryan who even has a specific physical appearance, to people's vague ideas on "human nature" which, as we know, "never changes." It is not only in order to deliver themselves from existential anguish that men are so ready to give up their individual characteristics to conform to a model, but also in order to enjoy the illusion of perfect communication with their fellows. We speak of the

[96] *Ibid.* Madame Moscardo, whom the Loyalists had left unmolested in Madrid, was the wife of the officer in command of the Alcazar.
[97] *L'Espoir*, NRF, 1948, p. 147.
[98] For this reason, Manuel's order to execute two of his men who had fled before the enemy, is one of the most important episodes of the book. (See pp. 277 and 290.)

"communion" of the faithful, which, in totalitarian countries has been replaced by the communion of mass demonstrations. It is true that such demonstrations serve a political purpose, but they could hardly be so successful if they were not to the people's liking. What we seek in passion, whether it be love or nationalism, is a more perfect union with other beings, the end of our solitude.

If there is no Self, there is no communication between Selves. In a universe which has lost the centre through which its radii could correspond with one another, man is thrown into an irremediable solitude. *La Condition Humaine* is one of the books in which human solitude has received its most poignant expression. It is "man's fate" to be alone and to pass his life trying to console himself for it: Kyo with his love for May, Gisors with opium, Ferral with eroticism. Katow speaks for all of them: "The one really necessary thing is not being alone."[99] But physical presence is a poor substitute for that of the spirit, and Gisors knew that "there is no knowledge of other beings."[100] Kyo has his voice recorded and, of course, fails to recognize it when it is played back. Malraux returns several times to this incident, for it symbolizes in a striking way our confinement within ourselves.

> Just as Kyo had not recognized his own voice because he had always heard it with his throat, in the same way the consciousness that he, Gisors, had of himself, was no doubt irreducible to that which he might have of another being, because it was not acquired by the same means. It owed nothing to the senses. . . . This total solitude—even the love he had for Kyo did not deliver him from it.[101]

If love plays so slight a rôle in the work of Malraux, it is for the same reason that the absurd plays so large a

99 *La Condition Humaine*, NRF, 1933, p. 245.
100 *Ibid.*, p. 75.
101 *Ibid.*, p. 82.

one—the conviction that Man's value depends upon a refusal to make terms with his lucidity. Love is not a solution to human solitude, it is a refuge from it. This is Kyo's discovery when May informs him that she had finally given in to the persistent solicitations of one of the men with whom she worked. The love of Kyo and May was to have borne the mark of human reason, like the society which the revolution was bringing into being. Theoretically, May was free to sleep with whomever she wished; theoretically, since her affections were not engaged, it should have made no difference to Kyo; actually he suddenly rediscovers himself alone, their spiritual union disintegrated into the meagre solace of bodily presence.

> "She escaped him completely. . . . The revelation of what he wanted finally dawned upon him—to sleep with her, to take refuge there against this dizziness in which all of her was lost to him. They did not need to know each other when they were using all their strength pressing themselves in one another's arms."[102]

Something else does survive, nevertheless, because for May alone Kyo is more than the sum of his acts, something more than his biography; the others ". . . are not the same as I am, they are the ones who look at me and judge me. . . ."[103] This conception of others as beings with whom our only communication is exterior, by "the gaze" (*le regard*), is one which, as we shall see, acquires great importance in *L'Etre et le Néant.*

The meaning of love is clearer in its less complex forms, where the failure to achieve its purpose is more evident. Ferral is more alone than Kyo, but his "dignity" as a white man, and a rich one, enables him to support it more easily. It is in what Malraux has written of love in its most elementary form—eroticism—that we find the most remarkable anticipation of *L'Etre et le Néant*, not only of certain details, but of its basic theme.

A solitude as terrible as that which afflicts the personages of *La Condition Humaine* is unthinkable apart from the absurd. We imagine the religious ascetic and the philosopher as solitary persons, but never as suffering from solitude. Indeed, the only really satisfactory cure for solitude is not intercourse with others, but the belief that there is a reason for our existence, that our presence on earth fulfils, in some way, a Purpose. Metaphysics and religion, however, are but half-way houses; and in love, according to Sartre, man makes the attempt, which necessarily fails, to "justify," or to "found" his existence in the immediate by being simultaneously the thing and its contemplator, the created and the creator. The lover seeks to be at one and the same moment himself and, through his partner, his own contemplator. In this way he will escape from the blindness consequent upon being "in the world" and, standing at a distance from himself, as his own creator, he is God; for the *ens causa sua* can only be God.[104] Malraux's reasoning takes precisely the same course. "All of eroticism is there," he writes in *La Tentation de L'Occident*, "to be oneself *and the other*. . . ."[105] Ferral's relations with women could, in almost every detail, be interpreted with reference to *L'Etre et le Néant*. Valéry ". . . was sure that he [Ferral] would derive most of his pleasure from the sensual transformation of her features."[106] Later, on another occasion, we understand why ". . . he would possess, through this Chinese woman who was waiting for him, the one thing he coveted— himself. He needed the eyes of others to see himself, the senses of others to feel himself."[107] It is Gisors, in a con-

---

[104] This longing of the for-itself to be in-itself-for-itself, or God, is what animates the Sartrean universe. Love is only one of the countless forms that this foredoomed ambition assumes. We shall return to this, of course, when we come to consider *L'Etre et le Néant*.
[105] Grasset, p. 102.
[106] *La Condition Humaine*, NRF, 1933, p. 142.
[107] *Ibid.*, p. 275.

versation with Ferral, who draws the conclusion: ". . . every man dreams of being God,"[108] or more precisely, it is ". . . man's dream—of becoming God without losing his own personality. . . ."[109]

For as long as there was an essence "Man," we all partook of it. We were all children of God, or rational beings, or products of class, and so forth. But if man is no more than what he does, if each of us is position and not thing, a position in respect to which matter orients itself and which is not itself oriented by matter, then clearly communication between individuals, to the extent once supposed possible, is out of the question. The more what we do is uncommon, the greater the distance we place between ourselves and other men. No one was closer to Tchen than Gisors, whom Tchen had always consulted in difficult moments, but it is impossible for Gisors to enter into the world of murder in which Tchen had unwittingly isolated himself. "Gisors could say nothing more: every word would have sounded false, frivolous, imbecile. . . . He felt how poorly he had brought to Tchen the help he was asking him for, what a solitary thing murder is. . . ."[110] Manuel, of *L'Espoir*, finally wins over a woman whom he had loved in vain for many years and suddenly finds her presence a burden—between his love and the woman's capitulation, the civil war had intervened.[111]

However, the extent to which our act separates us from certain persons, is the extent to which it draws us closer to others, to those with whom it was accomplished. And so Malraux discovers fraternity, the theme which recurs more frequently than any other in his books and upon which, consequently, we need not insist. It is in fraternity that man is least alone. Since man is act, it is by participating in the same act, and not the same essence,

---

[108] *Ibid.*, p. 271.
[109] *Ibid.*, p. 272. "A man who has never tried to make himself like the Gods, is less than a man." (Valéry, *Tel Quel I*, 1949, p. 34.)
[110] *La Condition Humaine*, NRF, 1933, pp. 74–5.
[111] NRF, 1948, p. 289. In Sartre's *Morts sans Sépultures*, Lucie ceases to love Jean because she has more in common with the men with whom she had been captured and tortured.

that he succeeds in communicating with his fellows. The characters of Malraux's novels are of all nations and races, but it is not in that way that they distinguish themselves from one another. How many of us are conscious, in reading *La Condition Humaine*, that Kyo is an Oriental? or that Hemmelrich is Belgian? Their action is the same, and therefore there is a resemblance and as a result a fraternity between them impossible with the two Europeans, Hemmelrich and Ferral. "What a mockery," writes Malraux, "to call brothers those who are merely of the same blood."[112]

A world of essences is a world of hierarchy. It is of the essence of a thing to be "better" or "worse" depending upon its distance from the "supreme essence," God or Truth. The practice of inductive reasoning, rather than replacing these hierarchical and anthropomorphological habits of thought, seems satisfied to cohabit with them; and if there are few who still believe that an aristocrat is in some way intrinsically better than a peasant, there are many quick to believe that a German is "better" than a Pole or that a worker is "better" than a bourgeois. No real fraternity is possible where men have not accepted to be no more than they do, where they do not wish to understand that the death of the "Supreme Essence" involves that of man.

Les Noyers de l'Altenburg was a radical departure from everything that Malraux had previously written; however, we should perhaps consider the change as having taken place less in Malraux than in the world situation. Fascism was no longer being opposed, as in Spain, with dynamite and a few antiquated aircraft, but with the resources of most of the world. The historical circumstances which made books like *La Condition Humaine* and *L'Espoir* possible have changed; it is not unnatural that Malraux's writings should change with them. It is the peculiar nature of Malraux's genius to be able to think with acts,

112 *Le Temps du Mépris*, NRF, 1944, p. 151.

and not merely with ideas, and one wonders whether, having ceased to act, his genius has not been cut off from a source of nourishment vital to it. It is too early to say; we shall have to content ourselves therefore with trying to decide what it is precisely that causes *Les Noyers de l'Altenburg* to resemble Malraux's previous books in many respects and yet to differ from them so radically.

Apart from the colloquy at the Altenburg, the novel is one about men at war. Its principal character, Vincent Berger, is, like most of Malraux's characters, an intellectual who has acquired through action a deep mistrust, when it is not contempt, for the purely cerebral activity of the orthodox intellectual. The colloquy gathers a number of the latter together, and Berger's (and to a certain extent Thirard's[113]) presence there enables Malraux to comment upon the realm of "pure ideas" in which the others move. "The thought which for the last hour had been developing itself in the presence of my father was exclusively a dialogue with culture. An idea was never born of a fact: always of another idea."[114] If, however, the action of Vincent Berger recalls that of other heroes of Malraux in the contrast it offers to the practical impotence of the intellectual, there is a difference perhaps more important than the resemblance. Berger is not a revolutionary. His action is not a protest against the absurd in the form of social injustice. There is in Berger far more acceptance than defiance, and it is ironical that although Malraux has been congratulated by some for having ceased, with the publication of *Les Noyers de l'Altenburg,* to be an "adventurer," of all Malraux's characters, Vincent Berger is closest to being an adventurer in the true sense of the word. This "acceptance" on the part of Vincent Berger and his son, the narrator, is closely bound up with a curious atmosphere of detachment, unique in the creative writing of Malraux. For the first

113 As for example, when he remarks: ". . . Its object [that of culture] has always been to found life on quality, . . . but that is something quite different from founding it on truth!" (NRF, 1948, p. 116.)
114 *Les Noyers de l'Altenburg,* NRF, 1948, p. 114.

time, in *Les Noyers de l'Altenburg*, Malraux is not *in* the action described, he is *above* it.[115] He has arrived at a vantage point which we must attempt to identify, noting, however, that it is as yet provisional and insecure: "Perhaps anguish will always be the stronger; perhaps the joy given to the only animal that knows itself not to be eternal is poisoned at the source."[116] Nevertheless, there is talk of joy.

Throughout *Les Noyers de l'Altenburg*, Malraux suggests that there is, after all ". . . a datum upon which the notion of man may be based,"[117] and he further suggests that this constant is to be looked for in the fact that man is what he *does* and not what he *thinks*. In what he does, a man rejoins not only his fellows, but men of the remotest past. For almost as long as there have been men, they have fished and hunted, tilled the soil, made war and suffered; and the extent to which we continue to do these things is the extent to which we communicate with the past to form a solidarity of man against everything that is not man. The faces of the prisoners in the cathedral of Chartres begin, as their beards grow, to resemble those of Gothic statuary; beneath the veneer of "modern man" appears the antique visage of a persecuted race which, used to misery, ". . . waits for it to wear off. . . ."[118] In the course of the colloquy, Mollberg remarks: "One can conceive a permanence in man, but it is a permanence in nothingness," but Berger asks, "Or in the fundamental?"[119] and his question is one of the keys to the book. This, then, is the "eternity" that has made its appearance in the philosophy of Malraux; it is one to which we can attach no religious significance for it is simply the "eternity" of what is fundamental in man—not his ideas, but his acts. There is more, however, in the secret, "simple and sacred," which is mentioned at the end of the novel.

115 With the possible exception of the brief scene in which the narrator goes into battle with an armoured column.
116 *Les Noyers de l'Altenburg*, NRF, 1948, p. 289.
117 *Ibid.*, p. 150.
118 *Les Noyers de l'Altenburg*, NRF, 1948, p. 25.
119 *Ibid.*, p. 145. See *Les Voix du Silence*, p. 272.

We should bear in mind that in *Les Noyers de l'Alten-burg,* Malraux disavows no part of what he had previously said and the book bears witness to the fact that the new view of man and the universe we have been discussing throughout this work can be joyful as well as sombre. Between *La Condition Humaine* and *Les Noyers de l'Alten-burg,* there has taken place somewhat the same evolution that carried Sartre from *La Nausée* to *Les Chemins de la Liberté,* and which was a result of the discovery that man is not a "victim" of the absurd. The fraternity of *La Condition Humaine* and the "work of art" of *La Nausée* are frail bulwarks indeed against the monstrous pressure of the inhuman which otherwise oppresses the atmosphere of these books. In *Les Noyers de l'Altenburg* and *Les Chemins de la Liberté,* however, man acts not *against* the absurd but *for* himself. The absurd is no longer an obstacle; it is, on the contrary, what enables man to be free. The absurd cannot be a force, it is merely a presence, and if man is act, that is if there is in him no element of the absurd, if he is pure "intention," he is free. Whatever the conditions of our existence, it is one we have freely assumed. Thus the suicide of Dietrich Berger is in no way incompatible with his remark that if he had another life to choose, he would choose his own. By taking his life upon himself, by refusing to "alienate" it, Dietrich Berger, in a sense, creates it; and his creation is not without analogy with that of the Greek sculptor, whose head of a young man is to be seen in the Acropolis Museum, and which Malraux calls "the first sculpture to represent a human face, simply a human face; liberated from monsters . . . from death . . . from the Gods. That day man also drew man out of clay."[120] Hence the indulgence, and even irony, with which an old woman, sitting in the sun, contemplates her death. Death, and the material world cannot prevail against the life which young Berger discovers for the first time the morning after the battle in which, his tank having fallen into a trench, he thought he was certain

[120] *Les Noyers de l'Altenburg,* NRF, 1948, p. 98.

to be killed. The proximity of death which in previous centuries caused men to withdraw from life in the hope of "saving" it, on the contrary strengthens Malraux's conviction that life is meaningful because death is not. The goodness of life consists in the fact that, in all the universe, *it alone exists*. Life is not "thing," it is perishable and "unjustifiable"; but for Malraux, as for Sartre, the "nothing" that is human life, is, at the same time, everything.

At first glance, it is indeed a distraught and divided epoch that produces on the one hand a *Les Thibault* and on the other *Les Nourritures Terrestres; La Nausée* and *Les Noyers de l'Altenburg; Voyage au Bout de la Nuit* and *Terre des Hommes*. Nevertheless, the authors of these books have their disbelief in common; to most of the unanswerable questions that life poses their attitude is the same. But the absurd is ambivalent—we may choose to be more impressed by the abandonment in which it leaves man, or by the freedom it makes possible; by the "ambiguity" of life, or by the total truth of appearance. "Know in order to be able," wrote Francis Bacon, and ever since we have been waiting for the final truth which would deliver omnipotence into our hands. But now we see that we already knew all that there is to be known, and that since it is absurd to suppose ourselves capable in some way of gaining a perspective on a world of which we are a part, the ambiguity must coexist with the truth—to know is not to be able. In *Les Noyers de l'Altenburg*, Malraux can accept the ambiguity because he has discovered the truth —life is its own answer, its only problems are those that men invent. "As though the world were a riddle," writes Gide, "to which we had to find the key!"[121] For the very reason that the universe is absurd, it has nothing to conceal from us.

A word in conclusion about *Les Voix du Silence*. It is a book in which Malraux remains true to his ideas, but abandons their habitual mode of expression. It is a book by the philosopher Malraux, and not the philosopher-

121 *Journal*, 9 September 1924.

novelist which is our main concern here. Its thesis is this: Greek art, and European art, which between the Renaissance and Goya may be considered in some degree derived from it, was "representational;" that is, it was commonly supposed that the primary function of art was to represent objects as faithfully as possible. This notion is still, except by artists themselves, very generally held. However, thanks to photographic reproduction, we are now for the first time in a position to study human art *in its entirety,* and we discover that the representational ideal in art is unique in human history. After demonstrating that the artist who distorts reality does so intentionally and not simply out of inability to imitate more accurately, Malraux is able to assert that art is not an attempt to copy nature but the creation of an entirely different nature. Art is not a submission to the objects the world proposes to us, but the creation of another world. Romanesque artists, for example, were not men incapable of a more accomplished reproduction of the human form. They had a quite different purpose. "This romanesque style, which drew out or twisted its faces in accordance with a ritual transfiguration, proclaimed that a system of organized forms refusing imitation can exist in the face of things like another Creation."[122] Considered in this way, the purpose of art is to transform human destiny into freedom;[123] art is ". . . man's eternal revenge."[124]

A theory as comprehensive as this, that aims at nothing less than to reduce so immensely complex a phenomenon as art to a single formula, however broad, cannot fail to expose itself to a number of serious objections.[125] The

---

[122] *Les Voix du Silence,* NRF, 1952, p. 105.

[123] *Ibid.,* p. 621.

[124] *Ibid.,* p. 635.

[125] It is as hard to imagine an artist not interested in copying nature as it is to imagine a philosopher not interested in the truth. The impressionists, for example, give Malraux a difficult time; he is obliged to assert that they only *thought* they were attempting a more faithful representation of nature, in reality they were in revolt against the tradition of representation (see p. 115). But surely the artist is to be relied upon to know what he is attempting, if not what he has actually accomplished. The wish to copy nature has probably always been fundamental in art. What changes is the opinion as to what constitutes nature; or, at least, the proper vantage point from which to represent

validity of the theory itself, however, is of less concern to us than its relation to the thought of Malraux as we have exposed it.

The function of art is precisely that of the revolution as Malraux envisaged it, except that the artist, instead of working "in the world" as does the revolutionary, creates a different world. In both cases, there is refusal to accept the absurd, but while the "revenge" of the revolutionary must be incomplete and temporary, that of the artist is total. Art is act, but act free from ambiguity because it has rejected all compromise with things. Art is action which instead of trying to "humanize" the absurd, simply replaces it. Modern art, furthermore, like the action of one of Malraux's revolutionaries, is "gratuitous." Modern art, according to Malraux, is a "sacred art," that is, nonrepresentational; but in contrast to all "sacred art" that preceded it, it is its own object—it is dedicated, not to God, but to itself. Not only does it evidence ". . . the very ancient desire to create an autonomous world . . ." but that will is ". . . for the first time reduced to itself alone."[126]

The reader will have remarked that the theory of art exposed in *Les Voix du Silence* is, in part, in contradiction with the "return to things" in art of which we spoke in connection with Cézanne and the cubists. The need to create in the artist, Malraux argues, is bred not of a contemplation of nature, but of works of art. Art is a "closed system," without indebtedness to the exterior world whose domination it is the very meaning of art to contest.[127] Human freedom could hardly be carried further. The revolutionary can only dream of becoming God, the artist in a sense succeeds, and through him, the rest of us. But the liberation has been effected at the cost of introducing

---

it. We now view nature as absurd, and it is this nature that cubism copies; although it is possible, as we have seen, and as Malraux argues, to regard the cubists as primarily engaged in creating objects of their own.

126 *Les Voix du Silence*, NRF, 1952, p. 614.

127 We need not go into a discussion of these two views of art. The reader will find the existentialist reply to Malraux in an article by Merleau-Ponty entitled *Le Langage indirect et Les Voix du Silence.* (*Les Temps Modernes*, No. 80, June 1950.)

a new kind of separation between man and his world; not that of an attempt on the part of mind to gain a perspective on matter, but that of a withdrawal into a *different* world. It should not be forgotten, however, that *Les Voix du Silence* is a book on aesthetics, not politics; and as there can be no *engagement* in the plastic arts that is not self-destructive, Malraux's philosophy of art with its "other world" need not enter into conflict with his philosophy of action.

Chapter 3

Saint-Exupéry

> ... à chacun de nos actes le monde
> nous révèle un visage neuf.
> SARTRE

THE WORK of Antoine de Saint-Exupéry is a mirror that reflects the firmament. It has the purity of a jewel, for in it the Self has ceased to exist. Gide's suppression of it remained for the most part theoretical, and in the novels of Malraux, especially the earlier ones, it is not the absurd alone that so darkens the hue of things. Malraux's dialogues are very often conversations with himself, whereas Saint-Exupéry simply mediates between his reader and *Man's Earth*, to use the title of one of his books. What we learn about him is no more than what he himself had just learned in a combat with the elements or with men. And yet Saint-Exupéry is neither "objective," nor a writer of adventure stories.

No more than Malraux does Saint-Exupéry write of his experiences for their own sake; he has only contempt for men who, like the toreador, make a profession of danger. However admirable Saint-Exupéry's account of what happened in the course of his mission to Arras, the subject of the book is not the flight itself, but what it taught him. Having narrowly escaped death over Arras, he turns home thinking: "There are heaps of things I'm going to understand,"[1] and ". . . there, we learned more about ourselves than we would have learned in ten years of meditation."[2] Such statements throw into striking relief one of the aspects of the intellectual evolution we have been tracing.

---

[1] *Pilote de Guerre*, p. 366. (Unless otherwise indicated, all our page references will be to the edition of Saint-Exupéry's complete works, published by NRF, 1950.)
[2] *Ibid.*, p. 376.

Saint-Exupéry comes to understand not only the meaning of the war and why he should risk his life in it, which is the subject of *Pilote de Guerre,* but also his whole understanding of men and things is the product not of reason but of participation; not of books, but of acts. Léon Werth has written of Saint-Exupéry that he read little and knew everything.[3] The variety and depth of his abilities make of him a kind of contemporary Leonardo, and even more than in the case of Malraux is it surprising that a man who could without any doubt have made of himself a great scientist or philosopher should have preferred to be an aviator. It is true that for us, Saint-Exupéry is first of all a great writer—but in his own eyes? The literature of the world offers no more amiable figure than Saint-Exupéry; but with the *littérateur* and the intellectual, he could be positively brutal. In *Citadelle,* they are referred to consistently as "ink spitters," and in *Pilote de Guerre* he writes scathingly: "The intellectuals hold themselves in reserve, like pots of jam, on the shelves of the propaganda service, to be eaten after the war."[4] Few French writers have frequented literary circles less than Saint-Exupéry, who dreaded nothing so much as the possibility that his literary activities estrange him from such comrades-in-arms as Guillaumet and Mermoz.

The "immaculate knowledge" of the scientist and philosopher at which Nietzsche scoffed no longer nourishes the deepest needs of men. We learn about the world only on condition of occupying a "position" in it, and that there should be no Self in the work of Saint-Exupéry does not mean that his writing is "objective." The productive labours of men are accomplished under *particular* conditions, they are a part of existence. Saint-Exupéry liked to compare his aeroplane to the peasant's plough; and, as we shall see, no peasant thinks of the world and of men more exclu-

---

[3] *Vie de Saint-Exupéry suivi de "Tel que je l'ai connu"* by Léon Werth, Seuil, 1949.

[4] p. 300. ". . . They [intellectuals] rush, not to serve, but to be seen, heard or admired as they execute their acrobatics. Having finished their gyrations, they put on in advance an air of modesty. . . ." (*Citadelle,* p. 915.)

sively in terms of his village and fields, than does Saint-Exupéry in terms of flight. Aviation was not a goal for him, but one of the elementary activities through which men are united with things and with one another; it was the particular "point of view" by which he acceded to universal truth. Saint-Exupéry was not an author who was also an aviator, but an aviator with a genius for literary expression. This is as true of *Citadelle* as it is of any of Saint-Exupéry's books, for the ideas it contains are but elaborations of those we find in the preceding novels; the merciless chieftain of *Citadelle,* for example, is a reincarnation of the implacable Rivière. These two figures alone are sufficient to cast a long shadow across the sweetness and light which is all many readers wish to retain of the message of Saint-Exupéry. While it is true that of the two faces of contemporary thought—the absurd and the truth of appearance—it is of the latter that Saint-Exupéry is most sensible, the lamp-lighter of *Le Petit Prince* is not a joyful image of man's predicament. Shortly before his disappearance in the course of a reconnaissance flight over France, Saint-Exupéry wrote to a friend: "If I am brought down, I shall regret absolutely nothing. The ant-hills of the future terrify me, and I hate their robot virtues."[5]

Saint-Exupéry was a prodigal son who never returned. *Courrier Sud,* his first book, is a comparison of two worlds —that of the *petit bourgeois* which he left, and that of the air, into which he entered. There is, at the origin of his career, the same revolt of action against possession that we discussed in Gide and Malraux. Saint-Exupéry had one other enemy besides the man of letters, the lamentable Robineau of *Vol de Nuit,* symbol of the fearful mediocrity of a civilization which places possession above sacrifice. The dangerous Voltarian *petit bourgeois* of Péguy has, in a generation, become a pitiable nonentity. Inhabiting a depressing world of material wealth that he does not enjoy and of principles in which he no longer believes, he has not

5 Published in *Confluences,* Nos. 12–14, p. 166.

been equal to the stress of the times. The revolution of which Saint-Exupéry is one of the prophets is (for the moment) a spiritual rather than a political one, but it is none the less uncompromising for that; in fact Saint-Exupéry's rejection of bourgeois civilization is more absolute than that of the marxists: ". . . Neither action nor individual happiness allow of being shared. They are in conflict."[6] The contrast, explicit or implied, between these two ways of life is constant in Saint-Exupéry, and *Courrier Sud* is the story of the failure of an attempt to conciliate them. There have been, traditionally, two means of reacting against the spiritual dry rot of middle-class values—love and religion, and authors no less illustrious than Stendhal and Péguy have demonstrated their possibilities. Neither one nor the other, however, can appease the unrest of Bernis in *Courrier Sud*. As for love, ". . . one risks very little of oneself in a caress."[7] Women represent a way of life alien to that upon which Saint-Exupéry had embarked. " 'To love, to love and nothing else—what a dead end!' Riviére vaguely sensed a duty higher than that of loving."[8] Love has come upon lean days in the literature of the present century, in striking contrast to the prosperity it enjoyed in the last where, like other ideals of that time, it served as a refuge. There is no refuge more destructive of the quality of man, however, no story more shameful than that of *L'Education Sentimentale*. Antoine Thibault thought that his love for Rachel had been what was best in his life, and there is no better record of the moral impasse into which the nineteenth century had led than *Les Thibault*. Here is Saint-Exupéry's judgment upon *Werther*: ". . . Behind that pleasant face [that of a young man who had committed suicide for love] under that human skull, there had been nothing, nothing at all. Except the image of some silly little girl like so many others."[9]

It is with men like Valéry, Malraux and Saint-Exupéry

6 *Vol de Nuit*, p. 132.
7 *Courrier Sud*, p. 38.
8 *Vol de Nuit*, p. 133.
9 *Terre des Hommes*, p. 180.

that genuine atheism begins, because with them religion is not a "problem," it is an irrelevancy. The nineteenth century was, in the broad sense of the word, a desperately religious one, and Gide's *Numquid et Tu . . . ?* belongs to it. Men like Taine and Renan are but superficially atheists; they were able to dispense with one God only because they had another to fall back upon. True irreligion is inseparable from the absurd. It is not compatible with a belief in solutions. Contemporary religion, however, appears to Saint-Exupéry as unsure of the light it proclaims as is unbelief itself. Bernis enters a church to listen to a sermon which seems to him a cry that has long since ceased to expect an answer: "What despair! Where is the act of faith? I heard no act of faith, but a cry of total despair."[10]

The secret of the poetry of flight which Saint-Exupéry created lies in the completeness with which he abandoned the world we have just described. Flight is never considered from the ground; it is the earth on the contrary which is always considered from the point of view of flight. Saint-Exupéry writes always ". . . in the light of a particular point of view,"[11] and *Terre des Hommes* announces the discovery of another world, which, although "particular," is no less real than that of men who have never left the ground. Guillaumet coached Saint-Exupéry for his first flight over Spain, and as he spoke ". . . the Spain of my map became, under the lamp, a fairy-tale country, . . . I marked out this farmer, these thirty sheep, this brook. I bore to her exact place this shepherdess the geographers had neglected."[12] The world seen from the air does not "appear" other, it is other; it is a "world in a show-case, too exposed, too much displayed, towns in order upon a rolled-up map that a slow earth bears toward him with the sureness of a tide."[13] From a plane, the ordinary affairs of

10 *Courrier Sud*, p. 55.
11 *Terre des Hommes*, p. 162. "I cannot refrain from contrasting these two universes. The universe of the aircraft and that of the ground." (*Pilote de Guerre*, p. 376.)
12 *Terre des Hommes*, p. 158.
13 *Courrier Sud*, p. 15.

men do not "appear" negligible, they are: "Carcassone where every woman that keeps a draper's shop relives the life of her ancestresses. Humble, penned-up happiness."[14] The image of a motionless plane and a moving earth recurs very frequently in Saint-Exupéry. As a plane nears the ground; "This unified world breaks up. Trees, houses, villages stand up out of a smooth horizon, then drift away behind him."[15] Fabien, caught in a storm over hilly country ". . . understood . . . that all the ground masses . . . were as though torn from their supports, unbolted, and were beginning to swerve drunkenly around him."[16] Looking down upon the Mediterranean from the *Cimetière Marin,* Valéry had seen that the sea was a "roof"; similarly, from a plane not flying too high, a point beneath is at the bottom of a funnel. "The English rock dug out a depression to the east. . . ."[17] "The wonder in face of the world" which is so characteristic of the author of *Le Petit Prince,* and to which we referred in connection with phenomenology, is due to Saint-Exupéry's instinctive understanding that the world is inexhaustible because it is what it appears to be. There exists a world of flight, as for Tchen there existed a world of murder.

Not only did Saint-Exupéry "live in the domain of flight,"[18] he understood that the condition of knowing anything at all about the world we live in, is to consent to being "closed up in it." "The world in whose order we live cannot be divined unless we are ourselves shut up in it."[19] The impotence of the intellectual is the impotence of one who prefers arbitration to participation, or who prefers to be a "spectator," believing that in that way one comes to see things *sub specie eternitatis.* Saint-Exupéry congratulates himself, in *Pilote de Guerre,* upon having been able,

14 *Ibid.*
15 *Ibid.,* p. 20.
16 *Vol de Nuit,* p. 135.
17 *Courrier Sud,* p. 61.
18 *Terre des Hommes,* p. 224. Saint-Exupéry writes that pilots come out of the sky: ". . . as strange peasants come down from their mountains." (*Vol de Nuit,* p. 95.)
19 *Terre des Hommes,* p. 244.

though a writer, to remain a flyer among others. "The rôle of spectator has always been my bugbear. What am I if I do not take part? If I am to be, I must take part."[20]

It is not only because the universe is not a rational one that it reveals itself to action and not to thought, but also because man has no "interior" considered either as a depository of "innate" truths, as a receptacle for facts acquired by perception and reason or as a set of clearly defined characteristics.[21] This is perhaps Saint-Exupéry's fundamental intuition. His awareness is always of something that is exterior to him. In anyone but Saint-Exupéry, the following would be a mere figure of speech: in the desert the nights are very cold, and "Toward three o'clock in the morning, our woollen blankets become thin, transparent."[22] "The green paradise" of childhood was not locked up within the child's fancy, it was ". . . a closed civilization, where every step could be savoured, where things had a meaning . . . ,"[23] and as a grown man, Saint-Exupéry found it again in the desert. During the years he worked at Cap Juby, before the complete submission of the Moroccan tribes, the raids of war parties transformed the very sand. "What a difference of substance between the conquered sand and the other!,"[24] and he who sensed that the mystery of the desert lodged in the things about him and not in himself ". . . was not the play-thing of an illusion. We did not deceive ourselves when we hastened after these discoveries."[25] Generalities alone are not part of the exterior world, because they do not exist:

20 *Pilote de Guerre*, p. 370.
21 In the past, philosophy has tended to render action as a means of acquiring knowledge doubly superflous by making of man a symbol of the cosmos as in the Middle Ages, or a microcosm as in subsequent centuries.
22 *Courrier Sud*, p. 86.
23 *Terre des Hommes*, p. 221.
24 *Ibid*. In Sartre's *Le Sursis* (NRF, 1947, p. 27), Odette, on a beach with Mathieu, looks out at the sea and thinks that even if there is a war, the ocean at least will not change:
    "That at least will remain," she said.
    "What?"
    "That, the sea."
    Mathieu shook his head.
    "No," he said, "not even that."
25 *Terre des Hommes*, p. 222. See also *Lettre à un Otage*, p. 410.

. . . I do not know man, but men. Not liberty, but free men. Not happiness, but happy men. Not beauty, but beautiful things . . . those who pursue an essence other than as a birth merely show their vanity and the emptiness of their hearts. And they will neither live nor die, for one neither dies nor lives by words.[26]

Saint-Exupéry called the aeroplane a "tool" with the aid of which man can come to grips again with all the "old problems."[27] It is about the problem of death that his experience taught him most, and there is no better way to understand what Saint-Exupéry has written on this subject than to remark his constant tendency to see in the feelings and generalities of subjectivity, qualities of things in the exterior world. In *Courrier Sud,* the son of Geneviève dies, but initially the death makes no impression upon her. Having left for a few hours the house where death was installed, she had left her bereavement itself.

She felt that over there the chill light of dawn was whitening on a huge catastrophe. The cold, tumbled bedclothes. Towels thrown on the furniture. A chair overturned. Her job was to make head against this breakdown of ordinary things. . . . It was her job to wear herself out in vainly putting back into their places the things that made a setting for life.[28]

In the same way, the death of Fabien in *Vol de Nuit* is not at once present to his wife. "For her . . . Fabien's death would scarcely begin to be actual next day—a day henceforth empty in every action and in every object. Fabien would take a long time to leave his house."[29] In *Pilote de Guerre,* Saint-Exupéry is more specific still: "When engaged on burial fatigues, we feel love for the man who has died but we have no contact with death. Death . . . is a

[26] *Citadelle,* p. 807. See also pp. 814, 866, etc.
[27] *Terre des Hommes,* p. 153.
[28] *Courrier Sud,* p. 40. See also p. 34.
[29] p. 141.

new arrangement of the world."[30] Such is the death of others—a different "arrangement of the world." But what of our own?

Life, Saint-Exupéry remarks, always gives the lie to the phantoms we invent,[31] and this is never more true than where men confront danger and death. The imaginings of literature have in this respect little relation to reality.[32] Saint-Exupéry asserts that, with one exception, he had never known a man really afraid.[33] He had on the contrary always encountered the most extraordinary indifference to death. It was while working as a reporter at Madrid during the Civil War that Saint-Exupéry met the sergeant of whom he writes in *Terre des Hommes*. An absurd attack in which the men taking part were almost sure to be killed had been ordered for the early morning. The sergeant, who is to be one of the first to leave the shelter, lies down to sleep, and upon being awakened a few hours later to prepare himself to leave: "It was then that the man's real self shone through, then that he gave the slip to the foresights of logic. The sergeant was smiling."[34] It is also in *Terre des Hommes* that Saint-Exupéry tells of how Guillaumet was miraculously saved after his plane had come down in the Andes. Showing incredible endurance, he struggled for five days through the snow with his extremities slowly freezing. But what drove him on was not fear of death—death would have been a release—but loyalty to those who were relying on him to do his best to return to them. On one occasion, having stretched himself out to rest, not caring whether he ever got up again, he remembered that unless his body was recovered there would be a delay of four years before his wife received any assurance. This in mind, he was able to carry on for two more days.[35] A few years later, Saint-Exupéry, forced down in the desert, was able

30 p. 288.
31 *Pilote de Guerre*, p. 361.
32 "Where are we to find that haggard lunacy invented by literary folk to dazzle us?" (*Ibid.*, p. 307.)
33 *Ibid.*
34 *Terre des Hommes*, p. 262.
35 *Ibid.*, p. 178.

to confirm for himself everything Guillaumet had told him. The one concern of Saint-Exupéry and of his mechanic was the distress of those who would have to wait day after day with slowly diminishing hope, and apart from that— nothing. With only a few hours to live "I find nothing left in me except a great dryness of heart. I am ready to drop, yet despair is an utter stranger to me. I do not even suffer. . . . When I am found, with my eyes burnt out, they will imagine that I had cried loud and long and suffered greatly."[36] The explanation of all this is simply that death does not exist until it has struck, until it has taken shape in things; it exists only for those who are left to grieve over the marks of its passage. If the sergeant could smile, it was because he was going out, not to meet death, but simply: "the discomfort of dying."[37] So conscientious is Saint-Exupéry in his adherence to things, even in his writing, that he has "nothing to tell." "Ten minutes ago, I came close to disappearing," he writes in *Pilote de Guerre,* "and I have nothing to tell. . . ."[38] We have already learned from *La Nausée,* that existence knows no adventures, but only commerce with things. For the purpose of story-telling, we arrange into intelligible sequences what is not intelligible, what is not really communicable. Thus, in *L'Homme et les Eléments,*[39] Saint-Exupéry tells of being caught by a cyclone while flying in Argentina, and although the experience was one of the most memorable of his life, he declares himself incapable of describing what really happened. "I have gradually come to understand," he continues, "the deep-set reason for this incapacity. If you fail in the attempt to evoke horror, it is because you have invented the horror after the event, as you lived your memories over again." The real is act—contact with things; all the rest is invention. The mission to Arras was not a "war-time adventure"—"War adventure? Where

[36] *Ibid.,* p. 254.
[37] *Ibid.,* p. 262.
[38] p. 309.
[39] A fragment published in *Confluences,* Nos. 12–14.

was it?"[40] There had taken place no more than the succession of acts necessary to bring the aircraft over Arras and to photograph enemy installations there.

What we have said of death is equally true of other abstractions such as "war" and "peace"—they are in things, not in us. Not until anti-aircraft shells began to burst around his plane did the war come into being for Saint-Exupéry. "We were at war. The war had to show itself sooner or later. When it did show itself, it amounted to no more than a few streaks of light."[41] In the second and third volumes of *Les Chemins de la Liberté,* Sartre adopts a "cinematographic" technique of narrative because he is writing about the war; that is, about something which, non-existent apart from things, can only be appreciated from *individual* points of view.[42] If the abstraction "war" existed, it could be satisfactorily seized by the novelist in the "subjectivity" of a single person, or by the historian in the correspondence of diplomats. Similarly, peace for Saint-Exupéry, is something quite concrete: ". . . peace means there being a point in biting into country bread and sausage on the banks of the Saône. . . . The sad thing for me is the sausage having no flavour any more. . . ."[43]

This "exteriority" of Saint-Exupéry is naturally accompanied by the idea that man is act and not essence. But whereas in Malraux the necessity of action derives largely from the absurd, in Saint-Exupéry the emphasis is rather on the nullity, almost the degradation of a sheltered life. Rivière remarks that *les petits bourgeois* "do not exist,"[44] and there is perhaps no better reason why many men prefer risk to safety—life is sustained by movement, not by a foundation. Fabien tired by hours of flying and with the prospect of bad weather for the next lap of his journey is tempted for a moment to believe in the repose and security

40 *Pilote de Guerre,* p. 309.
41 *Ibid.,* p. 356.
42 To understand the war ". . . one would have to be everywhere at once." (Sartre, *Le Sursis,* NRF, 1947, p. 255.)
43 Letter to Léon Werth, published in *Confluences,* Nos. 12–14.
44 *Vol de Nuit,* p. 102.

offered by the village where he has halted for ten minutes, but to obtain them ". . . he would have had to give up a life of action. . . ."[45] Pellerin, another flyer of *Vol de Nuit*, narrowly escapes death in the course of a flight, but instead of reaching safety with the relief and gratitude we might expect, he returns as a "prodigious messenger";[46] instead of learning the price of everything he had almost lost ". . . he has just learned its triviality."[47] Saint-Exupéry dying of thirst in the desert discovers not only that it is easy to die, but that it is somehow preferable to die in this way than to live as do the "populations of the suburban trains." "How, in their hours of freedom, do they fill up their absurd little Sundays?"[48] It is not a question here, any more than with Malraux, of being contemptuous of life, but of *redefining* it. "It is not danger I love," writes Saint-Exupéry, "I know what I love. It is life."[49] Life, however, is not what we possess, but what we win, and this is to be taken in the most literal sense. In *Pilote de Guerre*, Saint-Exupéry writes: "Anguish is due to the loss of a real identity,"[50] and it is only through action that an identity may be regained. While preparing for his mission to Arras, it seems to Saint-Exupéry that he is awaiting an "unknown self" which is coming toward him "from outside, like a fantom."[51] His mission completed, and this "unknown self" understood, Saint-Exupéry points the moral in words which recall those of Garcia talking about the "clergy" of intellectuals: "A Being is not of the realm of words, but of that of deeds. Our Humanism has taken too little notice of deeds. It has failed in its attempt."[52] Humanism nowhere more clearly "neglects acts" than in the importance it necessarily attaches to leisure without which cul-

45 *Ibid.*, p. 93.
46 *Ibid.*, p. 99.
47 *Ibid.*, p. 99.
48 *Terre des Hommes*, p. 251. "In the suburban train I feel my agony far more keenly than I do here. Here, all things considered, I am in clover." (p. 252.)
49 *Ibid.*, p. 252.
50 p. 293.
51 *Pilote de Guerre*, p. 294. "It would be a little too easy to borrow ready-made souls!" (*Ibid.*, p. 308.)
52 *Ibid.*, p. 393.

ture, as our society defines it, can probably not exist. The cultivated man is disappearing with the leisure class from which he is inseparable. If man is no more than what he does, however, this disappearance of a species cannot be considered a catastrophe. Culture has perhaps been too often less a means of enriching life than of compensating for its absence. "Work compels you to embrace the world,"[53] writes Saint-Exupéry, but culture, after the antique tradition, proposes to make us independent of it. But there is no existence that is not contact with things.

> . . . The only important and growth-producing part of life [we read in *Citadelle*], is that which involves you, which involves your hunger and your thirst. . . . Otherwise, you are merely playing at life, caricaturing life and caricaturing culture. For you become only in opposition to what resists you. And since leisure makes no demand on you . . . what, in order to exist, are you going to do if you do not yourself reinvent work?[54]

It is perhaps in this context that one of Saint-Exupéry's favourite ideas, that of "exchange," may be most fittingly placed. There could be no better illustration of the fact that, for Saint-Exupéry, man, reduced to himself alone, is "nothing." He exists only in so far as by an act he "exchanges" or embodies himself in a thing, or in a different arrangement of things. Saint-Exupéry, like Malraux, writes only of heroes; but this heroic humanity is pitiably frail, a blurred reflection of the stony immensity in which it is enclosed. The notion of exchange, like that of eroticism in Malraux, is an attempt to arrogate the "self-sufficiency" of matter without ceasing to be consciousness. We feel ourselves, as Sartre remarks, ". . . unessential in relation to the thing revealed,"[55] (by consciousness), hence the effort to acquire some of the indestructibility of matter:

53 *Citadelle*, p. 602.
54 *Ibid.*, p. 601.
55 *Situations II*, NRF, 1948, p. 90.

228 / Literature Considered as Philosophy

"... The uselessly high quality of the metal, the perfection of the design, the sweetness of the lines . . . serve no purpose unless it be to receive that part of us which we have exchanged and which lasts longer than the flesh."[56] We have come a long way from the "immortality" that pre-occupies the *littérateur*. The men of whom Malraux and Saint-Exupéry write efface themselves, like the anonymous masters of the Middle Ages, behind the work accomplished. The existentialist "we" has replaced the essentialist "I."

In Saint-Exupéry, the reversal of rôles between the intellectual and the man of action, the beginnings of which we detect in Gide's admiration for the latter, is fully accomplished. The model which Saint-Exupéry proposes to himself is not that of a great writer or philosopher, but that of Hochedé, a fellow pilot during the war. It is not that Hochedé was the most courageous flyer of the group, nor that he combined in a high degree culture (of which he had none) and practical ability, but that he was *pure existence.* "I would like to exist as fully as Hochedé exists. A tree is fine, solidly planted upon its roots. The permanence of Hochedé is fine. Hochedé could not disappoint."[57] Hochedé could never disappoint because he is what he does. A man disappoints when his acts fall short of a supposed identity. Hochedé's acts and his identity are one. His whole existence is a state which Saint-Exupéry achieves only over Arras where, in the thick of enemy fire, "you are lodged in your act itself. Your act is you. . . .You no longer find anything else in you."[58] This conception of the "complete man" is quite new to our civilization. Hochedé ". . . would not know how to throw any light upon himself. But he is constructed, he is complete."[59] We usually think of an "accomplished" man as one who

[56] *Citadelle*, p. 455. "You appeared to us eternal from being so closely bound up with things." (*Courrier Sud*, p. 28.)
[57] *Pilote de Guerre*, p. 372.
[58] *Ibid.*, p. 361.
[59] *Ibid.*

has somehow found time to bring to perfection both his mental and physical activities, who is both philosopher and peasant, or statesman and soldier. Hochedé, however, has no "inner" life, yet he lacks nothing; for what really exists, exists in things exterior to us and comprehensible in themselves.

Although, as we have just remarked, Saint-Exupéry is drawn to action rather by contempt for *petit bourgeois* non-existence than by Malraux's acute sense of the absurd, the latter, though in a slightly different form, is by no means absent from his work. We have seen the idea of the absurd acquire in Valéry and Malraux, by a contrast between the boundless reaches of the universe and the infinitesimal presence of human consciousness, a poetic and a tragic value. Saint-Exupéry has written the tragedy into *Vol de Nuit* and the poetry into *Terre des Hommes*. Rivière's remorselessness is due largely to a feeling that everything human is under a constant menace of obliteration. "It is curious how events get the upper hand, how a great and obscure force reveals itself, the same that raises up virgin forests, that grows, that forces growth, that wells up from everywhere around great works."[60] Rivière is possessed by this image of man engaged in a ceaseless struggle to avoid being engulfed and lost for ever. Like a hero of Malraux, he is in revolt against death, and imagines the great stone cities of the past to have been constructed to thwart it, to protect ". . . the species that the sea of sand was to blot out."[61] The exigencies of one's work transform the world,[62] writes Saint-Exupéry, for whom the world so often observed from the air became a vast arid crust where the settlements of men lay like patches of barely visible dust on the great sloping surfaces. "Where do men get this taste for eternity, precariously

60 *Vol de Nuit*, p. 117. In a preface to a translation of Anne Lindbergh's *Listen! The Wind (Confluences*, Nos. 12–14), Saint-Exupéry talks to a universe, "almost broken down," which only the furious efforts of human beings keep in motion. (p. 194.)
61 *Vol de Nuit*, p. 134.
62 *Terre des Hommes*, p. 167.

placed as they are upon a still warm lava, and already
menaced by the sands that are to come, menaced by the
snows? Their civilizations are but fragile gildings. . . ."[63]
Yet the very fragility of human consciousness, lost in the
mineral wastes of the universe, makes its mere existence
that much more miraculous. In *Terre des Hommes*, Saint-
Exupéry tells of landing upon a small plateau in the
Sahara, which was so high above the surface of the desert,
and whose sides were so uniformly perpendicular that the
summit could never before have been visited by man. He
was therefore able to pick up from the bare face of the plateau, since nothing through the millennia could have dis-
turbed them, a number of aeroliths; and he marvels that this
slow "rain" should have come to be reflected in a mind.
"On a bed of minerals a dream is a miracle."[64]

Saint-Exupéry was of a temperament to find more exaltation than despair in this notion of human existence as
barely a palpitation, infinitely inconsequential, in the
senseless ether; for if man is so abandoned he is alone
responsible for what he is, and Saint-Exupéry looked upon
such responsibility as more of an opportunity than a burden. "Each is answerable for all,"[65] he repeats in *Pilote de
Guerre*, and that responsibility both justifies and compels
action which would otherwise be but the recreation of brutes
that many intellectuals like to consider it. Refusal of responsibility, misfortunes that are "explained" by fatality,
by treason, etc., are misfortunes that have been accepted.
"But if I take the error upon myself, I claim the power
that is a man's. I can act. . . ."[66] An act must be a sacrifice
for other men. The greatness of Guillaumet's exploit in the
Andes was not his courage—there are few human qualities
more universal—but the fact that he considered himself
responsible. Responsible not only for the mail, not only
toward his friends who were waiting for him, but: "Responsible a little for the destiny of mankind, in the meas-

[63] *Ibid.*, p. 186.
[64] *Ibid.*, p. 189.
[65] *Pilote de Guerre*, p. 384.
[66] *Ibid.*, p. 385.

ure of his work."[67] Each of us is a sentinel, and ". . . every sentinel is responsible for the entire empire."[68] In these two phrases from *Terre des Hommes*, Saint-Exupéry expresses with admirable concision the nature of the moral revolution that the existentialists are seeking to bring about. It is essentially an attempt to replace the idea of *duty towards*, by that of *responsibility for*. Where there are no absolutes, there can be no duty to fulfil in respect to them; but the freedom so acquired entails a total responsibility.

This stern ethic of responsibility and sacrifice is an opportunity also because it holds forth the precious recompense of fraternity about which Saint-Exupéry is quite as eloquent as Malraux. "I feel this sense of community with quite extraordinary clarity—'We, of Group 2/33!' "[69] This is what Saint-Exupéry learns in the course of his mission to Arras, the consequences of which he develops in the final pages of *Pilote de Guerre*. The fraternity, which made of his flight group a single organism, must be extended to ever larger groups. The fraternity that men once enjoyed in God, they would now have to reconstitute in man himself; the fraternity of action must replace that of common origin; sacrifice must replace possession. This is the idea out of which *Citadelle* was hewn.

Citadelle is, on the face of it, a collection of platitudes. Its fundamental thesis appears to be simply the time-worn verity that happiness is not a state but an activity, that it is the reward not of possessing but of trying to possess. There is, to be sure, more in *Citadelle* than this, but unless we place ourselves in the proper perspective, we will not see it. On the surface, *Citadelle* proposes nothing very new. Actually it *proposes* nothing at all, it cites a number of concrete instances. Critics who have reproached Saint-Exupéry with dispersing his thought in too many images

---

[67] *Terre des Hommes*, p. 179. "To be human is precisely to be responsible. It is to know shame in the face of a poverty which did not seem to have anything to do with us." (*Ibid.*, p. 180.)
[68] *Ibid.*, p. 270.
[69] *Pilote de Guerre*, p. 369. "The greatness of a calling lies perhaps above all in uniting men." (*Terre des Hommes*, p. 171.)

have failed to understand this. *Citadelle* is a treatise on government which proceeds not by argument, but by illustration. It is a utopia without a plan, a cathedral upon which the work never ceases.[70] On the surface, little is new, and yet everything has changed. The features are the same, but the expression is different. For example, when Saint-Exupéry writes ". . . the road, the field of barley and the curve of the hill are different for a man according to whether or not they make up a property,"[71] we know now after what has been said previously that he does not mean that man's *attitude* towards these things has changed, but that they are really different. Saint-Exupéry is a writer who is implicitly if not explicitly no longer tributary to what Sartre calls the "digestive philosophy";[72] that is, classical epistemology which conceives knowing as in one form or another the process of taking things into the mind as the stomach takes in food. In this view of the mental processes, the mind is also a kind of store-house in which the end-products of the digestive activities are placed to await the moment of the great synthesis, the philosopher's Day of Judgment, when everything shall be made clear.[73] Historical periods show, when we look back upon them, a surprising homogeneity. This "possessive philosophy" which put aside principles with a view to acquiring one day a final one, accords itself very well with a society that believes man to live by possessions alone. The acquisitive society has its acquisitive philosophy. *Citadelle* is an attack upon both. It is part of that literature in which the existentialist may find confirmation of his theories—mind is not a "container," but act; and, correspondingly, the world is not rational, but inexhaustible. To the extent in which it is permissible to sum up a

---

[70] It is, therefore, in a sense appropriate that *Citadelle* should have been left unfinished. ". . . I have never completed my town. . . ." (*Citadelle*, p. 491.)

[71] *Citadelle*, p. 442.

[72] "Intentionalité dans la Philosophie de Husserl," *Situations I*, 1947.

[73] This is one of the most notable of the logician's illogicalities. "It is striking that transcendental philosophies of the classic type never ask themselves whether it is possible to effect the total explanation that they always suppose to be *already made somewhere*." (Merleau-Ponty, *La Phénoménologie de la Perception*, NRF, 1945, p. 74.)

book which contains no argument, we may therefore say that *Citadelle* is an attempt to point out the fallacies inherent in the great longing to possess, whether it be goods for the body or principles for the mind.

We need hardly insist upon this first point, that life is movement toward" and not material possession. No idea in *Citadelle* recurs more frequently. Happiness is the "warmth of acts;"[74] a civilization rests upon what it exacts from its people and not what it furnishes them;[75] life is a "permanent creation";[76] ". . . if I am no longer movement and action towards, then I am as dead";[77] etc. In a fine metaphor, Saint-Exupéry compares our society to a chess player who has ceased to play the game in order to devote himself to fondling the chessmen.[78] *Terre des Hommes* demonstrates that the aeroplane is not a goal, but a tool, and this is true of whatever we possess. It is not a question here of the venerable commonplace that material well-being corrupts. There is no exhortation in *Citadelle*, rather simply the conviction that to exist implies to act, and that those who have "alienated" themselves in what they own, have in some fundamental way ceased to be men. Ennui notoriously accompanies a too secure prosperity, and ennui, according to Valéry, is a "metaphysical sentiment."

Not only existentialism, but contemporary thought in almost all its branches, is abandoning the search for "Truth" by analysis in favour of the description of structure.[79] The long hunt for nature's "secrets" has caused us to overlook what is given with evidence. Having lost confidence in total explanations, we perceive with astonishment that there is nothing to explain, that the techniques of analysis create the very problems they set out to resolve. Anyone who proposes to comprehend life by trying to

[74] *Citadelle*, p. 461.
[75] *Ibid.*, p. 466.
[76] *Ibid.*, p. 512.
[77] *Ibid.*, p. 550.
[78] *Ibid.*, p. 837.
[79] See Bréhier, *Les Thèmes Actuels de la Philosophie*, Presses Universitaires, 1951.

penetrate beyond what is immediately given, is in somewhat the predicament of the physicist who studies phenomena so minute that any attempt to observe them causes a change in their comportment. Phenomenology is simply a belief in the possibility of seizing appearances *before* a conscious effort to observe has had the opportunity to alter them.

In the work of few creative authors is this tendency more faithfully mirrored than in that of Saint-Exupéry. No useful purpose is served by making of life an object of study, for there is nothing "behind" or "beyond" it, and if there were, we could not know it. ". . . Stones know nothing of the temple they compose and can know nothing of it."[80] The attempt to "possess" life in the capsule form of principles assimilable to the intelligence must therefore be as unsuccessful as that of the *petit bourgeois* to possess it in the form of the goods it offers.

We have referred to the harshness, so unusual in Saint-Exupéry, with which he speaks his mind about intellectuals. The life of the bourgeois is self defeating, it contains its own disillusionment. The intellectual, on the other hand, can rarely be undeceived. He has reached his conclusions by "objective" means, they are consequently irrecusable, and if his theories are never practically effective, it is because the times are rife with ignorance and selfishness. The intellectual is the only serious menace to the desert "empire" of *Citadelle* where he appears in two forms—as the moral perfectionist or the "squint-eyed one" and as the "geometer." The first wishes to eliminate evil and the second contradiction. But neither can be eliminated without destroying existence, of which they are essential constituents. "Your historians came, your logicians and your critics. They considered the material and, being unable to make anything of it, advised you to enjoy it. And you have refused the fast which was a condition of the feast of celebration."[81] This elementary notion of the "necessity

80 *Citadelle*, p. 636.
81 *Citadelle*, p. 836. See p. 696, etc.

of contradiction," which the intellectual and the moralist are compelled to eschew, is one of the corner-stones of *L'Etre et le Néant*, where what is (the in-itself) owes its existence in consciousness to what is not (the for-itself). In broader terms, we can perceive an object only thanks to the existence of what is not that object. Antinomies, which are problems for the reason, are sustenance for life. There is no truth without falsehood, no good without evil, no being without nothingness. Life cannot be thought, it has to be lived; but until the present, the great affair of the intellectual has been to discover what *makes life possible,* and not what it *actually is.* For Saint-Exupéry, as for Gide, existence has no problems except those that have been artificially created. In *Vol de Nuit,* Rivière, despite the disappearance of Fabien, refuses to cancel his night flights, and the act of sending another plane off into the night "resolves all the problems."[82] Saint-Exupéry, installed in his plane, and on the way to Arras, notes: "I experienced nothing but the physical pleasure of self-sufficient acts sustained by meaning."[83] An act, as we have already learned from Malraux, "bears within itself all its fatalities," among which inequalities and injustices which outrage the intelligence but which we suppress only at the price of ceasing to act. "Justice and equality. Such is death. But fraternity is found only in the living tree."[84] Fraternity forms a part of no system. It cannot be established by decree, for it is born of action and dies with it. It belongs to existence, not essence. Truth for Saint-Exupéry is that which exists, not what is "discovered" after what is merely appearance has been identified and eliminated. ". . . I know only one truth, which is life. . . ."[85] Truth is not the answer to a question, but

---

82 p. 148.
83 *Pilote de Guerre,* p. 297.
84 *Citadelle,* p. 693. See *L'Espoir,* p. 75, where Barca remarks that it is not equality that is the contrary to the humiliation suffered by the poor, but fraternity.
85 *Citadelle,* p. 512. "Newton did not 'discover' a law that had long been deliberately concealed, after the fashion of a riddle situation. Newton carried out a creative operation." (*Terre des Hommes,* p. 267.)

the realization that questions are superfluous: ". . . The whole progress of man lies in discovering . . . that his questions have no meaning . . . truth . . . came as the wiping out of a question."[86] And this is so because life is not a sphinx's question with our salvation hanging in the balance. "They confront me with the world as with a riddle, demanding that I explain it to them. But there is *no* explanation and the world has *no* meaning."[87] Saint-Exupéry starts out from a point on the other side of absurdity to which Gide and Malraux acceded only in the latter part of their careers—a fact which may explain how two authors, whose lives and ideas invite so many comparisons, could produce books so radically different in tone as those of Saint-Exupéry and Malraux.

The intellectual's confidence that the world has a sense is at the same time confidence in language to express it. Language has been the voice of the Self which was that of the Absolute. But in fact language "expresses" nothing, it *is*. A thought is said, and not "replaced" or "interpreted" by words; the words *are* the thought, just as a clenched fist is not an "expression" of anger, but the anger itself. Here again, there is nothing "within" us; language ". . . is something like a being"[88] which "lives" in the exterior world and which consequently only approximately corresponds to our needs. There can be no perfect correlation between meaning and word. Language does not resolve the ambiguity of life, it is part of it. The tool of the intellectual, his language, shares the limitations of the lesser tools of the carpenter or soldier—it is act, and one that is either directed and made effective by the exigencies of a given

---

86 *Citadelle*, p. 546.
87 *Ibid.*, p. 635. "At this point you will ask me by means of my logic to discover for you a system that will save you from danger. But there is no such system, none whatever." (*Ibid.*, p. 816.)
88 Merleau-Ponty, "Le Langage Indirect et Les Voix du Silence," *Temps Modernes*, No. 80, June 1950, p. 2118. On the same page we read: "Now, if we expel from our minds the idea of an *original text* of which our language is supposed to be the translation or a ciphered version, we shall see that the idea of a *complete* expression is nonsense, that all language is indirect or allusive. . . ." See *La Phénoménologie de la Perception*, Part I, Chapter VI.

historical situation, or emasculated by the requirements of a system. "Don't forget that your phrase is an act," writes Saint-Exupéry in *Citadelle*,[89] where he has much to say of the intellectuals' over-estimation of the capacity of language. "They imagine that the world is contained in words and that the language of man expresses the universe. . . ."[90] Existence cannot be compressed into the compartments of language; a statement is therefore not "more true or less true, but other";[91] it is not closer to or farther from "objectivity," it is a more or less faithful representation of a particular point of view.

There is in Saint-Exupéry the same mistrust of reason we found so prominent in the thought of Gide;[92] but while Gide usually had in mind reason as an invaluable aid to self-deception, Saint-Exupéry deplores it as concealing from us the "simplicity" of things that are.[93] Reason serves not only to create false Selves, as in Gide, but also rigid ideologies, ". . . the sanguinary insanity of ideas,"[94] for which the only cure is the autonomy of act—act as a direct response to things, and not act as an attempt to force the world into a rationality of which it has no need. This positive element of existentialist ethics, that an act must be free both from the dictates of the Self, which is necessarily spurious, and of systems, none of which can ever be comprehensive,[95] is more conspicuous in Saint-Exupéry than in Gide or Malraux—perhaps because Saint-Exupéry was further removed from the clergy of intellectuals than either Malraux or Gide. Hence the universal appeal of his books

[89] p. 731.
[90] *Citadelle*, p. 505.
[91] *Ibid.*, p. 507.
[92] "The art of reasoning which permits man to deceive himself. . . ." (*Ibid.*, p. 494.) "To be tempted, is to be tempted, when the mind is asleep, to yield to the reasons of the Intellect" (*Pilote de Guerre*, p. 300)—a sentence which might have been taken from some Gidean meditation on the Devil.
[93] *Citadelle*, p. 743.
[94] *Ibid.*, p. 551.
[95] In *L'Existentialisme est un Humanisme*, Sartre explains that there can be no rules of conduct, every act must be an "invention": "The one thing that counts is to know whether the invention is made in the name of freedom." (Nagel, 1946, p. 86.)

which none the less never betray an effort to "reach the masses." Saint-Exupéry several times compares himself to a peasant, for like the peasant his life was determined by the pressure of immediate needs and not by that of the great "problems." To concern oneself only about those questions which spring directly from the requirements of existence is to recognize the perfect adjustment of man to the world of which he is a part, an adjustment which he upsets by preferring to "think" rather than to "live" his environment, the elements of which do not fit together like the pieces of a giant puzzle, but simply "refer" to one another, or "imply" one another as the building stone "implies" the quarry. In this view, it is useless to ask why a thing is, or how it can be made to "fit" ". . . because it simply is,"[96] and consequently ". . . there is nothing to regret. Nor to reject."[97] This reconciliation of Saint-Exupéry with life, his conviction that evil can never be entirely suppressed, is the origin of the serenity with which, throughout his life, he kept company with tragedy. He accepted not only the absurd, but its necessity. The chieftain of *Citadelle* congratulates himself that God should remain inaccessible to him, for otherwise ". . . I have finished my becoming."[98] Men cease to become when they find a solution, in whose place Saint-Exupéry proposes a return to the perfect evidence of things that are.

It is not by the intelligence that we take cognizance of these evidences; in fact, intelligence often serves to obscure them. "There are truths," writes Saint-Exupéry in *Pilote de Guerre*, "which, although they cannot be formulated, are evident."[99] The dictates of reason are frequently in direct contradiction with those of what Saint-Exupéry calls Spirit (*L'Esprit*), the name he gives to the faculty that governs our immediate reaction to events, and whose resolutions common sense and prudence may unfortunately induce us

[96] *Citadelle*, p. 693.
[97] *Ibid.*, p. 562.
[98] p. 912.
[99] p. 350.

to abandon.[100] Saint-Exupéry cites the French declaration of war on Germany in 1939 as an example of the victory of Spirit over Intelligence. It was "illogical" for a nation to pit itself against a neighbour having twice its population and industrial capacity. Yet in the face of almost certain defeat, it was a war that had to be undertaken. In the same way it was unreasonable of Saint-Exupéry to expose himself to almost certain death during the war, since a man of his calibre would have been more useful behind a desk. "The demonstration was decisive,"[101] but there are certitudes that have no relation to logic. The persons who collaborated with the German occupiers of their country during the last war in the sincere belief that they were doing the best they could for their country under the circumstances, provide a notable example of the way in which reason may serve to becloud a number of truths perfectly evident to the less subtle. For a while after the fall of France, there was no reasonable cause to hope that Germany would ever be defeated. France could only be saved by collaboration. On the other hand, the barbarity of the Nazi régime continually offered immediate reasons for an uncompromising resistance; and given the inevitable un-

100 Opportunities of comparing some of the ideas we have been exposing to those of Stendhal are continually presenting themselves. If the heroes and heroines of Stendhal have a trait in common it is their contempt for common sense and prudence—fitting characteristics of the pompous nonentities which in the work of Stendhal precede by a century the gallery of Swine in *La Nausée*. The tragedy in Stendhal's novels rises out of the triumph of calculation over gratuity, possession over act; which is how one might also express the tragedy of *La Condition Humaine* and *L'Espoir*. There is a good deal of Fabrice del Dongo in Lafcadio; and, though more transformed by the passage of time, in the anarchists of *L'Espoir*. There is little difference fundamentally between Stendhal's contempt for the "great" of the earth and the contempt on the part of the authors we have been studying for the principles upon which the prestige of the great is based.

101 *Pilote de Guerre*, p. 300. We have referred to Saint-Exupéry's account in *Terre des Hommes* of how, his plane having come down in the Sahara, he almost died of thirst before being rescued. The rescue itself, however, was hardly more remarkable than Saint-Exupéry's decision to walk East when, according to his calculations, the only chance, however feeble, of finding a settlement was to walk West. The only reason he could discover for going East was that Guillaumet had saved himself in the Andes by taking that direction! Reasoning of a sort that lesser men would perhaps do well not to imitate.

certainty of the future, it is these reasons which should
have prevailed. Truth, according to Saint-Exupéry, is what
simplifies the world,[102] and the elaborate theories of historical and economic necessity with which a collaborator
might have justified himself would have been less "true"
than a determined hatred of the oppressor. Passiveness
requires justification; action, of the kind which concerns
us, never does. The baggage of principles and ideals, or
the quest for them, which is the business of the intellectual
has no place here. Saint-Exupéry, preparing himself for a
flight from which he has every chance of never returning,
does not think about the struggle of the West against the
Nazis: "I think in terms of immediate details."[103] The
Spanish sergeant, whom Saint-Exupéry met in an entrench-
ment on the Madrid front, was not fighting for his political
convictions of which he had none. If he had become engaged in the Civil War, it was because of a "truth which
he had not been able to translate into words, but whose
evidence had governed him."[104] We have already learned
from Gide that when someone begins to reason out a
course of conduct, he does so not, as he may sincerely
suppose, to discover the truth, but to conceal from himself
a disagreeable evidence. The truth never requires to be
sought out. "If I seek," writes Saint-Exupéry, "I have
found, for the mind desires only what it possesses. To find
is to see. And how could I look for that which, as yet, has
no meaning for me?"[105]

In the concluding pages of *Pilote de Guerre* and throughout *Citadelle,* Saint-Exupéry asks himself the same question, the only question that matters—how is the way of life
we have evolved in the West to regain its fervour without
giving up its lucidity? How is it to break out of the impasse
of possession which it takes to be the be all and the end
all? The "broken world" we have inherited must some-

102 *Terre des Hommes,* p. 267.
103 *Pilote de Guerre,* p. 289.
104 *Terre des Hommes,* p. 263.
105 *Citadelle,* p. 713. Compare with Merleau-Ponty: ". . . We need to know
what we are looking for, otherwise we should not be looking for it. . . ." (*La
Phénoménologie de la Perception,* NRF, 1945, p. 36.)

how be put back together again, but without making use of "eternal principles" to cement the fragments. The same images recur incessantly in *Citadelle,* that of the "Cathedral," the "Empire," the "Domain," which are not conglomerations of things or people, but entities. There exists, in addition to the sum of the parts, something which Saint-Exupéry calls "the divine knot" or "the meaning of things," the intangible something which transfigures quite ordinary words by virtue of their occurring together in the same verse just as it transfigures the stones which make up the cathedral. Saint-Exupéry is far from being the first to deplore the pulverization of our society into individuals who, lost to the ancient "meaning of things" and unable to find a substitute for it within themselves,[106] have been desperately manufacturing systems and lay religions ever since, as certain Italian city states of the Renaissance manufactured constitutions in an attempt to bring back the civic glories of the mediaeval republics. The diagnosis is easier than the remedy. Many are disappointed by the conclusion of *Pilote de Guerre.* In *Citadelle,* the chieftain talks repeatedly of his father's place where "every step had a meaning," but there appears to be no hint as to how this happy state of affairs is to be brought back to life.

The work of Saint-Exupéry is not an argument. It is an example. It is made up of events which are recounted to inspire, and not to persuade. However, our intellectual training is such that we are prepared to give our allegiance only to the logically coherent; but since existence is never logically coherent, our allegiance can never honestly be given without reserve—and at the same time we protect ourselves from the evidence of our responsibility. If we may cite Saint-Exupéry again: ". . . There is no explana-

---

106 The "Swine" is one who, to protect his own importance, is obliged to deny that the meaning has gone out of things. He does this by the exercise of "bad faith." He is compelled to declare that he "believes" in certain principles which, however, are but projections of self-interest. On the other hand, the genuinely religious person, for example, draws his importance from God, a principle exterior to himself. With the "Swine" the process is just the reverse, the principle existing for the sake of the Self, whether the principle involved is a religious one, racial "superiority," class, etc.

tion and the world has *no* meaning."[107] It is therefore vain
to seek a demonstration in *Citadelle*[108] whose purpose is
simply to confront us with a certain number of evidences
which we have grown accustomed to think of as "problems." One of these evidences is the necessity of act as
opposed to the superfluousness of system—and it is act
which creates the "Empire," it is act which provides the
"meaning of things." We are persuaded that action is inspired, then directed and disciplined by faith in a principle.
In reality it is the act which creates the principle. Thomas
Aquinas wrote at the end not at the beginning of the Age
of Faith. Louis XVI was not executed by the Revolution;
it was his execution along with a number of other decisive
acts which made the Revolution. Marxism came into being
not with *Das Kapital* but with the success of the Russian
Revolution, which, according to dogma, should never have
succeeded, given the weakness of the industrial proletariat.
Just as a man is the sum of his acts, an idea is the sum of
the sacrifices made for it; our mistake is to suppose that
the dogma, which is all that remains after the passage of
the intellectual, was the "cause" of the sacrifices.

Life will take on new meaning when we act to give it
one, but not before. ". . . At every one of our acts,"
writes Sartre, "the world shows us a new face,"[109] and it is
in these perpetually renewed aspects of the universe that
man must find his *raison d'être,* not in the theoretical common denominator which the intellectual has made it his
mission to discern. In *Terre des Hommes,* Saint-Exupéry
tells of the Arab chieftain who caused a number of French
lieutenants, his allies, to be murdered; for it was only with
peace that the Sahara had become really a desert, and
from this irreparable act ". . . a world will be born . . ."[110]
—just as a new world had come into being for Tchen. In
language which recalls that of Malraux's anarchist whose

107 *Citadelle,* p. 635.
108 ". . . We all know how deceptive reasoned arguments are. Those I was
watching . . . were not in the least drawn to conviction by the most com-
pelling proofs." (*Citadelle,* p. 504.)
109 *Situations II,* p. 90.
110 *Terre des Hommes,* p. 208.

words Vincent Berger found so apt, Saint-Exupéry tells of "This new appearance of the world after a difficult stage—these trees, these flowers. . . ."[111] This world, one view of which is no "truer" than any other, is to the world of science what expression is to the features of the face. In looking at a person's face, it is the expression, however transient or impalpable, of which we are *immediately* aware; it is, so to speak, the existentialist aspect of the face, which any attempt to analyse causes to disappear. "Intellectuals," writes Saint-Exupéry, "take the face apart, in order to explain it by its pieces, but they no longer see the smile."[112] The world has its "expressions" which, like those of the face, require no explanation, they simply are. They are the world's only "meaning"—the recompense of act, never of reason.

Protestantism, in those countries where it established itself, slowly destroyed religion as a public institution and substituted for it a more personal relationship between the individual and God. The result, depending upon the individual, was either a much more intense religious life, or total indifference. Gide knew both the religious exaltation and the unbelief, and it might be said that the object of his ethic was to reconcile one with the other, to unite unbelief with fervour. We called the gratuitous act a disinterested act; we could have used the word abnegation. The gratuitous act of Philoctetes is simply the abnegation of Alissa without God, the protestant dialogue with God having become one between man and himself. The heroism God no longer exacts we must learn to exact of ourselves. Gide's thinking about the Self was somewhat inconsistent, but Malraux and Saint-Exupéry by firmly suppressing it made possible a much more direct and sound approach to gratuity. If being is to be identical with action, then what is done can never have as its purpose to abolish the need for action. All action is gratuitous in the sense that it accom-

111 *Ibid.*, p. 171.
112 *Pilote de Guerre*, p. 301.

plishes nothing definitively. That this should be so is at once the tragedy and opportunity of our time; tragedy because, with a yearning for light nourished through the centuries, we have come to understand that none exists; opportunity if we grant not only that there are no unequivocal answers, but that there must not be any—in which case man is free at last to conduct his affairs in his own interests.

Apart from such considerations, the figure of Rivière in *Vol de Nuit* is incomprehensible. The importance of the work with which he is charged seems grotesquely out of proportion with the ferocious earnestness with which he accomplishes it. No officer responsible for the defence of a sector which, if lost, would open his country to the invader is more merciless with his men than is Rivière with his pilots and mechanics whose business it was to guarantee the delivery of what Saint-Exupéry contemptuously calls some "merchant's letter."[113] Rivière knew that it was "illogical" in the face of the rapidly increasing practicability of air travel to insist upon establishing air routes across the Andes and the South Atlantic, and to operate them at night as well as in the day-time, with planes that in a few years would seem ludicrously primitive. But Rivière also knew that the object of his labours was less the founding of an airmail service, than it was the creation of men. It was Mermoz who first found a passage through the Andes in the days when the maximum altitude of planes was less than that of the mountains, but his victory was not the discovery of the passage, it was ". . . the man who was born in him when he crossed the Andes."[114] Rivière cannot be sure that his work is of any value, in any case it is certainly not the postal network that justifies the sacrifice of his pilots: "Perhaps the goal justifies nothing," but, he adds, ". . . action delivers from death."[115] In *Citadelle*, Saint-Exupéry repeats that "one never arrives any-

[113] *Terre des Hommes*, p. 266.
[114] *Terre des Hommes*, p. 226.
[115] *Vol de Nuit*, p. 143.

where,"[116] and that consequently "I will trace out my furrow without previous understanding. I will simply go on. . . ."[117] This is precisely what Rivière was doing. We cannot foretell the future, and there is no immovable goal toward which we can direct ourselves; Rivière's one concern, therefore, is to prevent "acts and things from losing their meaning," for otherwise: "The emptiness around us shows itself. . . ."[118]

For Saint-Exupéry, as for Gide, the gratuitous act is the means by which man "surpasses" himself, but with Saint-Exupéry it is in the direction of other men. "The greatness . . . of my civilization," he writes, "is that in it a hundred miners feel bound to risk their lives in order to save a single buried miner. They save Man."[119] In Malraux, Saint-Exupéry and Sartre, the Gidean gratuitous act loses its ascetic purity and becomes a powerful means of practical accomplishment. Thus Rivière is able to think to himself: "I am surprised, sometimes, by my power;"[120] and there is in all of Rivière's meditations this apparent contradiction between the futility of human effort, and its omnipotence.[121] It is an omnipotence, however, which can only be exercised in the immediate ". . . toward what ought I to bend my efforts? Because goals have no significance. And my answer to you would be . . . that to prepare the future is merely to found the present."[122] But the present is existence, which is ambiguous and which resists. It is easier to withdraw into the peaceful isolation of the *clerc*, and to devote oneself to "founding" the future, accusing everything else of being vain and transitory; to which Saint-Exupéry replies: "As for those who are ready to reproach the chosen face for being gratuitous . . . my

116 For example, p. 571.
117 *Citadelle*, p. 817. Compare with Gide's: "As for me, I don't know where I'm going; but I am advancing." (*Journal*, 26 October 1924.)
118 *Vol de Nuit*, p. 142.
119 *Pilote de Guerre*, p. 392.
120 *Vol de Nuit*, p. 122.
121 "What lives upsets everything to live, and creates its own laws so that it may live. It is irresistible." (*Ibid.*, p. 123.)
122 *Citadelle*, p. 576. See also p. 492: ". . . If I make war to obtain peace, I establish war. Peace is not a state that one attains through war."

answer will be that any justification is more than we can expect."[123]

The "dispossession" that Gide preached, but which he practised imperfectly, Saint-Exupéry carried to its last extreme in the equanimity with which he continually risked his life. In *Terre des Hommes,* he concludes the account of his desert ordeal by speaking of a "plenitude" and of a "deliverance" which he experienced at the point of death. ". . . I thought I had plumbed the depths of despair, but, once I had accepted renunciation, I found peace."[124] There is no better example, if one is needed, of the fact that an existentialist ethic does not terminate in despair—it begins there. The problem is: "How can we help this kind of deliverance to grow in ourselves?"[125] How are we to deliver ourselves from our centuries of dead knowledge, our antiquated wisdom, our petty wealth? None of all that is of great use any more, for our culture has reached that point of disillusionment which, so far as we know, no preceding civilization went beyond.

We have the choice of considering our lucidity dangerous and of binding ourselves to a mast to ride out the difficult times, or we can use it as a starting point, as have the three authors we have just studied, for further ventures. Sartre has helped by providing a new metaphysics.

[123] *Ibid.,* p. 740.
[124] *Terre des Hommes*, p. 257.
[125] *Ibid.*

PART THREE

Chapter 1

Sartre

Etre, c'est ne pas être une chose.
CLAUDEL

L'ETRE ET LE NÉANT has acquired the reputation of being a very difficult book, and more often than not it is implied that its difficulty is due less to the novelty of many of the ideas than to their obscurity. This is the more curious inasmuch as informed philosophical opinion almost invariably admires the lucidity and coherence with which Sartre develops his thought. Campbell talks of the "solid timbering" of *L'Etre et le Néant,* and calls it "terribly, dangerously coherent";[1] Jeanson goes so far as to describe it as "an easy work";[2] for Varet, it is "a great and beautiful creation."[3] If we wish to suspect these men of being partisans of the new order in philosophy, we may turn to *Le Choix de Jean Paul Sartre* by Father Troisfontaines, where we will read that *L'Etre et le Néant* is "on the whole compact and simple."[4] Even though *L'Etre et le Néant* proves to be less "easy" for most laymen than for Jeanson, it is true that it is easy in the sense that with patience and determination we can come to learn in each instance precisely what Sartre means. The only difficult philosophy is one that is obscure; but that of Sartre is so little exposed to this accusation that some philosophers, on the grounds that existence is never clear, consider Sartre too faithful to the great Cartesian tradition of clarity in French thought.

When Husserl suggested that Truth might not be a hidden

---

1 Robert Campbell, *J. P. Sartre ou une Littérature Philosophique,* Pierre Ardent, 1947, p. 315.
2 Francis Jeanson, *Le Problème Moral et la Pensée de Sartre,* Myrte, 1947, p. 167.
3 Gilbert Varet, *L'Ontologie de Sartre,* Presses Universitaires, 1948, p. 4.
4 Aubier, 1945, p. 10.

249

absolute, but the very stuff with which we think and perceive, elusive not because of its distance from us but because it is so close that we habitually look beyond, he cleared the way for a philosophy which, assuming truth to be acquired, would be free to concentrate its whole attention upon its *utilization;* a philosophy which would be no longer an investigation, but an act; no longer a science, but an ethic. Such is the philosophy of Sartre. *L'Etre et le Néant* bears the subtitle: *Essai d'ontologie phénoménologique.* It is an "ontology," that is to say, it is concerned with determining the precise nature of what Sartre terms "human reality."[5] But, as we shall see, the essence of that "reality" is to be without essence—man's only Being is one which he acquires for himself. Consequently, as Sarte remarks, ". . . it goes without saying that ontology can in no way be separated from ethics. . . ."[6] Sartre's entire philosophy is devoted to the problems of human conduct, and it is perhaps this fact which best accounts for the widespread opposition, from whatever quarter it issued, which greeted the appearance of *L'Etre et le Néant.* Sartre is usually "not clear" for three groups of people: the "absolutists" of left and right, who had grown used to being alone in disputing the soul of the general public, and the philosophers of the old school, who were frequently unaware that Sartre was not primarily interested in "making a contribution to knowledge."[7]

[5] Scientific procedure is just the reverse. It is interested exclusively in facts. However, facts do not organize themselves, they simply accumulate; and if they are ever to receive a *significance*, they must be considered in their relation to "human reality." See *Esquisse d'une Théorie des Emotions*.)

[6] "Lettre-Préface" to Jeanson's *Le Problème Moral et la Pensée de Sartre*. If Jeanson's is the only book on *L'Etre et le Néant* in which Sartre, as he says in his "Lettre-Préface," has been able to recognize his philosophy, it is partly because Jeanson, like Sartre, is convinced that ethics is ". . . the real and unique philosophical question." (p. 34.)

[7] A. J. Ayer well represents the attitude of the orthodox philosopher toward Sartre. In his articles on *"L'Etre et le Néant"* which appeared in *Horizon* (July and August 1945), he described that book as being: ". . . always difficult and often obscure." We understand why if we consider that elsewhere Ayer has written of philosophy's "contribution toward the growth of human knowledge" (*Language, Truth, and Logic*, Gollancz, London, 1949, p. 153), and of the possibility of the problems of philosophy being "definitively answered." (*Ibid.*, p. 133.) We are dealing, in other words, with a system which, though generally known as "empirical," is in reality theological. Existentialism is

At the same time, the phenomenologists accused Sartre of perverting the new discipline. *L'Etre et le Néant* is not only an "ontology," it is a phenomenological ontology; but many continental philosophers hold that the terms are contradictory. Whatever consciousness encounters exists, and inversely, what we have no consciousness of does not exist. Thus material things exist but, it is argued by the phenomenologists, "materiality"[8] or what Sartre calls in-itself (*en-soi*) does not. The purpose of the much criticized introduction to *L'Etre et le Néant* is to assert the independent existence of the in-itself in addition to its individual appearances. ". . . The being of what *appears* does not exist *only* in so far as it appears,"[9] but also in its own right. Consciousness is born in contact with a Being other than itself, and this is what Sartre calls the "ontological proof." The affirmation of the existence of Being, which Varet calls "sensational"[10] and which the layman will find less sensational, does not appear for the first time in *L'Etre et le Néant*. It is the subject of *La Nausée*, where the transcendent reality of Being is not demonstrated philosophically but directly experienced. It is through "nausea" that Antoine Roquentin has existence revealed to him; not the clearly-defined "humanized" existence of this or that thing, but existence in itself, the "stuff" out of which our craving for order has made up the familiar objects that surround us and to which they are capable of reverting.[11] "A menace hovers over the city," Roquentin cries to a passer-by. What if we should cease to be able to hold existence at bay, as has already several times happened to Roquentin? What if it should begin to "flow" like lava and fill up the spaces with

---

based upon the *evidence* of the *cogito*; empiricism upon *faith* in the existence of a supreme order. Empiricism maintains its faith in progress towards "definitive answers" by avoiding encounters with existence; according to Ayer: "The philosopher must be content to record the facts of scientific procedure." (*Ibid.*, p. 98.)

8 As we shall see in a moment, this term is not quite accurate.

9 *L'Etre et le Néant*, NRF, 1949, p. 29.

10 Gilbert Varet, *L'Ontologie de Sartre*, p. 172.

11 ". . . The light crust of the meanings we attribute to things sometimes melts, revealing the raw material of reality which has no meaning." (Sartre, *Saint Genêt*, NRF, 1952, p. 239.)

which our logic marks off one thing from another? Being
is not a vast series of hard-contoured essences, dependent
one upon the other, supremely reasonable; nor the substance in which qualities inhere, nor the equivalent of what
appears, but the viscid mass of everything that *is*, "nau-
seous" in its amorphous gratuity. Sartre has been invited to
retract his rash ontological proof so that much that is precious in the remainder of *L'Etre et le Néant* might be
saved,[12] but we suspect that he has not particularly troubled
himself over the purely technical debate that this question
has aroused—moral issues alone have importance for him.
This does not mean that Sartre has had to sacrifice philosophical rigour to achieve practical effectiveness; on the
contrary, his greatness as a thinker lies precisely in the
consummate skill with which he demonstrates the dependence of one upon the other. A further examination of *La
Nausée* will serve as an example of this.

Although there is no objectivity in the absolute, each historical context brings with it its own objectivity, its own
particular truth, with the aid of which we are able to direct
our acts.[13] These truths, however, being transitory, being *in*
time and not *above* it, are not more clear to the logician
than to the labourer. Since we are all necessarily of a given
epoch as much as of a given race or family, its truths and
falsehoods are unmistakably known to us, they are part of
us. We may, however, prefer to ignore them. In other
words, a man's thought is inseparable from his moral
choice. Our personal philosophies serve not to discover the
truth, which is perfectly evident,[14] but to justify the moral

12 See, for example, Jean Wahl's articles in *Deucalion*, Nos. 1 and 2, 1946–7,
p. 239.
13 Between existentialism and Anglo-Saxon philosophy there is no common
ground because the former accepts only subjective and the latter only objective criteria. But when the traditionalist declares himself to be "not interested"
in a school of thought which bases its reasoning upon subjectivity, he forgets
that the existentialist has not suppressed objectivity, he has changed its nature.
An objective truth is not an eternal but a temporary one, and it is one that
is evident (or subjectively known) to all of us.
14 See particularly Sartre's *Saint Genêt*, where we frequently find such statements as the following: ". . . It [the Good] is evidence itself" (p. 153), and
"The impossibility of Evil finds an exact counterpart, on the level of knowledge, in the impossibility of consciously deceiving oneself." (p. 308.)

attitude we have taken toward it. (Hence the importance for Sartre of "bad faith," which in his philosophy replaces "faulty reasoning," "moral turpitude," etc. We do not "fall into error," we choose it.) Roquentin's experience of the fundamental meaninglessness, or gratuity, or absurdity, or whatever term one prefers, of all that exists, is one that lies in wait for all of us;[15] although, of course, it need not take the form which Sartre gives it in *La Nausée*. And because it is so constant a menace, we need to protect ourselves against it. This is the purpose of the work of art that Roquentin envisages at the end of *La Nausée*, for the work of art is characterized by an interior necessity, so much so that it is precisely the degree of its necessity which seems to determine that of its perfection. Art, however, which makes use of matter, can only fulfil itself through the annihilation of matter; we either look at the canvas and paint of a picture or we look at the image itself, in which case we move into the imaginary; we cannot do both at the same time. Art, to the extent to which it seeks to be a law unto itself, is consequently a form of evasion, and Roquentin will find it no more effective a barrier against the absurd than was his research into the career of Monsieur de Rollebon. But there is worse than evasion, there is the possibility of denying altogether the reality and significance of an experience such as that of Roquentin's, there is the possibility of exercising bad faith (and we shall see shortly why bad faith is not always a cynical recourse, but a trap into which most of us readily fall at one time or another) by talking of eternal truths, of Right and Wrong in the absolute, etc. This is the attitude adopted by the people to whom Sartre refers as "Swine," those who will cling to order, any order, to avoid ". . . the great metaphysical fear that contingency and freedom inspire."[16] *La Nausée* is already literature that is

---

15 ". . . In apprehending ourselves by ourselves, we appear to ourselves with the distinguishing marks of a fact that cannot be justified." (*L'Etre et le Néant*, p. 122.)

16 Sartre, *Saint Genêt*, p. 113. William Faulkner has written of these people in the following terms: ". . . it is . . . what we call the prime virtues—thrift, industry, independence—that breeds all the vices—fanaticism, smugness, meddling, fear, and worst of all respectability." (*The Wild Palms*, Chatto and

engagée. It is in part a sort of analysis of a mentality capable of turning away from the "blinding light"[17] which indicates the good of a given political situation in order to speak of "Rights" to which all the rest must be sacrificed. One of the purposes of Sartre's "sensational" affirmation of Being is now clear. As long as it is believed that there is a natural and necessary order and hierarchy in the external world, it will appear that these qualities are essential as well to the smooth conduct of human affairs. And they no doubt are. But the natural laws or the "teleology" of the exterior world are the free constructions of human intelligence, they are neither necessary nor eternal, and it is therefore illegitimate to argue that man should conform to certain determinisms of the world he inhabits, since these determinisms do not exist; or rather, are of his own making. Here again, existentialism brings to completion the revolution begun and then abandoned by rationalism. The relativity of the moral law so much talked about on and off during the eighteenth and nineteenth centuries could never be taken seriously as long as the laws that governed the material world were considered to be absolute;[18] however, if what exists is formless and arbitrary, or *de trop,* as Sartre writes in *La Nausée,* it follows that we are ourselves superfluous. Roquentin's encounter with existence is necessarily an encounter with his own nothingness—there is no more a "moral law within" than a natural law without.

Thus the existentialism of Sartre, perhaps more than any previous philosophy, is simultaneously an account of the nature of the world we live in and an ethic. Such a develop-

17 *Saint Genêt*, p. 149.

18 Communism is the supreme example of "scientific" law having reimposed a belief in moral law. On the other hand, Merleau-Ponty outraged French opinion by pointing out (in *Humanisme et Terreur*) that Boukharine was really the traitor he was tried for being; in other words, that political philosophies are relative and that of the West is not the only conceivable one. (What really made the trials objectionable, Merleau-Ponty argues, was that everyone pretended not to know that most of the accused had sincerely worked for what they thought to be the good of the revolution.)

ment was only possible with the advent of a genuine atheism. Thinkers who believed in gods—the God-Essence of classical philosophy, the God-Man of religious philosophy and the God-Objectivity of scientific thought—had a double task, that of defining its deity and that of recommending the conduct best calculated to propitiate it. But in the case of Sartre, the world is what man makes of it, ontology and morality are one.

Writers like those we have considered who deny all efficacy to contemplation and whose art consequently aims at something beyond itself, create, in many circles, an intolerable malaise. The distinct lack of sympathy with which the orthodox philosopher encounters the work of Sartre is paralleled by the discomfort of the aesthete (not to mention that of the Absolutist), who honestly interprets the writings of Gide, Malraux and Saint-Exupéry. By seeking to suppress the Self and in denying the existence of an Order with which the Self might commune, our authors place themselves in the position of a priest who would deny the effectiveness of prayer—they fall outside the community. They are revolutionaries in the true sense of the word; any communication between them and the society they have renounced is based upon indifference or upon a misunderstanding.

The genuine revolutionary brings into question not the distribution of wealth, or the privilege of class, but the validity of the ideology to which the group in power owes its hold upon the minds of men. His criticism is philosophical rather than political. The *Philosophes* attacked social injustice and intolerance only as manifestations of the deeper ill that was the decay of feudalism. A régime is sound to the extent to which men are prepared to give intellectual or emotional assent to the more or less clearly defined metaphysical assumptions from which the political are derived. Now, far from forming an autonomous and rival cultural system, leftist political philosophy has from its inception actually been performing a function within the framework of capitalist democracy. It came to fill a place prepared for it by rationalist political thought which declares that every national group has a right to governmental representation and to legal protection from possible intolerance on the part of other groups. To be sure, much has changed since 1914, by which time socialism had become a respectable and perfectly innocuous institution. The success of the Russian Revolution brought into existence everywhere political parties sincerely interested in the overthrow of democratic government. What we must remember, however, is that the communist revolution does not effect the replacement of one culture by another, rather it is to be regarded as an attempt to complete the revolution of 1789 rendered abortive by the concentration of wealth in the hands of the bourgeoisie. It is in vain that occidental communist parties exalt the culture of the "people" to the detriment of that of the middle classes. Whatever may be the case in Russia, in the West, the people's culture based upon the material independence of rural areas has ceased to exist and it will eventually disappear in Russia also before the progress of industrialization. To express this conception differently, it might be said that communism represents the "success" of the pluralistic ideal of government and not the triumph of one culture over another alien to it. Consequently, all that is left for the proletariat to aspire to is the universalization, not of its way of life, but of that of the bourgeoisie. One immediately senses that the communist, despite his efforts, lives more or less within the culture he seeks to overthrow, when one considers that the possibility of intellectual accord between him and the bourgeois still exists, and that very often their disagreement is the result of bad faith on one side or the other and not of a misunderstanding. Lenin or Aragon speak the language of the bourgeois; in their time, Stendhal and Baudelaire did not; today, the cubists and the surrealists do not. The bourgeois is perfectly able, though he may deny it, to sympathize with the demands of the proletariat, because they were, or are, his own; he is quite unable to sympathize with, or perhaps even to understand, Breton's attitude toward insanity.[19] He may intelligently discuss an editorial in the *Daily Worker,* but not *Corydon,* not *La Nausée;* and if these two books are "revolting" or "difficult" reading, it is precisely because they attempt to dissipate the intellectual atmosphere of classical rationalism which is that of the bourgeoisie. François Mauriac has asserted that the writings of Sartre make him want to vomit. There is little doubt, on the other hand, but what his reactions to the books of Maurice Thorez remain intellectual rather than physiological. The toleration which the bourgeois has written into his creed extends to other political systems, not to other conceptions of the nature of the universe and of man.[20]

What is the most nearly succinct expression we can give to the metaphysics of bourgeois rationalism in opposition to which there has come into being a tradition of thought that we have traced from Stendhal and Baudelaire to the present and in which we see the only genuinely revolutionary movement since the eighteenth century?

The philosopher's initial premise is that part of his thought which he is least eager to discuss; and indeed the modern rationalist often appears to have forgotten (perhaps because in this his thought does not differ from that of all of human history) that he has assumed the existence of an Order, conceived as being exterior to man (materialism) or within him (idealism). The rationalist Order differs from the theological in that it is "discoverable" in all essential details. It is utilizable for the purpose of human progress. In brief, it can be possessed. The price, which at one time could be considered modest indeed, that the rationalist pays for this acquisition is the suppression of the subjective, as being the source of the irrational.[21] The price, however, is increasingly coming to be found too great, and what we have been discussing throughout these pages is, in a sense,

19 We exclude, of course, the bourgeois who is a professional intellectual.
20 The communist prefers not to recognize that there is a profound contradiction between his alleged atheism and his faith in an ordered universe. Thorez is no more an atheist than is Mauriac.
21 The idealist is not a "subjectivist"; for although he reduces matter to mind, the mind remains, as we have seen, a thing, and one that is common to all men.

the affirmation of the rights of subjectivity. Both bourgeois and communist societies, since they share the same philosophical parentage, refuse to tolerate the subjective. The great trials of Moscow were not more unfair or cruel than the treatment suffered in the West by the insane and by those given to practising the various sexual "aberrations." The Moloch of historical law may be more spectacular, but it is no more terrible than that of economic, psychological or religious law.

Laws are plagued by their exceptions, but while the exceptions to the laws governing matter may eventually be absorbed into a more comprehensive law, the exceptions to social "laws" are men themselves, who may, by an *exigency of sincerity,* deny the existence of law since they find no evidence of it within themselves. Subjectivity rather than objectivity becomes the source of truth. When Stendhal wrote: "Above all, I want to be true,"[22] he associated himself with a current of French thought which has culminated in Sartre's "evidence of the cogito." The need for sincerity, which places a greater strain upon our courage than upon our intelligence,[23] and which is so characteristic of Gide, Malraux and Saint-Exupéry, leads not to ever increasing self knowledge, but to the conclusion that the search is in vain. Stendhal decided that all he could know of himself was what he liked and what he disliked. The next step was to accept the fruitlessness of introspection, not as an indication of personal incompetence in that exercise but as an evidence, incontrovertible in its immediacy. There is nothing more characteristic of Stendhal than his irreverence—in a nation of *frondeurs,* he is one of the greatest; and this because he knows that his own indetermination is necessarily shared by the captains and the kings. However, it was not only the reactionary bore who annoyed Stendhal. The jargon of the

[22] *Souvenirs d'Egotisme,* Le Divan, 1950, p. 57.
[23] Hence the attention that cowardice receives in the work of Sartre, who would argue that the government of the Nazis, for example, was the result not of their ignorance or stupidity, but of their "metaphysical cowardice"; it being impossible for them to accept the nothingness within that absolute sincerity reveals.

liberals who aimed at replacing one objectivity by another was as suspect to him as were the attitudes of the distinguished. Stendhal's position in respect to the politics of his time was precisely that which Malraux was to adopt in his. Julien Sorel is the nineteenth century's Garine.[24]

As time went on, it was discovered, as we have seen, that one of the certitudes of subjectivity is the absurd. There is what we might call the "aesthetic" absurd, or the chaotic world of sensation which had been that of Stendhal (hence his "égoisme"), of Valéry and in part of Gide (*Les Nourritures*), the political and social absurd, a barrier to thought, but to act—a promise, and the "physical" absurd of *La Nausée,* the cubists, Valéry, etc. The "immediate" (or the "things-in-themselves" which make up the world as revealed by subjectivity) for Julien Sorel was his own interest; for Malraux and Saint-Exupéry, living in a different historical context, it was necessarily the interest of man. In the words of Saint-Exupéry: "We do not discover the truth, we create it."[25] In the ordered world of the rationalist, Truth awaits discovery; in the absurd world of today, it awaits creation.

Before turning back to Sartre, here is a schema of the situation as he will find it.

There are two schools of rationalist thought: first, that which assumes Order to be exterior to man. Philosophically, this is known as materialism, and politically, it is associated with bourgeois democracy, out of which has grown a number of pseudo revolutionary movements, among which is communism. This Order, existentialism refuses, for it considers matter to be totally inorganized or absurd. The second school considers Order to be interior to man. Philosophically, this is known as idealism, and existentialism opposes to it the suppression of the Self. One takes cog-

24 One is tempted also to contrast Balzac and Stendhal in somewhat the way in which we have contrasted Proust and Gide. The characters of Balzac may be described as "interior" and those of Stendhal as "exterior," in so far as the characters of Balzac do because of what they are, while those of Stendhal are because of what they do.
25 *Carnets,* NRF, 1953, p. 135.

nizance of the Order of rationalism by assuming an objective point of view, existentialist thought is based upon the evidence of subjectivity. To use the word "existentialist" here, instead of "Gide, Malraux and Saint-Exupéry" is clearly to beg the question. It therefore remains for us to show how these three conceptions—the absurd, the suppression of the Self, and the evidence of subjectivity— which we have already disengaged from the tangle of contemporary thought and art have been utilized by Sartre, not as details of his philosophy, but as the very basis upon which *L'Etre et le Néant* has been made to rest.

The "world picture" we have been building up is, for the moment, in a state of anarchy. It requires the intervention of a philosopher who will answer such questions as: How literally are we to take the statement that the world is absurd? If there is no Self, what constitutes the unquestionable unity of character? How does thought take place? If man is no more than what he does, are we not driven to the apparently absurd conclusion that besides matter there is nothing? But how could this be, since we have spoken of the "affirmation of the rights of subjectivity, etc.?"

We have already seen how Sartre, hypothesizing the absurd, goes on to point out that if there is no Order in the exterior world, philosophy is not a discovery, but a choice; in other words an ethic. He thus joins his efforts to those of Gide, Malraux and Saint-Exupéry in the revolutionary attempt to discredit the concept of Order which underlies modern thought in its entirety and which renders an ethic of *conduct* superfluous; for if Order already exists, then it is attained by *thought,* and conduct becomes a simple matter of conforming to regulations. Let us return then, for a moment, to Sartre's affirmation of being. It will be best to use Sartre's term in-itself because such words as "being," "materiality," etc. are insufficiently comprehensive, the in-itself being *everything that exists,* not only material things, but everything of which there is consciousness—a pain, a dream, a memory, as well as the objects that fill the "exte-

rior" world.[26] All that can be said of the in-itself, as Sartre
repeats again and again throughout *L'Etre et le Néant,* is
that it is, and this is the way in which he expresses the idea
of the Absurd. The in-itself is absurd (or contingent, to use
Sartre's language) because all that can be said of it is that
it exists; and thus we arrive at a definition of one of the
concepts that has occupied us throughout this study. A
philosophical statement that would originally have appeared
nonsensical can now be appreciated as a perfectly natural
development. However, if all that can be said about the in-
itself is that it is, we can leave it at once in order to see what
consequences follow from our premise.

Since everything that exists is in-itself, there is no
"room" in the universe, which must be imagined as "solid"
and "full" like the inside of a stone, for the existence of
anything else. Yet the very fact that we are able to speak
of the in-itself indicates that there has to be something else,
for the recognition of a given object as such is only conceivable in the case where what is not that object also exists.
For example, if everything that exists were white in colour,
we could not know it unless the colour black also existed. To
put this in another way, imagine a chequer-board, every
space of which is occupied. No movement is possible. This
is the in-itself. If, however, we remove one of the pieces,
that is, if we create a "hollow," or a "void" somewhere in
the fullness of the board, all the pieces become mobile.
Monism, of whatever nature, is philosophically untenable,
because if everything were one (as the in-itself is one),
there could be no consciousness of it. In precisely the way
that Good cannot exist without Evil, materiality (if we may
again make use of this inaccurate term) cannot exist without immateriality—the in-itself could not exist without
nothingness, and the Sartrean universe is, in one sense, a
great duality—*L'Etre et le Néant.* We say "in one sense,"
because although by far the greater part of *L'Etre et le
Néant* is devoted to a description of nothingness (*le Néant*),

---

[26] Here it will be recalled that according to intentionality, the mind can
"intend" nothing that is not exterior to it.

nothingness does not exist, and therefore Sartre's philosophy is in another sense monism. It is this impossibility of satisfactorily classifying the thought of Sartre which has enabled the marxists to label it "idealist," and the Catholic philosophers "materialist." We might also remark in passing that the "return to things-in-themselves" of which we have had so much to say can now be carried no further, since apart from things-in-themselves, there is nothing.

The nature of our reasoning has, thus far, in no way differed from that of orthodox philosophy; indeed, the mere fact that we have reached our conclusions by a process of reasoning rather than by simple observation and description indicates that we have departed for a moment from the method which has been that of all our authors; philosophically it is called intentionality, and elsewhere we have variously named it the "return to things," "immediacy," "evidence of the subjective," etc. Needless to say, that method is also the one utilized by Sartre and we may now turn to consider the way in which he makes use of it to establish the existence of nothingness as an evidence in every subjectivity; for the essential of the "Copernican Revolution" that is phenomenology is the belief that, as we have seen, truth is not the object but the condition of thought. It will be noticed that we have used the apparently antithetical expressions "return to things" and "evidence of subjectivity" together, as though their meaning were much the same, and indeed it is. We have now reached the point where it will be possible for us to explain how nothingness may be considered to exist; how we can think of there being no distance between man and things, and at the same time speak of subjectivity. Man, we remarked in a previous chapter, is both everything and nothing; and the problem of understanding *L'Etre et le Néant* is that of understanding how such an assertion can be literally and philosophically true.

To illustrate briefly the way in which a subjective evidence may be utilized philosophically, let us try again, making use of intentionality, this time, to understand why we must accept the real existence of nothingness.

We have seen that consciousness is always consciousness of something. It is equally important to note that that of which there is no consciousness does not exist. This identity of appearance and existence is the bed-rock of Sartre's existentialism. The final appeal is always to consciousness, and not to logic. The empiricists, for example, talk about "sense data," about the "sensation" of green; but all that we are aware of is "green," there is no sensation, nothing that "mediates" between us and the green object. Philosophers have deduced something, the existence of which the *cogito* refuses to confirm. ". . . Sensation," consequently, ". . . is a fantasy of the psychologists. . . ."[27] We shall, of course, have much to accept from consciousness that logic will not absorb; much that is not deduced, but which simply is. Sartre speaks of those facts which ". . . can neither be deduced nor proved, but which simply 'let themselves be seen'. . ."[28] Bearing this in mind, we discover that consciousness at the very beginning presents us with an absolute contradiction; namely, that consciousness, or, to use Sartre's term, the for-itself, both exists and does not exist. Consciousness is always consciousness of something. A consciousness that would not be consciousness of anything is inconceivable. Furthermore, consciousness is always consciousness not only of the object it "intends," but also of itself as consciousness of the object in question. But the for-itself is never conscious of itself apart from the in-itself; in attempting to seize itself it inevitably falls back upon the object of which there is consciousness. There is consequently nothing for it to

27 *L'Etre et le Néant*, p. 378.
28 *Ibid.*, p. 594. Compare with G. E. Moore's article "A Defence of Common Sense" (in *Contemporary British Philosophy*, Vol. II, Allen and Unwin, London, 1925), where we read: "I have, I think, no better argument than simply this—namely, that all the propositions in (1) are, in fact, true." Or again: "In answer to this question, I think I have nothing better to say than it seems to me that I *do* know them, with certainty." Intentionality provides a sound basis for such assertions.

264 / Literature Considered as Philosophy

seize; since, as we have just seen, it is pointless to talk about anything of which there can be no consciousness. We are therefore tempted to identify the for-itself with the "void" we made in the chequer-board.

The for-itself, however, although a nothingness, is not what Sartre calls an "absolute nothingness,"[29] it is a nothingness of a very particular kind; and the best introduction to a study of it is Sartre's *L'Imaginaire*.

The purpose of *L'Imaginaire* is to fix the precise nature of the mental image. Its first part is entitled "The Certain," the second, "The Probable." What is certain about the mental image is what each of us may learn about it by reflecting upon his own. ". . . What is given in reflexion is certain,"[30] while what the psychologists *deduce* from their "observations" of the mental images of others can only be probable. Reflexion will yield us the essence of the mental image, the basic information which will permit us to orient effectively our psychological research which would otherwise continue to be a compilation of facts impossible to organize and therefore of uncertain utility.

Three characteristics of the mental image which Sartre calls certain and which are important to us are first: the image is the entire consciousness, it is not "in" consciousness, it *is* consciousness. It should be remarked that the word image is not very satisfactory, because we are conscious of a given *object* and not of an *image*.[31] Second: the object of the image is given from no particular point of view. We know it exhaustively; we need not observe it for we can learn nothing from it. It cannot possibly "surprise" us. This image, unlike real objects, is only as rich as we make it. Its identity always corresponds precisely

[29] *L'Etre et le Néant*, p. 558.
[30] *L'Imaginaire*, NRF, 1948, p. 14.
[31] Except, of course, reflexively. We spoke of the certitude of the results yielded by reflexion; but there are two reflexions, "pure" and "impure." This is a point, however, which will not be fully elucidated until Sartre has completed his book on ethics. See *L'Etre et le Néant*, p. 201 and the footnote on p. 111.

to the intention, which it never precedes.[32] This is what Sartre calls the phenomenon of "quasi-observation." Third: the object of a mental image is posited as being not actually present; the image ". . . gives its object as not being";[33] or " . . . one can say that the image envelops a certain nothingness."[34] We only imagine what is not there; and yet since there is nothing in consciousness, it is necessarily the object itself which appears—but it is intended as "absent." The object of the mental image is, with equal certitude, both present and absent; or as Sartre puts it, " . . . I really see something, but what I see is nothing."[35] Alain was so struck by the absence of the mental image that he denied its existence. If we form an image of the Parthenon, however clearly we see it in our imagination we will be unable even to begin to count the columns. What we see before us is invisible; and Sartre can say of the object of an image that ". . . what is present is, in a way, its absence."[36]

We can appreciate now the precise nature and the full measure of what separates existentialism from previous

[32] It is important to note also that the intention does not precede the image. There is no more striking characteristic of mental imagery than its spontaneity. The mental image, nevertheless, continues to be "intended" in the sense that its object is "recognized." If someone suddenly holds before our face a photograph of a friend, it is the result of an "intention" that we recognize it as such; otherwise we perceive a piece of paper with dark patches upon it. In the same way: "The intention is what causes the image of Peter to be consciousness of Peter." (*L'Imaginaire*, p. 79.)

[33] *Ibid.*, p. 26.

[34] *Ibid.*, p. 25.

[35] *Ibid.*, p. 70. See also p. 98, where the following sentence appears entirely in italics: ". . . The essential characteristic of the mental image is a certain manner the object has of being absent in the very midst of its presence."

[36] *Ibid.*, p. 116. The reader will recall that we declared a memory to be *in-itself*, and he may wonder why the image of a past event should be considered any less a nothingness than that of, say, a person in the next room. In *L'Imaginaire*, Sartre writes that in the act of imagining we can posit the object of the image in four ways only: as inexistent, as absent, as existing elsewhere, or the act can remain "neutral," i.e. not posit the object as existing. When we recall a past event, none of these four possibilities applies, because the object is posited as existing presently although "in the past," or "given now in the past." (*L'Imaginaire*, p. 230.) When the object of an image is a living person, the person is posited as existing elsewhere, etc., but when the image is that of a person who has died, that image, or memory of him, is his only existence. The "intention" is realized as fully as it is possible for it to be. And so Faulkner can write: "The past is never dead. It's not even past."

philosophies. Within reasonable limits, philosophers have always been permitted to proceed as far as they wished, or were able, from their initial premise on the condition of never contradicting themselves; and here at the very root of the philosophy of Sartre stands a flagrant contra-diction.[37] But it is a contradiction which, since it appears to consciousness, exists; it is, as Sartre writes, though in a slightly different context, ". . . the subject of the most concrete of experiences."[38] We have to choose between a contradiction that exists, and a logical construction whose result does not; between existence and essence.

The mental image is the whole of consciousness, it is what Sartre will eventually come to call the for-itself, or nothingness. We have seen that the for-itself is not a nothingness in the literal sense of the word. But even so, its existence is of the most shadowy and tenuous kind; al-together improper in appearance to account for the vast-ness of what is to be laid to man's enterprise. And yet Sartre has been able with astonishing completeness to ac-count for human activity entirely in terms of the inter-relation of Being and Nothingness. *L'Etre et le Néant* is a philosophical demonstration made entirely without re-course to immanence. It has abolished the Self as a philo-sophical necessity. The source of the unity of experience is not the Ego, but the in-itself; it is the unity of the "at-titude" or "project" which the individual has adopted *vis-à-vis* the in-itself. In Sartre's article *La Transcendance de l'Ego* which is an ideal introduction to his work as a whole, we find: "In a sense it [consciousness] is *nothing* . . . but this nothing is *everything*,—since it is *conscious-ness of* all these objects."[39] But the question remains, how can the for-itself, this bizarre "tangible absence" we have just discussed, be consciousness of anything? Conscious-

---

[37] It is this contradiction, and another we shall come to in a moment, which probably causes most of the difficulty encountered by the layman who under-takes to read *L'Etre et le Néant.*
[38] *L'Etre et le Néant,* p. 23.
[39] p. 117, *Recherches Philosophiques,* Vol. VI, 1936–7.

ness not only of the fact that this is a house, but that it dates from the last century, that it is well or ill planned, etc. etc.? The entire complex apparatus of epistemology has to be abolished because no element of it is directly experienced. Within us we are conscious of nothing whatever, at least nothing in the nature of an identifiable thing, such as the association of ideas, the judgment, etc.; and since what exists is absurd, it is out of this inner void and its commerce with the in-itself that everything must be created. It will be helpful once again to begin with *L'Imaginaire.*

In *L'Imaginaire,* Sartre is intent upon examining the mental image itself and upon demonstrating the absolute incommensurability between the imaginary and the real; for classical philosophy had confounded the two in considering the image a kind of "internal perception," the judgment perceiving the image as the eye perceives an object. The study of the rôle the imaginary plays in perception was reserved for *L'Etre et le Néant;* however, toward the end of *L'Imaginaire,* there are several indications of the direction in which Sartre was to expand his ideas. Fixing the eyes and attention upon a specific object causes everything else in the field of vision to "recede," to become a kind of backdrop upon which the object of interest appears in relief. The world becomes what Sartre calls a "nihilated backdrop" *(fond néantisé)* for that which is the centre of attention.[40] All that which has been in this way "nihilated" can be said to be *neither truly absent nor truly present*—precisely the case of the mental image. The entire world with the exception of the object perceived has been nihilated, that is "affected with nothingness" so to speak, and *not* annihilated, *néanti* and *not anéanti.* We may, if we wish, imagine the object perceived as a white

40 The same phenomenon occurs even when the object of attention is a mental image, and this is one of the arguments that Sartre uses to prove the real existence of nothingness. If I am looking for a friend in a café, even though he is not there, the café appears as a backdrop or *fond néantisé* to the image I have of him, just as it would have done had my friend been physically present. (See *L'Etre et le Néant,* p. 44.)

spot, but one which can be recognized as such only after a "muff" of blackness has been placed around it. The massive and compact existence of the in-itself can only be made perceptible if isolated by a halo of nothingness. Furthermore, the more absolute the nothingness, the closer it approaches total absence, the greater becomes the "relief" of the object until we reach the point of its maximum presence which we call fascination. The readiness with which we identify objects of perception is due not to the functioning of some mental machinery of analysis, but to the "presence-absence" of the entire world of our past experience. No object is comprehensible in itself, but only as an element of that of which it is a part.[41] A world is implied by the existence of a given object, and the presence of that world is essential to the understanding of the object; but since it is unthinkable that it be physically present, its presence must resemble that of the imaginary. It will be recalled that according to the principle of "quasi-observation," the mental image is an exhaustive representation of its object, it presents instantaneously all we know about the object: " . . . The object of the image is delivered to us all at once by all our intellectual and affective experience."[42] The "nihilated world" which organizes itself as a backdrop behind the perceived object is the total of our "intellectual and affective experience" which enables us to recognize the object for what it is. To be sure, the nihilated world is not necessarily present to the same degree as is the object of a distinct mental image; its presence is often implicit (or as Sartre will say in *L'Etre et le Néant* "non thetic"), not explicit. ". . . The imaginary represents at each moment the implicit sense of the real," and " . . . all apprehension of the real as world implies a hidden recourse to the imaginary . . . all consciousness of the world calls for and motivates an imaging consciousness enabling us to grasp the particular *sense* of the

[41] But since that of which the object is a part is necessarily always present as a "nihilated backdrop," we have been able to argue previously that objects are comprehensible in themselves.
[42] *L'Imaginaire*, p. 122.

situation."[43] It would be difficult to exaggerate the importance of these words for the understanding of *L'Etre et le Néant*. Nothingness, far from being simply the void, is the shadowy "presence" (in the way in which the object of the mental image is present) of a world, and to nihilate an object, or to perceive it, is to situate it at the centre of this vast presence which is yet an absence—a nothingness. The for-itself is everything which is not physically present, and yet whose presence is essential to perception and understanding. It is the intangible immensity whose presence-absence surrounds the hard core of the in-itself to render it intelligible.

The ideas fundamental to Sartrean thought, we already possess; they differ from those that have preoccupied us from the very beginning only by a greater precision, and *L'Etre et le Néant* will carry that precision still further by a minute investigation of the relations that obtain between in-itself and for-itself. A thorough analysis of so huge a book as *L'Etre et le Néant* being out of the question,[44] we shall restrict ourselves to remarks of a general nature centred on the chapter entitled: *Les Structures Immédiates du Pour-Soi*, which is the most difficult of the book, but which must be clearly understood if the rest of *L'Etre et le Néant* is to make sense.

Sartre begins with incredibly little. Of the in-itself all we know is that it is, and the Self has become a nothingness. It is clear, therefore, that *L'Etre et le Néant* will not be concerned with the in-itself and the for-itself taken in themselves, but with their interplay, which will necessarily be of considerable complexity. In appearance, by far the greater part of *L'Etre et le Néant* is devoted to the for-itself, but we must never for a moment forget that while in one sense the for-itself exists, in another, only the in-itself exists. This means that in one breath, Sartre will be able,

43 *Ibid.*, p. 238. See also p. 230 ". . . To perceive this or that real thing (*donné*) is to perceive it against the background of total reality as a whole. This reality is not the object of any special act of my attention but it is co-present as the essential condition of the reality actually perceived."
44 The best is that of Francis Jeanson, *Le Problème Moral et la Pensée de Sartre*, Myrte, 1947.

for example, to speak of "the in-itself that the for-itself is" (since the for-itself is nothingness) and in the next breath refer to the for-itself as something quite different from the in-itself (since the for-itself is a nothingness that exists). This bizarre duality of the for-itself is of such importance that it constitutes a definition: Sartre defines the for-itself as something which "is what it is not, and is not what it is." Let us imagine that we are looking at a building. The building will be perceived as such thanks to the presence around it of a "muff" of nothingness—the for-itself, or the presence-absence of the entire world and way of life that the existence of this particular building implies and which is essential to its recognition. The for-itself "is what it is not"—the for-itself *is* the building, since besides the in-itself there is nothing, and yet it "is not what it is"— the for-itself cannot *be* the building because in that case the in-itself could not be known, there would be no consciousness.

The expression "duality of the for-itself" of which we have just made use must be carefully qualified. The for-itself is not two, but one. And yet not only must we recognize that the for-itself is in some way divided but also that the division may occur *within itself*. (From this point forward, the Appendix may be consulted for a more detailed treatment of what follows.) In other words, the for-itself can be its own nothingness; it is capable of nihilating itself. Thus we are faced with another contradiction—a separation within a unity; but again, it is a contradiction whose existence is attested to by subjectivity. We have all, at one time or another, "fooled ourselves." Indeed, there are people who do so for years at a time, like the pastor of *La Symphonie Pastorale,* and others who never cease to do so, like Gide's Robert. When we say: "he is deceiving himself," only one person is involved, yet a kind of scission is implied. More concretely, it is quite common for a man to be, for example, a coward and at the same time *sincerely* to believe that he is not. Such a situation can only be explained by postulating a consciousness that is *within itself,* separated from itself. What occurs is that a person in order to "perceive himself" as a coward, must effect a nihilation involving the notion "courage" without which that of "cowardice" could not exist. At one and the same moment and within itself, the for-itself is what it is not (cowardly) and is not what it is (courageous). It is in this way that Sartre disposes of the problem of sincerity which has interested or tormented so many contemporary writers. In order to be one thing, we are necessarily another; and, in any case, the whole system is a nothingness. "I am not, I become," wrote Gide; and Sartre, . . . "nothingness is not, it nihilates itself." If we are to mistrust "good sentiments" as Gide advised, it is because they are sustained by the evil sentiments that the for-itself at that moment is. Few are more concerned with evil than the uncompromisingly virtuous.[45]

The for-itself is, therefore, within itself separated from itself; it is "present to itself." Let's us remember, however, that at the same time, the for-itself is necessarily present to the in-itself without which it could not exist. The for-itself comes into being as the nihilation of a *particular* in-itself. There being no objective point of view or absolute truth, the for-itself can only exist "engaged" in matter, focused upon this or that individual in-itself. But things taken in themselves in this way are absurd, and what gives the Sartrean universe its "animation" is the attempt on the part of the for-itself to suppress the absurdity (or contingency) that it *is,* by suppressing the division within itself; that is, by becoming at once in-itself and for-itself, by becoming at once a thing, and sentient. We are here at the "core" of *L'Etre et le Néant;* it might, therefore, be well to proceed more slowly.

The in-itself that the for-itself is going to attempt to become will, clearly, not be the contingent in-itself imperfect and *de trop.* There is, however, another; it is part of the

---

[45] The reverse, of course, is also true; and Sartre's interest in Jean Genêt is consequently not evidence of a perverse attachment to evil, as Sartre's critics are eager to assert, but of interest in the good, by which Genêt has, for the greater part of his life, been obsessed.

nihilation which renders objects intelligible to us. The perfect in-itself (or what we call "value") exists in the presence-absence which isolates momentarily the imperfect object of consciousness. We appreciate at this conjuncture the importance of the fact that the for-itself is its own nothingness; since the only way for the for-itself to "realize" this ideal in-itself is by another nihilation, this time of itself. Let us take the example of thirst. As part of the nihilation which constitutes our consciousness of the in-itself (thirst) is an ideal thirst (absent in-itself and, therefore, for-itself) which the for-itself seeks to be. However, to achieve this, another nihilation is necessary, the chief element of which will be "non-thirst," that is, the act of drinking. Needless to say, the fusion that the for-itself seeks and which will abolish the division within itself can never be consummated for (in the present case) the act of drinking, instead of perpetuating the in-itself thirst as a self contained system, at once thing and consciousness, has brought into being a different in-itself, satisfied thirst, with the nihilation, the division, that necessarily accompanies it. Consciousness implies separation from, or as Sartre says, a "nihilating recoil" *(recul)*. Consciousness is unthinkable apart from the existence of what is not the thing of which there is consciousness. Man acts because he desires, and what he desires is the impossible repose of "thinghood," without however sacrificing consciousness; the for-itself does not seek its own extinction. What man desires, in other words, as Malraux had seen, is to become God; for only God is "his own cause"— simultaneously thing and consciousness, what Sartre calls in-itself-for-itself. Man is this perpetual longing, impossible of fulfilment, to "rejoin himself," to establish a cause and, therefore, a justification for his existence by "knowing himself," without the introduction of what is not himself. It is for this reason that man is, in the words of Sartre, "a useless passion."

None of the authors we have studied before coming to Sartre troubled himself to enquire whether man were free;

for them the eternal debate had lost its interest. If we will refuse to be impressed by the many forms of scienticism that continue to befog the intellectual atmosphere of the times, we will discover that we know we are free with the same certitude that we know what we like and what we dislike. It is the business of the philosopher, however, to demonstrate, and once again we find Sartre clarifying for us a notion which, up to the present, we have simply taken for granted. If man is a "useless passion" as far as achieving definitive results in any field of activity is concerned, he is nevertheless free in the immediate to attempt and usually, if he is determined enough, to achieve whatever he undertakes.[46] We shall have to go more deeply into this question.

It is characteristic of much of existentialism to appear at once new and yet strangely commonplace. This is due to its being less a school of thought than a movement which, as such, is not without relevance for every aspect of human life. It is due also to the way in which the existentialists, as a form of "reduction," utilize the "obvious" to philosophical ends. A striking example of this is the place the word "freedom" occupies in the writings of Sartre. It is disconcerting for those unfamiliar with *L'Etre et le Néant* to observe that the word recurs as frequently in the books of Sartre as in the orations of the merest politician where it no longer has any meaning whatsoever. It is for this reason, even though freedom is the very keystone of Sartre's thought, that we have avoided using the word until a precise meaning could be attached to it. But of course if that were possible it is because we have been using another word that means the same thing, and that word is for-itself. Man does not "possess" freedom, he *is* free. The for-itself *is* freedom.

---

[46] One of the most frequent objections raised against *L'Etre et le Néant* is that Sartre makes human freedom so absolute as to deprive it of all value and meaning. Yet Sartre makes it perfectly clear that man is not at all times free to accomplish whatever he sees fit. "The technical and philosophical concept of freedom, the only one we are considering here, signifies simply: autonomy of choice." (*L'Etre et le Néant*, p. 563.) The prisoner is free, not to escape, but to plan to escape.

With the acumen of hind-sight, we can look back to
L'Imaginaire and see that even at that time Sartre was
singularly preoccupied to establish that the mental image,
along with its other characteristics, is rigorously undeter-
mined. "There is no causal relationship between two con-
sciousnesses."[47] A few schematic lines disposed in a certain
manner on a piece of paper do not "cause" by association
the mental image of a man running. On the contrary, we are
aware of ourselves creating and continually renewing the
image.[48] Even in the case of a portrait of someone known to
us, the portrait does not summon into our minds an image of
the person represented. We *make use of* the portrait to recall to ourselves the appearance of the person involved.[49]
Deterministic psychology is obliged to conceive of the mind
as in some way material; but once we accept it as a nothingness, or as Sartre says in *L'Imaginaire,* capable of posit-
ing "a thesis of unreality," there is no longer any reason
to suppose it submitted to the determinism which is one
aspect of the existence of things. We cannot simultaneously
imagine and perceive; to imagine is to *separate* oneself
from reality, to cause the world to "recoil."[50]

To adopt the language of *L'Etre et le Néant,* the for-
itself is self-presence—it is not the in-itself that it is. But
the freedom of the for-itself is not the purely negative freedom to disengage itself from matter; for that portion of the
for-itself that is what it is not, is that which *determines
precisely what the nihilated in-itself shall be.* A mountain,
for example, is nothing "in the absolute." What it is depends entirely upon the "absent totality" which the for-
itself is and which determines the mountain as being a barrier for advancing soldiers, for vacationists a means of
obtaining a view, for the geologist an object of study, etc.
We are not less free because a mountain is able to frustrate

47 *L'Imaginaire,* p. 41.
48 See *L'Imaginaire,* p. 51.
49 See *ibid.,* p. 37.
50 "For a consciousness to be able to imagine, it must by its very nature escape
the world. It must be able to derive from within itself a position of 'withdrawal' in relation to the world. In a word, it must be free." (*L'Imaginaire,*
p. 234.)

our attempts to flee across a frontier, since it is our own project of escape freely arrived at which constitutes the mountain as an obstacle. *"There is no state of things—satisfying or not—except by the nihilating power of the for-itself."*[51] The world is *ours*. It is no more than the totality of objects to which the for-itself has given appearance and meaning as a consequence of utilizing them in its attempts to rejoin itself.

Phenomenology made of Cézanne a "scientist" as well as an artist, and existentialism consecrates the right of literature to speak with an authority equal to that of science and philosophy about the nature of the world and of man. The world is what it appears to be and man is what he does; to philosophize, consequently, is simply to speak about what *is* and about what is to be done.

The absurd is what remains after we have denied the existence of everything not directly experienced—for example, the perspective that Cézanne eliminated from art; and the "immobile" point of view which disappears in cubism; for we do not contemplate things, we use them and move about among them. Gide had no experience of either a scientific or moral law; indeed his sexual propensities were in direct conflict with both. However, instead of denying the validity of his personal experience, instead of sacrificing the certitude of the *cogito* to a hypothetical Order, Gide rejected the Order for the sake of the evidence of the absurd; that is, the sensations by which things are revealed to us when taken in themselves. Malraux had no more experience of an Order in society than had Gide of a natural or religious dispensation indicating certain acts as good and others as bad. On the contrary, what is most evident about societies and governments is the impossibility of rationally justifying most of the procedures that obtain, with the poverty and injustice that result. Submission to the social "order" is submission to the absurd, to the inhuman; that is, to death. We live to the extent in which we

---

51 *L'Etre et le Néant*, p. 511.

refuse to ignore what *is* in exchange for an "explanation" that is not. Saint-Exupéry instead of reducing the world seen from the air to the "objective" world of the rest of us (as Gide might have reduced his desires to aberration or sin) considered that he had discovered another world, and that there are as many more as we have the courage, by our acts, to bring to light. *La Nausée* carries to the last extreme this destruction of systems and absolutes which follows from our modern incapacity to believe what we cannot see or feel. In *La Nausée* even the categories of colour are abolished, for we cannot say of an object that it is brown but only that to a greater or lesser extent it approaches brown. For Sartre, not only is there no sense in matter, but we inhabit a world in which things "shade off" one into the other, and which are kept apart, not by any natural necessity, but simply by the particular attitude that man adopts towards them. All that we can say of the in-itself is that it exists.

As Malraux had seen, the death of God is necessarily followed by that of man. Gide, in deciding that conduct should be a response to the solicitations of individual things rather than obedience to an alleged law, rendered the Self—the invisible counterpart of an invisible Order—gratuitous. It is apparent to everyone that modern art constitutes an extraordinarily decisive and comprehensive disavowal of the whole past of representational art. But the change would have been far more extraordinary had it restricted itself to art alone. The "dehumanization" of which one speaks in connexion with modern art, and which is simply the artist's refusal to interpose a factitious Ego between his eye and the object, occurs conspicuously in Malraux and Saint-Exupéry who denounce the intellectuals' eternal attempts to interpret things in preference to changing them; that is to say, their tendency to construct a world which will answer to the requirements of their intelligence rather than to change the world in accordance with their needs. Because the world is absurd, in other words *changeable,* man is not what he thinks but what he does.

L'Etre et le Néant has made it practicable for philosophy, after art and literature, to dispense with the Self. We have just seen how Sartre accounts for perception and act entirely without the use of immanence considered as a thing. A man is the sum of his acts and not the elusive Self supposedly at their source. If we are able to predict with a high degree of probability what a man's conduct will be under certain circumstances, it is not because he possesses a character which "causes" him to act in certain ways under certain conditions, but because a man's choice of himself usually remains constant throughout his life. In regard to the world and other people, each of us nourishes a "project," which determines the way in which things and people appear to us (hostile, friendly, indifferent, etc.), which determines our character in other words, in precisely the same way that a nihilation determines the identity of an object. The project is a supreme nihilation; man, therefore, in addition to the acts which that nihilation inspires, is nothing.

The revolution that is existentialism, like all successful revolutions, destroyed nothing that was not already on the point of collapse. During the past half century, science, and rationalism in general, have been so severely shaken that the existentialists had only the rubble to clear away before beginning to construct. Hence the bewilderment of many readers of *L'Etre et le Néant* who find themselves suddenly confronted by a new world before anyone had told them why the old could no longer be kept in a state of repair. This is one of the reasons why, even in university lecture halls, existentialism (and it is particularly important at this point to bear in mind that we refer exclusively to that of Sartre) is presented as a philosophy of destruction, as a philosophy of despair, anguish,[52] the absurd, abandonment, etc. But these notions are destructive only of values which have ceased to function; they signify spiritual paralysis only for the rationalist; for the existentialist, as for Gide, Malraux and Saint-Exupéry, they are parts of

52 ". . . it [anguish] is . . . altogether exceptional." (*L'Etre et le Néant*, p. 73.)

a new edifice. The thought of the three authors we have studied does not terminate with the discovery of the absurd; on the contrary, they regard it as a necessary condition of human freedom; a condition without which our acts are "stolen" from us as were those of Gide's Oedipus; without which the careers of Garine and of Rivière would have been nonsensical. Historically considered, the idea of the absurd is the natural end-product of an evolution which begins when certain Renaissance philosophers, in the interests of science, abolished the supernatural from matter. But the supernatural, whether religious or simply a primitive animism, was still human in that its appearances were motivated, they signified something; while the establishment of the impersonal scientific fact which signifies nothing was the first step towards the gradual separation of man from his environment which, passing by fideism, by deism and the various natural laws, culminates in Sartre's assertion that not only the isolated fact, but the entire material universe signifies nothing, it simply is. It will be recalled that Vincent Berger's experience of anguish was not that of this totally non-human universe, but that of the limitless and inalienable freedom which results. Sartre gives a concrete example of such an experience. The dread that sometimes seizes us at the edge of a precipice is the way in which we apprehend the fact that nothing prevents us from throwing ourselves over; there is no Self (instinct of conservation, etc.) which causes us to draw away from the edge. The sense of the situation is not "preconstituted"; it is created by a nihilation which, as we have just seen, we ourselves are (the for-itself is what it is not).[53] The absurd, therefore, involves anguish not because it deprives man of a number of spiritual comforts to which he has been accustomed but because it bestows a freedom so unencumbered that it amounts to a total responsibility; and yet it is a responsibility of which he can

[53] See *L'Etre et le Néant*, p. 69. "It is precisely the consciousness of being one's own future in the mode of not-being that we will call *anguish*."

never rid himself because the world, being absurd, offers no solutions.

However, if the world is absurd when, like Malraux's "clergy of intellectuals," we attempt to think it as a totality, it begins to make sense once we consent to form a part of it, once we have returned to things-in-themselves, because then it appears not as an enigma to be resolved, but as a succession of tasks to be accomplished.[54] European humanism, as Saint-Exupéry remarked, neglected the act; and it did so because it conceived the world as "exhaustible"—as amenable to thought. Gide broke decisively with this tradition by coming to consider thought as either superfluous or harmful depending upon whether it is turned outward or inward. Things have no meaning more deep than the sensations to which, taken individually, they give rise; and subjectivity is, or at least should be, no more than a "gratuitous" response to these sensations. Hence Gide's often repeated assertion that we are to take literally that passage of scripture, according to which the after life begins here and now; for an act undeformed by theory and dictated by the immediate, is a fulfilment; while thought is merely the contemplation, or in the case of scientism, the anticipation of a fulfilment. Gide, however, although he had abandoned solutions in what concerns the individual continued in spite of himself to think of politics in terms of completely satisfactory arrangements. As a result, the gratuitous act was turned inward, and Gide failed to see that the real function of gratuity must be to enable us to dispense with theory or faith so that we may see the Real which always presents itself in the form of tasks requiring our immediate attention.[55] Thus, most of the heroes of

[54] See *ibid.*, p. 250: ". . . this world is a world of tasks."
[55] If, as Gide remarks in *Les Nourritures*, books tend more to obscure than to enlighten, it is because the intellectual, seeking *to be* rather than *to do*, treats the Real of a given situation as a consequence or a cause rather than as a summons to act. This process is often carried so far, that the Real has to be rediscovered—such is the object of Sartre's articles entitled "Les Communistes et la Paix," in one of which he remarks: ". . . I am trying to understand what is going on in France, today, under our eyes." (*Les Temps Modernes*, October-November 1952, p. 753.)

L'Espoir are, as Sartre remarks, ". . . on the level of the *act.* . . ."[56] for, having renounced the "ontological" longing to be, their acts assume a value here and now in themselves as the satisfaction of an immediate need.[57] The heroes of Saint-Exupéry also, Mermoz looking for a pass through the Andes, Rivière creating his aerial service, live in the realm of act, and find it vain to look beyond the task that their situation in the world proposes.

We have seen how Sartre, in the interests of the practical effectiveness of philosophy, took what was for a philosopher the bold step of declaring that the in-itself exists independently of its individual appearances. Intentionality had offered philosophers the hope of being able to abolish the problems of epistemology, and if Sartre's affirmation of Being appeared so serious a matter to many of them it was because it was the first step not toward mitigating but toward intensifying the mind body duality which is the source of the trouble. And indeed no difference is more irreducible than that between Being and nothingness, in-itself and for-itself. But it is because of the very absoluteness of their opposition that the for-itself cannot exist without the in-itself. Already in *L'Imaginaire,* Sartre was anxious to establish their interdependence.[58] As always with Sartre, the first concern is to obtain as high a degree of effectiveness in ethics as is compatible with philosophical rigour. Thus, in the case of the question at hand: Sartre considers consciousness inconceivable apart from separation, but this separation is effected in such a manner as to make impossible, on the one hand, the idealist's retreat into mind and, on the other, the empiricist's submission of the human to

---

[56] *L'Etre et le Néant,* p. 507. The heroes of *L'Espoir* begin at the point attained by Sartre's Goetz only at the end of the play, which Goetz concludes with the words: "There is this war to be fought and I'll fight it." (*Le Diable et le Bon Dieu,* NRF, 1951.)

[57] This should not lead, as it has done in the case of Camus, to the idea of revolt for its own sake. The absurd is not incompatible with constructive action which is content to be of limited scope. If existentialism is so conscientious a return to the Real, it is precisely so that it may construct effectively. Camus's "revolt" is a form of defeatism; hence the very decisive rupture which recently took place between Camus and Sartre.

[58] See pp. 234 and 235, NRF, 1940.

the non-human. In other language, Sartre has sought to render philosophically indefensible the *refusal to act*. Attempts to arrive at a satisfactory theory of knowledge have almost invariably led to the reduction of mind and body to either one or the other. But since for Sartre there is only the in-itself mind being nothingness, he is able to retain the epistemological advantages of the reduction of mind to body without the moral paresis to which it ordinarily leads; for if there is no mind, the humanist of Saint-Exupéry and the intellectual of Malraux can no longer take refuge in it, and if mind though not a thing is nevertheless more present than ever before as act, then the marxist must abandon his contempt for subjectivity. The philosophy of Sartre might be called that of the "authentic act," for in seeking to change the world and not to think it, it does not hope to effect changes which will gradually abolish the need for change. We need not, however, be content with generalities. We have seen that man is desire, and that what he desires is the impossible fusion of in-itself and for-itself; he desires to become a thing, self-caused and justified thanks to its ability to contemplate itself without introducing the separation which consciousness inevitably entails. On the political and social level, this "useless passion" of the for-itself to overcome its contingency translates itself into a faith in Absolutes; an Absolute being an in-itself-for-itself invented by reflexion to compensate for or to explain the absurdity of existence.[59] Life, however, is necessarily ambiguous because consciousness is always nihilation of a *particular* thing or group of things, since the for-itself in order to be must know precisely what it is not; or, in the language of *L'Imaginaire,* ". . . all apprehension of the real . . . is always . . . a free nihilation of the world and that always *from a particular point of view.*"[60] The backdrop of the world which is part of every nihilation cannot exist without the concrete thing or things to which it gives a meaning. To live, therefore, is to be "situated,"

[59] See *L'Etre et le Néant,* p. 133.
[60] NRF, 1940, p. 235.

to be at grips with the particular. Life is passage from one individual thing to another. Consequently, man must accept ". . . not to *regain,* but to flee from himself, not to coincide with, but to be always at a distance from, himself,"[61] since, as we saw, the for-itself is both the particular thing and those absent things essential to its intelligibility. The usual means adopted to put an end to this perpetual unrest that is the for-itself is to imagine value (another word for the absent total in-itself) as something imposed from without and which man will eventually rejoin thereby overcoming the blindness to which his dependence upon the particular condemns him. But value *is* the for-itself; it is part of the nihilation which makes meaningful a given thing or situation, and to elevate it to the status of an immutable goal or ideal is to sacrifice the concrete to the abstract, the existent to the non-existent.

The great contemporary philosophy of despair is, therefore, in reality a philosophy of action considered as a response to the immediate. The word "immediate," however, must not be taken too literally. Existentialist political thought is founded upon marxism, considered not as the "Truth" but as the most satisfactory description of the realities of the present historical context. Action, therefore, although inspired by the immediate, nevertheless inserts itself within a trend that we may call progressive, not in the sense of movement toward a fixed goal, but in the sense of an amelioration of the present.

It is one thing to establish, as we have tried to, the precedence of action over contemplation, but quite another to determine what that action shall be at any given time; and while this question has no place here, it might be well to say a few words about it in view of the bitter controversy to which it has given rise in France since the end of the war.

We called communism a "pseudo-revolutionary" movement on the grounds that authentic revolutions are cultural

61 *L'Etre et le Néant,* p. 722.

as well as political. On the other hand, conservatism has nothing to offer—it never has, it being by definition non-creative, interested only in the maintenance of what is, even though this is never possible without recourse to oppression. Granted the obsolescence of the classical notion of objectivity, granted the principle that the intellectual as well as other men exists only in so far as he makes his weight felt in society, the problem of the cold war years for Sartre and his followers was to act in the absence of complete sympathy with any organized group, and for Sartre this involved throwing in his lot with the communists while withholding his intellectual allegiance to communism as a philosophy. Such conduct pains and mystifies the orthodox intellectual for whom intellectual assent is an indispensable prerequisite to active participation. But here one of two things occurs, either he is lucid enough to withhold assent, in which case he never acts, or the thirst of the Absolute overcomes his scruples and eventually he is bitterly disillusioned. This is what happened between the wars. But the absolutist cannot live without the Truth, and for people like Koestler, the Truth, after having been communism, became anti-communism. These intellectuals have become a danger, for we may expect them to resist for as long as possible any suggestion that communism may not be totally evil, as it was once totally good. The absolutist *needs* to believe that stalinism and communism are one. Sartre refused to accept this view, and in full knowledge of such barbarities as the Soviet labour camps, he preferred working with the communists to doing nothing at all which is the usual choice of the intellectual.[62]

62 Since this was written, the Hungarian revolution has taken place, and Sartre, adapting as always his thought to the situation rather than the situation to his thought, has broken with the communists.

The only hope for any decisive improvemen in French politics is the formation of a new *front populaire*, but during the past twelve years this would have been unthinkable without the participation of the largest single party in the country—the communist. Hence Sartre's attempt to co-operate with it. But recently, the party's persistent refusal to "destalinize," its approval of the Russian intervention in Hungary, and its bargaining with Mollet over the North African situation may sufficiently discredit it with the workers as well as with the intellectuals to give some faint hope for the formation of a new party or of a new left. It is to this task that Sartre will now apply himself.

Nothing prevents us from refashioning marxism to suit our needs, and to such a refurbished marxism, the right has absolutely nothing to oppose. The superciliousness with which the Anglo-Saxon intellectual speaks of a political philosophy which has produced two of the most considerable events in human history—the Russian and Chinese Revolutions—is simply comic. We cannot replace marxism. Our work must be to make it a cultural as well as a political revolution. This may one day come to be regarded as the greatest achievement of Sartrean existentialism.

Conclusion

IN THE broadest possible terms, we may say that existentialism is an attempt to utilize philosophy. It is an effort to tear philosophy away from its contemplation of an order that does not exist, so that it may participate in the confusion that does; it is the substitution of a living ambiguity for a dead absolute. Inasmuch as philosophy has, from the earliest times and without interruption, been a quest for a total explanation, it is clear that existentialism represents a break with the past which could hardly be more radical. For such a revolution to have been practicable, it was necessary to show how final principles could be dispensed with, how the absurd could be thought. Husserl believed that intelligibility is not the *goal* of thought, but the *condition of its possibility*. The truth is implicit in all intellection, and the function of the phenomenological reduction is to render it explicit by an examination of consciousness which is an "absolute" in the sense that there is existence only in so far as there is consciousness of existence. Existentialism grew out of an impatience with phenomenology for what it retains, not of classical philosophy itself, but of the classical philosopher's cast of mind. In general, the phenomenologists continue to regard *knowing* as the condition of *acting;* and with them, as in the past, the latter is effaced by the former. The existentialists are reproached with jeopardizing the growth of phenomenology by utilizing it while it is still in its infancy. The existentialists answer that if we possess the truth, then it is infinitely more important to make use of it than to elucidate its functioning in the activities of consciousness. The reduction as employed by the phenomenologists will, in theory, lead eventually to a clear understanding of the "essences" which make it possible for appearance to be Reality. The reduction as Sartre uses it is the stripping away of the verbiage of the intellectuals, of their "explanations" and of their theories so that we may see what really is. ". . . How can you fail to see that work is a kind of *suffering*"[1]—such is the fundamental truth about human labour; but it is one which intellectuals, including the marxists, have to an extraordinary degree succeeded in overlooking. We are all empiricists. So deeply rooted is our mistrust of metaphysics that it seems extravagant that the author of *L'Etre et le Néant* should be of all philosophers the one who strives most unremittingly to see things as they are. It is not easy for many of us to cease to equate knowledge and scientific knowledge, to see that faith in science was the "subjectivity" of an epoch. What the scholastics frequently objected to in science was its abandonment of the solid ground of *a priori* reasoning for the logical uncertainties of experimentalism. The experimentalists now reproach the new philosophy for quitting the solid ground of scientific method for the metaphysics of the *cogito*. However, the solid ground of the scholastics, and now that of the experimentalists, is suspended in the air because the certitude of which each boasts is arrived at only at the cost of not taking into account the essential —human existence.

Since the truth, if we will lay aside our theories and our principles, is there for us to see, it is as much the domain of literature as of philosophy. There is no more striking characteristic of great literature than its "ambiguity"—one does not "explain" Dostoievsky or Faulkner. If we are often uncertain of exactly what they intend, it is not because the best art expresses emotion rather than idea, but because it expresses the truth, the nature of which is to be ambiguous. Its *presence* is undeniable: but either it is in itself contradictory (like Sartre's mental image) or it fits into no ready-made compartment in a great harmonious scheme (like the fact that the work of the proletariat,

---

[1] Sartre, "Réponse à Lefort," *Les Temps Modernes*, April 1953. This entire article is an excellent illustration of the point we wish to make. Sartre says: ". . . It appeared useless to me . . . to formulate a theory of the proletariat." What is necessary is not another theory, but an effort to *see* what *at this moment* really exists.

which the intellectual transmutes into statistics, is first of all a form of human misery). There is, consequently, an underlying sympathy between existentialism and great prose art which is founded upon their mutual adherence to the Real, however refractory to logical organization it proves to be. Rationalism, as always, approaches the question of literary creation by dividing the indivisible; art consists of form and content; but since truth is scientific truth, the content of art will come to be considered of secondary importance. Art is primarily form. *L'Education Sentimentale* is the supreme product of this aesthetic—a gloomy monument, compared to which the books of a Céline or a Malraux are light-hearted, commemorating the belief that art is a philosopher's stone transforming whatever it touches into pure gold. Such a notion responds perfectly to the requirements of "objective" studies in literature. *What* a novelist has to say is of less moment than the influences which "caused" him to say it and the technique with which it is said. *What* is said is subjective and therefore without relation to the Truth which remains the preserve of science.

It is not one of the least of the existentialist "reductions" to recall that prose *says something,* that a writer is first of all a man with something to say; and it is on that basis that he is to be judged, since, as Gide and Malraux saw very clearly, the aesthetic value of prose is all but inseparable from the soundness of the thought it expresses. However, a thought remains sound for a given period only—a Bossuet or a Pascal would be unthinkable today, and it is not by chance that Claudel is a poet, or that de Maistre and Bloy excite only academic interest.[2] On the other hand, it is possible for an admirable prose to say nothing at all, as in the case of Montherlant, and the badly-written *Cahiers* of Péguy will be read long after Montherlant has ceased to be anything but a name.

2 In his *Religion de Rabelais,* Lucien Febvre has shown that in the sixteenth century men were still incapable of not believing. During most of the following century, this was to a great extent still true.

But there is a more important reason why a writer is to be judged upon what he says rather than upon how he says it; namely, that the truth of a given historical context is perfectly evident, and it is the business of the writer to prevent it from being obscured by fear or selfish interests.[3] The truth, being known, must be manifested. "The time has gone by," writes Malraux, "when it was thought that understanding would come later."[4] Nevertheless, *engagement* need not result in the usurpation of literature by journalism; for there is a metaphysical as well as a practical truth, a fact which permits writers who diverge from one another as widely as do a Kafka and a Saint-Exupéry to express themselves in perfect freedom.

We have just traversed a period during which literature had nothing to say because science already had or eventually would say the essential. However, if philosophy is not, like science, an investigation but a "manifestation," then to say that existentialism seeks to utilize philosophy is but another way of saying that literature has been given back its content.

[3] The expression "between the wars" came to be used in France *before* the outbreak of the second world war. In his *Les Conséquences Politiques de la Paix* (written in 1920), Jacques Bainville quite clearly foresaw the events of the next two decades. History offers few more remarkable spectacles than the passivity of the world's intelligentzia before what was a perfectly obvious threat to its very existence.
[4] *Les Noyers de l'Altenburg*, NRF, 1948, p. 130.

Appendix

THE MIND is not only perception of things, it "perceives" itself—as honest or dishonest, thrifty or extravagant, etc. The for-itself, therefore, must be capable of being its "own nothingness," of nihilating itself. But how is this possible and what does it teach us about the for-itself?

There exists a conduct in which the for-itself asserts itself to be something which it is not, an examination of which should yield some useful information. It is the act of lying to oneself which we call bad faith. The problem presented by bad faith is that of understanding how within the same consciousness and at the same moment there can exist nevertheless a kind of duality, that of the deceived and the deceiver. To avoid this logical impossibility, psychoanalysis hypothesizes the existence of a subconscious which, inaccessible to ordinary introspection, is responsible for the extraordinary confusion which greets those with the courage and leisure to undertake a thorough *examen de conscience*. Thus the duality of liar and lied to is re-established and the possibility retained of considering man an essence rather than an existence. However, psychoanalytic theory fails to explain how the conscious portion of the mind can repress movements emanating from the subconscious without knowing what it is repressing. How can the patient recognize as exact the psychoanalyst's diagnosis of his trouble without being already aware of it himself? "Can one conceive," writes Sartre, "a knowing that would be ignorant of itself?"[1]

It is quite common for people to succeed throughout their lives in not seeing a fact detrimental to their self-esteem even though they are perfectly aware of its existence—like the hero of *Death of a Salesman*. How is it possible for a homosexual to acknowledge his acts and yet at the same time deny without a trace of cynicism that he

[1] *L'Etre et le Néant*, p. 91.

is a homosexual? Having refused the explanation of a consciousness divided into two different parts, given the absolute "translucidity" of consciousness, we are obliged to recognize that, at the same time, the for-itself both "is and is not what it is."[2] Let us take the example of a coward unable to recognize that he is one. In order that a man become aware of himself as a coward, a nihilation must take place, the principal ingredient of which will be courage. Courage is the "presence-absence," the nothingness which renders the notion "coward" meaningful. One cannot be a coward as a table is a table. Cowardice exists only to the extent to which there is consciousness of it, and consciousness implies a "nihilating recoil," the introduction of what Sartre calls a *négatité* (in this case "non-cowardice" or courage) which is essential to the understanding of the situation. Consequently it may be said that man "is not what he is" (the coward exists only in so far as he can sustain himself as such by the act of consciousness, ". . . act sustains being"[3]) and "is what he is not" (he is the nihilation, or courage, by which he gives existence to his cowardice). Bad faith can be explained only if consciousness ". . . at the same time, and in its being, is what it is not and is not what it is."[4]

Thus, as in the case of *L'Imaginaire,* an outrageous contradiction stands at the base of *L'Etre et le Néant;* and again, instead of trying to elude it, Sartre exploits it. Another way to express the curious duality within unity we have just found in the for-itself is to say that the for-itself is "self-presence," a kind of "decompression" of the solid plenitude of the in-itself. A belief, for example, is more than a belief, it is awareness of belief. In the "prereflexive *cogito,*" the for-itself is its own witness. The for-itself, unlike the in-itself, does not "coincide with itself" and yet what separates it from itself is *nothing.* If we try to seize a

---

[2] ". . . I must, originally and simultaneously, be and not be what I am." (*L'Etre et le Néant,* p. 106.)
[3] *L'Etre et le Néant,* p. 102.
[4] *Ibid.,* p. 111.

belief in itself, we encounter only our consciousness of belief; if, on the contrary, we try to fix our attention upon this "consciousness of," we are left with the belief itself. It is natural, of course, that we should be unable to locate the for-itself, since nothingness, as Sartre says, "is not, it nihilates itself." Consciousness is always elsewhere; it is a "play of mirrors," a "reflecting-reflection," perpetual instability; in brief, incapacity *to be*. It is, therefore, impossible to attribute to consciousness, as does classical philosophy, the "highest" or the "noblest" form of being. Plenitude and self-sufficiency are for the for-itself an aspiration, not a fact, because it is separated from itself.

At the same time, however, it must not be forgotten that the for-itself exists. The for-itself is necessarily present to what is not itself; it must be "supported" by the in-itself, otherwise it is an "absolute nothingness." But the in-itself is absurd, or to use the term preferred by Sartre, contingent; that is, the for-itself is present to or nihilation of a particular thing or things, from a particular point of view. Each of us is born into a given situation, and if the existentialists talk of our being "abandoned" in the world, it is because the situation we occupy can never be shown to exist by necessity, it is always contingent.[5] The for-itself is "a being not founded in itself, which, as a being, could be other than it is in the measure to which it fails to explain its being."[6] We can neither choose nor explain our situation, yet we are totally responsible for it, since its only existence is that which our consciousness gives it.

Further light upon the for-itself, therefore, reveals that far from possessing "the highest dignity of being,"[7] it suffers from a number of serious ontological deficiencies, and we begin to suspect that the Sartrean universe, as yet a static one, will receive its animation as the result of attempts on the part of consciousness to remedy those

---

[5] "Why is this particular being such as it is, and not different?" (*L'Etre et le Néant*, p. 122.)
[6] *Ibid.*
[7] *Ibid.*, p. 119.

deficiencies. Sartre must find a way to escape from the "instantaneity" of the *cogito*, but without losing the benefits of immediate communication with it.

The for-itself then is divided from itself (it both is and is not what it is) and it partakes of the contingency of the in-itself that it necessarily is if it is to exist. The for-itself, therefore, is going to attempt to suppress the division within itself, to "coincide" with itself; for if it succeeds in so doing, it will have at the same time suppressed its contingency. The in-itself that the for-itself is, will have become a self-sufficient totality—"self-caused," and therefore justified. The for-itself will have ceased being *de trop*. But how can such an attempt be made and what will be the results?

The for-itself is essentially an insufficiency of Being. In the act of nihilation, the for-itself *denies* that it is the in-itself, and this is what Sartre calls "internal negation." The for-itself is a perpetual refusal of the in-itself that it is, a "decompression," a "recoiling from." However, for this refusal to be possible, the for-itself must know precisely what it is refusing to be; that is, as part of the nihilation, there must exist a perfect in-itself which the for-itself determines itself as not being. "The concrete and real in-itself is in its entirety present in the heart of consciousness as that which consciousness determines itself not to be."[8] For example, the recognition of a quarter moon as such is conceivable only if the full moon is present as part of the nihilation. A totality which is *not* present reflects back to give meaning to the particular in-itself that is: ". . . it is what is not that determines what is. . . ."[9]

This perfect being that the for-itself is "in the form of not being it" is what the in-itself (considered as the in-itself that the for-itself *is*) aspires to be in its attempts to "found itself," to achieve self-containment; in other terms, it is the self that the for-itself seeks to rejoin in its efforts to

---

8 *L'Etre et le Néant*, p. 128. "Knowledge" is not involved in this process, see *L'Etre et le Néant*, pp. 138 and 224.
9 *Ibid.*, p. 130.

suppress the division within itself. It is this *"Self as an abortive being-in-itself* which constitutes the meaning of human reality."[10] "Human reality" is a foredoomed attempt to fuse into one being both for-itself and in-itself. The absence which "haunts" the for-itself (the full moon which renders the quarter moon intelligible) is itself become in-itself; it is itself, no longer divided but possessing the plenitude of the in-itself as well as consciousness of itself. But since consciousness is necessarily *separation*, the synthesis of in-itself and for-itself is impossible; the for-itself can only become in-itself at the cost of ceasing to exist as for-itself.

Let us work out this argument with a concrete example —that of suffering. There is nothing in consciousness since consciousness is a nothingness. Suffering, consequently, is an in-itself of which there is consciousness; that is, an in-itself in attempting to found itself has succeeded only in "giving itself the modification of the for-itself," it has succeeded in founding not the perfect Being or in-itself-for-itself, but only nothingness. Nothingness, however, exists; it exists as the presence-absence of all that is necessary to our recognition of suffering as such. It exists, that is to say, as a nihilation. Consequently, the for-itself *simultaneously* is suffering, since besides suffering there is nothing; and is not, since it is the "recoil" that makes possible consciousness of suffering. The for-itself "is not what it is," it is not the in-itself that nevertheless it necessarily is since consciousness, to exist, is consciousness of something; and it "is what it is not," it is the *négatité* which constitutes the sense of the situation but which also constitutes nothingness. The in-itself failed to suppress its contingency; that is, the for-itself is nihilation of this particular suffering, or "self-presence" since it both is and is not the in-itself. But there remains, as the meaning of the attempt, as its goal, as an element of the nihilation, the perfect suffering in-itself that the for-itself determines itself as not being and that *at the same time* is the self from

10 *Ibid.*, p. 132.

which the for-itself is separated. This absence and un-realizable in-itself-for-itself is what Sartre calls value. It will at first glance seem paradoxical that the object of suffering should be to realize a "perfect" suffering. However, Sartre considers "posterior and reflexive" the belief that suffering, thirst, sexual desire, etc., seek their own suppression. "Thirst and sexual desire, in their naïve and unreflecting state, seek the enjoyment of themselves. . . ."[11] It will be recalled that according to Sartre, an emotion is not something we undergo, but a conduct. The sufferer's tears and exclamations represent an attempt *to be* suffering, to realize the ideal suffering of the statue or the tragic mask, instead of which our suffering ". . . is like a degraded approximation of this suffering in-itself which haunts our own suffering."[12] To the person unfortunate in love, the thought that his suffering will one day cease is an additional source of suffering.

Nevertheless, we seek to quench our thirst and to find a remedy for our suffering. How does this fit in with what has gone before?

If the in-itself is absolute plenitude of being, the for-itself which exists only to the extent to which it refuses the in-itself, is a lack (*manque*) of being; and, indeed, there is no more conspicuous and universal characteristic of man than desire. The *cogito* reveals nothing with greater certitude than that man appears to himself as an imperfect being, and he feels his imperfection in the presence of the perfect being or in-itself-for-itself, or the self become in-itself. What the for-itself lacks to coincide with itself is more for-itself; that is to say, if the absent totality is to be realized, if it is to be rendered present, it must become the object of a nihilation—the prerogative of the for-itself. Let us take the example of thirst. We have seen that the totality "self-

---

[11] *L'Etre et le Néant*, p. 146.
[12] *Ibid.*, p. 135. The absent in-itself that haunts the for-itself is, as we have said, value; but it is also the object of artistic creation. The joy or suffering depicted in a painting is joy or suffering in-itself; but it is an *in-itself* that, while having escaped from its contingency, has at the same time ceased to exist except as an "absent." "The real," as Sartre remarks in *L'Imaginaire*, "is never beautiful." (p. 245.)

thirst" haunts my consciousness of thirst as what remains in the for-itself of the in-itself's attempt to found itself; in other words as part of the nihilation which makes consciousness of thirst possible. But if this absent in-itself-for-itself is to become present, it must in its turn be nihilated (we have seen that the for-itself is its own nothingness); that is, it must be confronted by the *négatité* "non-thirst," or satisfied thirst, if its identity as thirst is to be established. That which the for-itself lacks to realize itself as in-itself-for-itself is what Sartre calls the possible of the for-itself— in this case, the act of drinking. To be more precise, what happens is the nihilation of a nihilation, the second of which (needless to say, there is no sequence, all this occurs instantaneously and for the most part non-thetically) is consciousness of drink, but being a nothingness it must be sustained by an in-itself, in this case a glass of water to be drunk. ". . . The emptied glass haunts the full as its potential, and constitutes it as a glass for drinking from."[13]

It might be well to test the accuracy of what we have learned by taking from *L'Etre et le Néant* two of the many passages which at first glance seem a deliberate mystification. They should by now make sense to us. On page 111, we read: "Fleeing by the 'not-being-what-one-is' the in-itself that I am not in the mode of being what one is not, bad faith, which denies that it is bad faith, aims at the in-itself that I am not in the mode of 'not-being-what-one-is-not.' " "Fuyant par le 'non-être-ce-qu'on-est' l'en-soi que je ne suis pas sur le mode d'être ce qu'on n'est pas, la mauvaise foi, qui se renie comme mauvaise foi, vise l'en-soi que je ne suis pas sur le mode du 'n'être-pas-ce-qu'on-n'est-pas.' " The person of bad faith is not content to deny that he is this or that, he asserts at the same time that he is something that he is not; that is: "Fuyant par le 'non-être-ce-qu'on-est' (the for-itself is not what it is) l'en-soi (for example cowardice) que je ne suis pas sur le mode d'être ce qu'on n'est pas (the for-itself is what it is not) la mauvaise foi, qui se renie comme mauvaise foi, vise l'en-soi (that is, 'non-cowardice') que je ne suis pas sur le mode du 'n'être-pas-ce-qu'on-n'est-pas' (the for-itself cannot *be* what does not exist)." The following sentences appear on pages 131–2:

> The for-itself, as the foundation of itself, is the springing up of negation. It founds itself in so far as it denies *of itself* a certain being or manner of being. We know what it denies or nihilates, it is the being-in-itself. But not just any being-in-itself: human reality is above all its own nothingness. What it denies or nihilates of itself-as-for-itself, can only be *itself*. And, as its meaning is constituted by this nihilation and this presence in it of what it nihilates as thing nihilated, it is the *self-as-an-abortive-being-in-itself* which constitutes the meaning of human reality.

> Le pour-soi, comme fondement de soi, est le surgissement de la négation. Il se fonde en tant qu'il nie *de soi* un certain être ou une manière d'être. Ce qu'il nie ou néantit, nous le savons, c'est l'être-en-soi. Mais non pas n'importe quel être-en-soi: la réalité humaine est avant tout son propre néant. Ce qu'elle nie ou néantit de soi comme pour-soi, ce ne peut être que *soi*. Et, comme elle est constituée dans son sens par cette néantisation et cette présence en elle de ce qu'elle néantit à titre de néantisé, c'est le *soi-comme être-en-soi* manqué qui fait le sens de la réalité humaine.

This idea results from a closer examination of the structure of a nihilation than that which Sartre conducts in his chapter on bad faith. The first three sentences mean simply that the for-itself founds itself (but as a nothingness and not as Being) in the act of denying that it is a given in-itself (internal negation). "But not just any being-in-itself. Human reality is above all its own nothingness." (The being-in-itself in question is the perfect being that came into existence as part of the nihilation of the original or contingent in-itself. It is, therefore, *absent*; that is, part of the for-itself.) "What it denies or nihilates of itself as for-itself can only be *itself*." (The absent being-in-itself being part of the for-itself is simultaneously the being-in-itself that the for-itself determines itself as not being and the self of the for-itself.) Consequently the signification of human reality is to attempt to give existence to a Being which would be a synthesis of the in-itself and for-itself.

With the termination of the chapter "Les Structures Immédiates du Pour-Soi," the remainder of *L'Etre et le Néant* follows from what has already been established.

What we call the "world" is simply the sum of the obstacles which the for-itself encounters in its attempts to rejoin itself. It is what Sartre calls "the correlative in-itself of nothingness;"[14] that is, those in-itself which sustain the for-itself engendered in the nihilation of the absent in-itself-for-itself.

The for-itself is a "hollow always in the future" because it *is* the in-itself with which it attempts to coincide to realize the in-itself-for-itself. This in-itself, being part of the for-itself, is a nothingness, hence a "hollow," and it is one that is always future because the inevitable failure of the act whose aim is the realization of the in-itself-for-itself creates other absent in-itself with their particular "lacks" and possibilities. The act of drinking brings about not the impossible repose of a thirst that would be at the same time both a thing and sentient, but *consciousness of* a satisfied thirst; that is, another nihilation with all that implies. This perpetual "pursued-pursuit" is what we call time.

Sartre is *par excellence* the philosopher of intentionality. He alone has accepted uncompromisingly everything inherent in the principle. If consciousness is always consciousness of something, there is no subjectivity as classical philosophy understood it. But if there is no Self, how can there be "consciousness of"? We have seen that Sartre's answer to this question is the for-itself—a nothingness

14 *Ibid.*, p. 149.

that exists. It is easy to see that Sartre is now well placed to deal with the problems of epistemology—he has eliminated them by eliminating one of the two terms whose relationship with one another it is the purpose of epistemology to elucidate. "There is no other knowledge but intuitive,"[15] writes Sartre, and by "intuitive" he means the immediate and entire presence of the object to consciousness. All that can be said of the in-itself is that it is; it conceals nothing. Knowledge, consequently, is simply the presence of the object.

There is no better illustration of the way in which existentialism gives philosophical prominence to those questions most intimately connected with daily existence than the importance it attaches to the presence in our world of other people. Classical philosophy etherealizes the question of human relations into idle discussions for or against solipsism, or into ethical recommendations utterly without practical effectiveness except possibly for the philosopher himself. The first concern of the existentialist is, as we should expect, to describe the situation as it really exists. Such a description, being ontological, will at the same time more or less explicitly constitute an ethic. Sartre does not have to prove the existence of others, the *cogito* provides certitude on this score. His problem is to enquire how this certitude comes about, and he does so by examining the experience of "shame" since it is one that cannot occur without the presence actual or implied of other persons. If, for example, for one reason or another, I am brought to look through a keyhole, I can do so without the slightest embarrassment; but if I am discovered in the act, the result is an immediate and intense feeling of shame. The difference, according to Sartre, is the result of my being in the first instance, on the level of the "prereflexive *cogito*," that is, a nothingness;[16] whereas being seen by

15 *L'Etre et le Néant*, p. 220.
16 It is *reflexively* that we appear to ourselves as things, as possessing an Ego, etc.

another has the effect of "freezing" my subjectivity into a *thing*, and furthermore a thing forever characterized as being capable of such conduct. The gaze (*regard*) of another person has for a moment the power to transform us into in-itself, of making us the object of a nihilation which confiscates our possibilities to the advantage of the other. This is the sense in which another is always an enemy; not an enemy because he is necessarily hostile or to be mistrusted, but because for him we are an *object*—selfish, for example, as cats are animals with four legs; and if we are hurt by this judgment, it is because it is true (we are what we are not) and yet we are justified in rebelling against it (we are not what we are).

It is this theory of the "gaze" which provides the basis for Sartre's description of a certain number of comportments, to which, he believes, the others may be reduced. We will briefly examine that of love.

There are three ways in which the for-itself may attempt to coincide with itself, to become in-itself-for-itself. The first we have already discussed at length, the second (which we need not go into here) is by the aid of reflexion, the third is through our relations with others. In the case of love, the lover constitutes himself as an object in the subjectivity of the loved one. Now, while love exists in a great variety of forms, it is difficult to imagine a lover whose ambition is not to be loved in his turn, and this indicates on his part an attempt to recuperate the in-itself that he is in the subjectivity of the loved one by becoming master of the for-itself that created it, and so achieving at once the fullness of being and consciousness thereof— the in-itself-for-itself.[17] In love, however, as in everything

17 See Michel Leiris, *L'Age d'Homme*, NRF, 1946, p. 191. "Love—the only possibility for the subject and object to coincide . . . ," etc. *L'Age d'Homme* and the two volumes of *La Regle du Jeu*, NRF, *Biffures* (1948), and *Fourbis* (1955) are rather remarkable examples of existentialist psychoanalysis practised by an individual upon himself. One will notice that for Leiris, as for Valéry and Sartre, the Self is a "thing apart." It is not given, but reflexively created by the person concerned.

else, man is a "useless passion." If the lover succeeds in making himself loved, the result is simply a reversal of rôles, the loved one ceasing to mirror the other as in-itself to become in-itself in his turn for the subjectivity of the lover.

Bibliography

Our Bibliography for phenomenology and existentialism is offered as a guide to the most reliable works on these subjects and not as an exhaustive listing. In the case of Gide, Malraux and Saint-Exupéry, complete bibliographies will be found in the books of Justin O'Brien (*Portrait of André Gide*, Secker and Warburg, 1953), W. M. Frohock (*André Malraux and the Tragic Imagination*, Stamford University Press, 1952), and Jean Claude Ibert (*Antoine de Saint-Exupéry*, Editions Universitaires, 1953).

PHENOMENOLOGY

Farber, Marvin. *The Foundation of Phenomenology*, Harvard, 1943.

Bréhier, Emile. *Histoire de la Philosophie*, Presses Universitaires, 1941.

Transformation de la Philosophie Française, Flammarion, 1950.

Les Thèmes Actuels de la Philosophie, Presses Universitaires, 1951.

Levinas, Emmanuel. *La Théorie de l'Intuition dans la Phénoménologie de Husserl*, Alcan, 1930.

Berger, Gaston. *Le Cogito dans la Philosophie de Husserl*, Aubier, 1941.

Problèmes Actuels de la Phénoménologie, Desclée et Brouwer, 1952. (A collection of articles by some of Europe's most eminent phenomenologists.)

Waelhens, Alphonse de. *Phénoménologie et Vérité*, Presses Universitaires, 1953.

Lyotard, Yvon. *La Phénoménologie*, Que sais-je?, 1954.

Jeanson, Francis. *La Phénoménologie*, Téqui, 1951.

Merleau-Ponty, Maurice. *La Phénoménologie de la Perception*, NRF, 1945.

EXISTENTIALISM

Levinas, Emmanuel. *En découvrant l'Existence avec Husserl et Heidegger*, Vrin, 1949.
De l'Existence à l'Existant, Vrin, 1949.

Wahl, Jean. *Les Philosophies de l'Existence*, Colin, 1954.
Esquisse pour une Histoire de l'Existentialisme de Kierkegaard à Kafka, Editions de l'Arche, 1949.

Mounier, Emmanuel. *Existentialist Philosophies*, Rockliff, 1948.

Blackham, Harold John. *Six Existentialist Thinkers*, Routledge and Kegan Paul, 1952.

Campbell, Robert. *Existentialism*, Foucher, 1953.

Ajoux, Georges. *L'Attitude Existentialiste*, Gabalda, 1949.

Foulquié, Paul. *L'Existentialisme*, Que sais-je?, 1946.

Grene, Marjorie. *Dreadful Freedom*, University of Chicago, 1948.

Jolivet, Régis. *Les Doctrines Existentialistes*, Fontenelle, 1948.

Lukacs, George. *Existentialisme ou Marxisme*, Nagel, 1948.

Beauvoir, Simone de. *L'Existentialisme et la Sagesse des Nations*, Nagel, 1948.
Pour une Morale de l'Ambiguité, NRF, 1947.
Pour et Contre l'Existentialisme (a debate, with a text by Sartre), Atlas, 1948.

Allen, E. L. *Existentialism from Within*, Routledge and Kegan Paul, 1953.

SARTRE

I. BOOKS BY SARTRE

La Nausée, NRF, 1948.
L'Imagination, Presses Universitaires, 1938.
Le Mur, NRF, 1939.
L'Imaginaire, NRF, 1940.
Esquisse d'une Théorie des Emotions, Hermann et Cie., 1940.
Les Mouches, NRF, 1942.

L'Etre et le Néant, NRF, 1943.

Huis Clos, NRF, 1944.

L'Age de Raison, NRF, 1945.

Le Sursis, NRF, 1945.

La Putain Respectueuse, Nagel, 1946.

Descartes (Introduction and Choice of Texts by Sartre), Les Trois Collines, 1946.

Morts sans Sépultures, Marguerat, 1946.

Réflexions sur la Question Juive, Morinien, 1946.

Les Jeux sont Faits, Nagel, 1947.

Baudelaire, NRF, 1947.

Situations I, NRF, 1947.

Les Mains Sales, NRF, 1948.

L'Engrenage, Nagel, 1948.

Visages, Seghers, 1948.

Situations II, NRF, 1948.

La Mort dans l'Ame, NRF, 1949.

Entretiens sur la Politique (in collaboration with G. Rosenthal and D. Rousset), NRF, 1949.

Situations III, NRF, 1949.

Le Diable et le bon Dieu, NRF, 1951.

Saint Genêt, NRF, 1952.

Kean (Dumas, adaptation by Sartre), NRF, 1954.

Nekrassov, "Les Temps Modernes," May, June, July 1955.

II. BOOKS ON SARTRE

Murdoch, Iris. *Sartre, Romantic Rationalist,* Cambridge, 1953.

Jeanson, Francis. *Sartre par lui-même,* Seuil, 1955.
   Le Problème Moral et la Pensée de Sartre, Myrte, 1947.

Campbell, Robert. *J. P. Sartre ou une Littérature Philosophique,* Pierre Ardent, 1945.

Albérès, R. M. *Jean-Paul Sartre,* Editions Universitaires, 1953.

Varet, Gilbert. *L'Ontologie de Sartre,* Presses Universitaires, 1948.

WORKS OF GIDE, MALRAUX, SAINT-EXUPÉRY AND SARTRE WHICH HAVE BEEN TRANSLATED INTO ENGLISH

GIDE

Strait is the Gate, Vintage, 1956.

The Immoralist, Vintage, 1954.

Journals, Secker and Warburg, 1951.

Logbook of the Coiners, Cassell, 1952.

Marshlands; and Prometheus Misbound, Secker and Warburg, 1953.

Return of the Prodigal, preceded by five other treatises and *Saul,* Secker and Warburg, 1953.

Robert and *Geneviève,* Cassell, 1953.

The Vatican Cellars, Cassell, 1953.

The Coiners, Secker and Warburg, 1950.

Four Socratic Dialogues [*Corydon*], Secker and Warburg, 1952.

Dostoievsky, Secker and Warburg, 1949.

Two Symphonies [*La Symphonie Pastorale* and *Isabelle*], Cassell, 1949.

Fruits of the Earth, Secker and Warburg, 1949.

If it Die, Secker and Warburg, 1950.

Et Nunc Manet in Te and *Intimate Journal,* Secker and Warburg, 1952.

Notes on Chopin, Philosophical Library, 1949.

Oedipus and Theseus, Secker and Warburg, 1950.

Oscar Wilde, Kimber, 1951.

Imaginary Interviews, Knopf, 1944.

Afterthoughts, a sequel to Back from the U.S.S.R., Secker and Warburg, 1937.

Recollections of the Assize Court, Hutchinson, 1941.

Travels in the Congo, Modern Age, 1937.

Back from the U.S.S.R., Secker and Warburg, 1937.

Montaigne, Liveright, 1929.

MALRAUX

The Royal Way, Modern Library, 1955.

Voices of Silence, Secker and Warburg, 1954.

Man's Estate, Methuen, 1948.
The Psychology of Art, Pantheon Books, 1951.
Walnut Trees of the Altenburg, Lehmann, 1952.
Days of Hope, Routledge, 1938.
Days of Contempt, Gollancz, 1936.
The Conquerors, Cape, 1929.

SAINT-EXUPÉRY

Flight to Arras, Heinemann, 1955.
Letter to a Hostage, Heinemann, 1950.
Wind, Sand and Stars, Harcourt, 1949.
Wisdom of the Sands, Hollis and Carter, 1952.
The Little Prince, Heinemann, 1945.
Night Flight, McClelland, 1932.
Southern Mail, McLeod, 1933.

SARTRE

Literary and Philosophical Essays, Criterion Books, 1955.
No Exit and three other plays, Vintage, 1955.
In the Mesh, Dakers, 1954.
Kean, Hamilton, 1954.
Existential Psychoanalysis, Philosophical Library, 1953.
Lucifer and the Lord, Hamilton, 1952.
Baudelaire, Horizon, 1950.
Intimacy and other stories, Nevill, 1949.
The Chips are Down, Rider, 1951.
The Diary of Antoine Roquentin, Lehmann, 1949.
The Psychology of Imagination, Rider, 1951.
Three Plays, Hamilton, 1949.
Iron in the Soul, Hamilton, 1950.
What is Literature?, Methuen, 1950.
The Age of Reason, Hamilton, 1947.
Portrait of the Anti-Semite, Secker and Warburg, 1948.
The Emotions, Outline of a Theory, Philosophical Library, 1948.
Existentialism and Humanism, Methuen, 1948.
The Flies, Hamilton, 1946.
The Reprieve, Hamilton, 1948.

Index

Index

310 / Index